# Philosophy of Medicine

D1548476

What kind of knowledge is medical knowledge? Can medicine be explained scientifically? Is disease a scientific concept, or do explanations of disease depend on values? What is "evidence-based" medicine? Are advances in neuroscience bringing us closer to a scientific understanding of the mind?

The nature of medicine raises fundamental questions about explanation, causation, knowledge and ontology – questions that are central to philosophy as well as medicine. This book introduces the fundamental issues in philosophy of medicine for those coming to the subject for the first time, including:

- Understanding the physician–patient relationship: the phenomenology of the medical encounter.
- Models and theories in biology and medicine: what role do theories play in medicine? Are they similar to scientific theories?
- Randomised controlled trials: can scientific experiments be replicated in clinical medicine? What are the philosophical criticisms levelled at RCTs?
- The concept of evidence in medical research: what do we mean by "evidence-based medicine?" Should all medicine be based on evidence?
- Causation in medicine.
- What do advances in neuroscience reveal about the relationship between mind and body?
- Defining health and disease: are explanations of disease objective or do they depend on values?
- Evolutionary medicine: what is the role of evolutionary biology in understanding medicine? Is it relevant?

Extensive use of empirical examples and case studies are included throughout the book, including debates about smoking and cancer, the use of placebos in randomised controlled trials, controversies about PSA testing and research into the causes of HIV. This is an indispensable introduction for those teaching philosophy of medicine and philosophy of science.

**R. Paul Thompson** holds appointments as Professor in the Institute for the History and Philosophy of Science and Technology, the Department of Ecology and Evolutionary Biology, and the Department of Philosophy, University of Toronto, Canada.

**Ross E.G. Upshur** is a physician, and Professor in the Department of Family and Community Medicine and Dalla Lana School of Public Health, University of Toronto, Canada. He is also Head of the Division of Clinical Public Health, Dalla Lana School of Public Health, University of Toronto, Scientific Director, Bridgepoint Collaboratory for Research and Innovation, and Assistant Director, Lunenfeld Tanenbaum Research Institute, Sinai Health Systems.

# Philosophy of Medicine

An Introduction

R. Paul Thompson and
Ross E.G. Upshur

Routledge
Taylor & Francis Group

LONDON AND NEW YORK

First published 2018
by Routledge
2 Park Square, Milton Park, Abingdon, Oxon OX14 4RN

and by Routledge
711 Third Avenue, New York, NY 10017

*Routledge is an imprint of the Taylor & Francis Group, an informa business*

*British Library Cataloguing-in-Publication Data*
A catalogue record for this book is available from the British Library

*Library of Congress Cataloging-in-Publication Data*
Names: Thompson, R. Paul, author.
Title: Philosophy of medicine : an introduction/ R. Paul Thompson and
Ross E.G. Upshur.
Description: New York : Routledge, 2017. | Includes bibliographical references
and index.
Identifiers: LCCN 2017005902 | ISBN 9780415501071 (hardback : alk. paper) |
ISBN 9780415501095 (pbk. : alk. paper)
Subjects: LCSH: Medicine—Philosophy.
Classification: LCC R723.T47 2017 | DDC 610.1—dc23
LC record available at https://lccn.loc.gov/2017005902

ISBN: 978-0-415-50107-1 (hbk)
ISBN: 978-0-415-50109-5 (pbk)
ISBN: 978-1-315-15984-3 (ebk)

Typeset in Bembo
by Apex CoVantage, LLC

MIX
Paper from
responsible sources
FSC
www.fsc.org    FSC® C013056

Printed and bound in Great Britain by
TJ International Ltd, Padstow, Cornwall

For Aria Victoria Hylton
The world is yours; grasp what it offers with vitality.
Paul

To Kim, Olivia and Sara for their love and unwavering support.
Ross

# Contents

# Illustrations

## Figures

# Preface

Despite the difficulty for physicians like myself, unused to the language of philosophical discourse, I believe I am correct that a new understanding of medicine will not be possible without a return to basic philosophical issues.

(Eric Cassell 2004)

Philosophy of medicine is an emerging field. The philosophy of specific sciences was dominated until the late 1950s by philosophy of physics. Beginning in the late 1950s with Morton Beckner's *The Biological Way of Thought*, biology began to receive attention. Philosophy of biology is now a mature field of philosophical enquiry. Since the Renaissance, aspects of what today is analytic philosophy of medicine have received sporadic attention. Only in the last twenty or so years has a consolidated field of enquiry emerged. One of the catalysts was the rise of evidence-based medicine. Its commitment to randomised controlled trials (RCTs) as the gold standard of evidence and meta-analyses of related RCTs as the strongest basis for clinical decision-making attracted the attention of a number of philosophers. Among the trailblazers are John Worrall, Nancy Cartwright, John Dupré and David Papineau. They focussed initially on the logic of RCTs and the causal claims supposedly generated by them, based on Ronald A. Fisher's arguments in *The Design of Experiments* and the work of Jerzy Neyman and Karl Pearson.

Today, philosophy of medicine is a burgeoning field. During the last decade, numerous PhD theses have been defended in this field, a clear sign that it has found its place within philosophy of science. This book attempts to capture the growing enthusiasm for, and coalescing of, this field. It covers a number of the standard issues within philosophy of science – causality, determinism, reductionism, and theories and models, for example – with a focus on these within a medical context. Some topics are more specific to philosophy of clinical medicine – RCTs and biostatistics more generally, and phenomenological aspects of clinical practice, for example. Other topics are more relevant to philosophy of bench medicine; there is no other non-loaded term for this area, which includes human genetics, immunology, physiology, biochemistry and neurosciences. There are no doubt topics that some would have liked to see included and, contrariwise, topics some would have recommend excluding. This is an evolving field.

As we explain in the introduction and Chapter 1, we consider philosophy of medicine to be a sub-field of philosophy of science. As a result, the main analytic areas of philosophy involved are epistemology, metaphysics and logic; ethics is not central. It is clear that values permeate all of our claims to know and our investigations of the world around us. Exploring that recognition, although important, is only tangentially connected to philosophy of medicine. It cannot be ignored but is not its central focus.

As always, there are more debts to friends, colleagues and students than can ever be listed. One debt worthy of special mention is what we owe to the graduate students in our philosophy of medicine course over many years, especially Jon Fuller, Aaron Kenna and Mat Mercuri. Those we have worked with at Routledge: Taylor & Francis Group have been patient, helpful and encouraging – originally Tony Bruce and more recently our editor Rebecca Shillabeer, editorial assistant Gabrielle Coakeley and copy-editor Anna Carroll. Anonymous reviewers of the book proposal and the penultimate draft provided insightful and valuable comments. Throughout our careers, our families have been a source of unwavering support. We celebrate our good fortune.

# Introduction

Analytic philosophy is by its nature a critical enterprise. Ideas, claims, commitments and organised structures from theoretical to social are turned around; each facet is examined for clarity, brilliance, flaws and promise. This critical stance is a guiding principle for this book. That inevitably means that there will be readers who disagree with some of our expositions, analyses and critical appraisals. Our hope, and in part our goal, is to engender constructive criticism; it is a method of advancing knowledge and understanding. The expositions, analyses and critical appraisals offered in the book are not idiosyncratic or fringe perspectives as the numerous references should make clear. Indeed, they reflect a growing chorus of reflections and alternative views.

One obvious gem and promise of contemporary medicine in English-speaking and European countries (hereafter the Anglo-European world) is that contemporary medicine has mended broken bodies, ameliorated the lives of the chronically ill and offered hope to the mentally distraught with a success never rivalled before in the history of the world. There are still many disappointments, flaws and challenges to meet but the achievement is impressive. But, for large swathes of the Anglo-European world, physicians today, in many respects, have replaced the religious priesthoods and pastors of previous millennia. This success, as well as the flaws, and the increasingly dominant role of medicine in contemporary society make it an ideal subject for enquiry: sociological, economic, historical and philosophical to name only a few.

In this volume, we examine medicine philosophically. Given medicine's pivotal role in contemporary society, it is remarkable that philosophy of medicine has been a long neglected field. Until recently, philosophers of science have taken little interest in medicine, and the attitude of physicians, with a few notable exceptions, has ranged from disinterest to hostility toward philosophical examination of their enterprise. The interest of philosophers, however, has increased substantially in the last two decades, but why has it taken so long? The emergence of physics was interconnected with philosophy, and what today we call philosophy of physics has a long, and continuing, history. Moreover, interest in the philosophy of biology emerged about 60 years ago, and today it is an integral part of philosophy of science. There is no systematic enquiry into the delay in interest in medicine but there are some elements of a hypothesis that can be sketched.

First, medicine emerged as an applied discipline – from Hippocrates onward. Physics from the time of the late medieval scholars (the Merton school of mathematicians at Oxford University[1] around 1310, John Buridan, rector of the University of Paris around 1330, and Nicole Oresme around 1335, for example), who began to challenge Aristotle's physics and cosmology, was a mathematical/theoretical enterprise as well as an empirical one. Copernicus and Galileo built on this tradition. Galileo's famous passage (1623) expresses well this mathematical/theoretical orientation:

> Philosophy is written in this grand book, the universe, which stands continually open to our gaze. But the book cannot be understood unless one first learns to comprehend the language and read the letters in which it is composed. It is written in the language of mathematics, and its characters are triangles, circles and other geometric figures without which it is humanly impossible to understand a single word of it; without these, one wanders about in a dark labyrinth.

Bradwardine also expressed this orientation around 1330:

> it is [mathematics] which reveals every genuine truth, for it knows every hidden secret, and bears the key to every subtlety of letters; whoever, then, has the effrontery to study physics while neglecting mathematics, should know from the start that he will never make his entry through the portals of wisdom
>
> (Thomas Bradwardine,
> *Tractatus de Continuo*, c. 1330s)

Clinical medicine in the twentieth century became somewhat more mathematical, employing, however, mostly statistics. Its theoretical foundation remained underdeveloped. The theoretical foundation of physics was deep and elegant after Newton and Leibniz and the theoretical foundation of biology was secured by Darwin – *On the Origin of Species* is a masterpiece of philosophical sophistication and theoretical depth – and mathematised by the 1930s. There were, and remain, interesting and challenging philosophical dimensions in both fields. Philosophers saw considerably less interesting dimensions in clinical medicine. We think they were wrong and hope that by the end of the book you will agree. Note that this paragraph is about "clinical" medicine.

There is another significant area of medicine, which, for lack of a better term, we call bench medicine[2] (genetics, immunology, haematology, biochemistry and physiology, for example). Its use of mathematics is richer and its theoretical sophistication impressive. It does use probability and statistics but that is but one of an array of mathematical tools and its use of them is not the same as in clinical medicine. It, however, is very allied to the experimental methods, model building and theorising and reasoning of physics, chemistry and biology. To philosophers, these are basic sciences focused on humans. They require little special attention from philosophers of science beyond the attention given to physics, chemistry and biology. Chapter 3 addresses a feature of bench medicine, which has almost no analogue in clinical medicine: the structure and role of theories and models. Contrariwise, Chapters 7, 8 and 9 explore features of clinical medicine that rarely make an appearance in bench medicine. Those three chapters draw out what we claim are philosophically interesting features, albeit the examination is critical.

A third element *might* be a greater requirement of public confidence in clinical research and practice. Part of therapeutic interactions rely on trust. Beyond a few "magic bullets" (vaccination, antibiotics, water purification, food inspections and so on), uncertainty in clinical medicine is unavoidable, as we shall see. Philosophers tend to expose vulnerabilities in methods, reasoning, knowledge claims and actions. Clinical medicine may be more concerned about such criticisms eroding public confidence, leading to a chilly response to philosophers of science poking around.

A compelling analysis of the delay in interest by philosophers of science may include none of these elements but that requires further investigation. What we find exciting is that philosophers of science have finally focused on medicine. We think that is beneficial to philosophy of science and to medicine and signals a maturing of medicine.

Chapters 7 and 8 focus on aspects of biostatistics and experimental design in clinical research. They are, as a result, moderately technical. We have attempted to focus only on those elements that inform expositions, analyses and criticisms. Chapter 5 sets out important philosophical issues involved in the understanding and interpretation of probability and randomness. Probability, and statistical methods derived from it, play a significant role in clinical research and practice, which warrants some familiarity with them by philosophers of medicine. Randomness is far more complex than is often thought – philosophers and mathematicians excepted. Yet, it is a cornerstone of reasoning (drawing inferences) in contemporary clinical research, as the emphasis on randomised controlled trials makes clear.

We made a conscious decision not to devote a chapter to evidence-based medicine (EBM), although both of us have written on it. We consider it a variety of medicine, albeit one that has received a lot of attention recently. The substantive underpinnings of EBM are randomised controlled trials and systematic reviews; those we discuss in detail. The various injunctions of EBM about how to assess evidence and apply it are more akin to other varieties of medicine we identify: evolutionary medicine, and precision and personalised medicine, for example. Hence, we discuss it in the same chapter. Some may think we have provided too little on the topic; others (its strong critics) will think that we have given too much space to it. Those who have their interest piqued by our comments can find numerous comprehensive treatments of EBM.

## Notes

1 Thomas Bradwardine was in the forefront of the work of this school, along with his colleagues John Dumbleton, Richard Swineshead and William Heytesbury.

2 Some have used the term "medical science" for this area but that seems to pre-judge whether clinical research is science. We want to leave that question open for now. Some have used "medical biology" but that pre-judges whether clinical medicine is biological. "Bench medicine" is not ideal because not all research in this domain is laboratory based but the vast amount of it is. In this respect, as pointed out many times in the book, it is much more like physics and biology than clinical medicine but its importance to clinical practice is clear.

# 1 Philosophy of medicine

## Its scope and subject matter

Three domains of philosophy are principally embraced by philosophy of science: epistemology (i.e. how knowledge is acquired and what it is to "know" something), metaphysics (i.e. the role and nature of cause and effect, and space and time) and logic (i.e. the nature of scientific reasoning and the logical structure of models and theories). The examination of some aspects of science draws on more than one of these domains; examining the role of models and theories, for example, involves exploring their logical structure as well as their role in knowledge acquisition and expression. Philosophy of medicine, like philosophy of biology and philosophy of physics, is a branch of philosophy of science and, hence, also embraces these three domains of philosophy.

The fourth domain of analytic philosophy is ethics. During the last 50 years or so, increasing attention has been paid to ethical issues in medicine with an attendant increase in articles and books on ethical aspects of medicine. This enterprise is known as bioethics. Opinions differ about whether bioethics is a full-fledged discipline or a sub-discipline of ethics. Its practitioners include lawyers, theologians, sociologists, physicians, philosophers and others. Given the array of backgrounds of its practitioners, the lack of a common set of requirements and no common methodology, we suggest that it is not a discipline.

Whatever the resolution of that issue, in this book, we treat philosophy of medicine as a branch of philosophy of science. Consequently, ethics does not play a large role. There are occasions, however, where it does have tangential relevance; values may be influencing research methodology or medical knowledge may have obvious ethical implications. Fortunately, there are a large number of books and articles on these matters; hence, we need not digress from the central foci of philosophy of science. Where appropriate, we refer readers to the existing literature.

This description of the philosophical domains involved in philosophy of medicine is somewhat abstract. Examining two historically important medical events will illustrate the nature of a philosophical analysis of medicine in a more concrete way and will more sharply characterise the matters with which philosophy of medicine is concerned.

In 1753, James Lind, a Scottish physician, described his experiment on the treatment and prevention of scurvy. Today, scurvy is known to result from a deficiency of vitamin C (ascorbic acid); the name ascorbic derives from the Latin name for scurvy, i.e., scorbutus. It is a debilitating and ultimately fatal disease if not treated. In Lind's time, it was the scourge of seamen on long voyages. The symptoms include inflamed and bleeding gums, bleeding into the skin, joints and body cavities, weakness and fatigue.

Lind described his experiment in his (1753) *A Treatise of the Scurvy. In Three Parts. Containing An inquiry into the Nature, Cauſes, and Cure, of that Diſeaſe* (the "ſ" today is rendered "s"). The relevant passage, in more modern English, with italics as in the original, is:

> On the 20th May, 1747, I took twelve patients in the scurvy on board the *Salisbury* at sea. Their cases were as similar as I could have them. They all in general had putrid gums, the spots and lassitude, with weakness of their knees. They lay together in one place, being a proper apartment for the sick in the fore-hold; and had one diet in common to all, viz., water-gruel sweetened with sugar in the morning; fresh mutton-broth often times for dinner; at other times puddings, boiled biscuit with sugar, etc.; and for supper barley, raisins, rice and currants, sago and wine, or the like. Two of these were ordered each a quart of cyder a day. Two others took twenty-five gutts of *elixir vitriol* three times a day upon an empty stomach, using a gargle strongly acidulated with it for their mouths. Two others took two spoonfuls of vinegar three times a day upon an empty stomach, having their gruels and their other food well acidulated with it, as also the gargle for the mouth. Two of the worst patients, with the tendons in the ham rigid (a symptom none the rest had) were put under a course of sea-water. Of this they drank half a pint every day and sometimes more or less as it operated by way of gentle physic. Two others had each two oranges and one lemon given them every day. These they eat with greediness at different times upon an empty stomach. They continued but six days under this course, having consumed the quantity that could be spared. The two remaining patients took the bigness of a nutmeg three times a day of an electuary recommended by an hospital surgeon made of garlic, mustard-seed, *rad. raphan.* balsam of *Peru* and gum myrrh, using for common drink barley water well acidulated with tamarinds, by a decoction of which, with the addition of *cremor tartar*, they were gently purged three or four times during the course. The consequence was that the most sudden and visible good effects were perceived from the use of the oranges and lemons; one of those who had taken them being at the end of six days fit for duty. The spots were not indeed at that time quite off his body, nor his gums sound; but without any other medicine than a gargarism or *elixir vitriol* he became quite healthy before we came into *Plymouth*, which was on the 16th of *June*. The other was the best recovered of any in his condition, and being now deemed pretty well was appointed nurse to the rest of the sick.
>
> (pp. 192–193)

Lind's experiment has a sample of 12 scurvy sufferers. He was satisfied that their cases were sufficiently similar that any outcome of his interventions would not be due to differences in the severity, duration and so on of the disease. He also attempted to ensure that the physical environment was the same for all and the general diet was the same for all. The only thing that varied was an addition to their diet. He created six groups of two people. Each group had a different dietary supplement. His, now famous, result was that the group whose diet was supplemented with two oranges and one lemon improved quickly and dramatically.

The obvious immediate question is, was he just lucky? Twelve is not a large sample size; two individuals per group is very low; assessing the similarity of disease conditions was a subjective judgement by one person. Moreover, the choice of two oranges and one lemon for one group seems fortuitous. Why did he try that supplement and why in those quantities? These questions probe the adequacy of his experimental design, his methodology and his conclusions. Assessing the adequacy of these falls within the scope of philosophy of medicine. Other issues need probing as well. Does the experimental result justify any claims about causes of scurvy or the efficacy of this "cure"; if it does, then what kind of causal claims are they? The experiment seems to provide some "evidence" of a link between citrus fruits and amelioration of the symptoms of scurvy. What kind of "evidence" is it and how adequate is it for drawing conclusions regarding treatment? Surely, dose and timing of the treatment will matter. If so, what further work is needed to reveal the answers? Would subsequent treatment of those with symptoms of scurvy be important? Would similar remarkable recoveries strengthen the belief that this is an effective treatment? Given that differential diagnosis (distinguishing diseases based on symptoms) is complicated, and more so in the eighteenth century, some people with symptoms of scurvy may have some other ailment. That they will likely fail to respond to the therapy is not surprising but how should the data be interpreted? Examining these matters also falls within the domain of philosophy of medicine.

Then there are some larger matters that arise from Lind's discovery that fall within the scope of philosophy of medicine. Can his discovery – the link between citrus fruit and recovery from scurvy – be integrated with other knowledge in medicine at the time? Does it need to be? Can a model be developed that quantitatively describes features of the relationship Lind uncovered; for example, the relationship of the quantity of citrus fruit ingested and the speed of recovery? Are such models useful? Given the importance of models in modern science, it would be surprising if a model, even a simple model, were not to be important here. To underscore this point, consider a twentieth-century example, one that one of us has used before (Thompson 2011a): Bolie's model (1960) of the relationship of glucose and insulin. The model is important in the understanding and management of diabetes.

The principal role of insulin is to mediate the uptake of glucose into cells. A deficiency of, or a decreased sensitivity of cells to, insulin results in an imbalance of glucose uptake, resulting in severe physiological problems, which if untreated lead to kidney, eye and nervous system deterioration and ultimately to death. In some cases, treatment can be based on a dietary regime; in others, daily doses of insulin are required. Insulin is a protein. The sequence of DNA that codes for the production of the human insulin protein has been mapped and constructed. This DNA segment is inserted into a region of a plasmid in a bacterium; the bacterium then becomes a bio-factory for the production of insulin. Today, virtually all insulin used in rich countries is produced by genetically modified bacteria. Understanding the dynamics of the regulatory system allows considerable refinement to a therapeutic regime of insulin.

Bolie's model is very simple; it assumes only three entities (glucose, insulin and extracellular fluid) and identifies nine variables:

| | |
|---|---|
| Extracellular fluid volume | $V$ |
| Rate of insulin injection | $I$ |
| Rate of glucose injection | $G$ |
| Extracellular insulin concentration | $X(t)$ |
| Extracellular glucose concentration | $Y(t)$ |
| Rate of degradation of insulin | $F_1(X)$ |
| Rate of production of insulin | $F_2(Y)$ |
| Rate of liver accumulation of glucose | $F_3(X,Y)$ |
| Rate of tissue utilisation of glucose | $F_4(X,Y)$ |

$F_1(X,Y)$ through $F_4(X,Y)$ are functions of $X$ and $Y$ at specific times. Bolie's dynamical system has equations:

Insulin:   $dX/dt = (I - F_1(X) + F_2(Y))/V$ [the expression $dX/dt$ = the change in $X$ with respect to change in time – change in $X$ per unit time]

That is, the change in extracellular insulin concentration with respect to time equals the rate of insulin injection minus the natural rate of its production minus the rate of its degradation, all divided by the volume of extracellular fluid. The division by the volume of extracellular fluid means the change in insulin is expressed as a change per unit volume of extracellular fluid.

Glucose:   $(dY/dt) = (G - F_3(X, Y) - F_4(X, Y))/V$

That is, the change in extracellular glucose concentration with respect to time equals the rate of glucose injection or ingestion minus the rate of liver accumulation of glucose minus the rate of tissue utilisation of glucose, all divided by the volume of extracellular fluid.

Lind's discovery of the connection between citrus fruits and the prevention of scurvy would have been enhanced if a mechanistic account such as Bolie provides for the dynamics of insulin were known. Today, of course, we know the effective agent, L-ascorbic acid (aka vitamin C), and its function and the dynamics of its action. Although this knowledge confers significant benefits with respect to the prevention and treatment of scurvy, Lind's works demonstrates that simple experiments can yield successful medical interventions.

Turning to a different event in the history of medicine – the discovery of a smallpox vaccine – provides an additional illustration of the foregoing philosophical matters arising in medicine and also draws out others. Smallpox (*variola*) inflicted misery and death on hundreds of millions of people; those who survived the horrors of the symptoms were left disfigured and often disabled, with loss of vision for example. Jennifer Lee Carrell in her historical fiction, *The Speckled Monster: A Historical Tale of Battling Smallpox* (2004), captures this eloquently:

> For all our current fears, we are inestimably lucky to live in a world in which the threat of smallpox has shifted from ordinary to extraordinary. Paradoxically, in the absence of smallpox as an everyday enemy, it is hard to realise just how lucky we are. Sheer numbers may help. By the time the disease was vanquished in 1977, it had become far and away the most voracious killer ever to stalk the human species. With a victim count in the hundreds of millions, smallpox killed more people than the Black Death and all the bloody wars of the twentieth century put together.
>
> (p. xiv)

Jared Diamond in, *Guns, Germs, and Steel* (1999), holds that smallpox arrived in Rome around 165, presumably from Asia, so it is also a very old disease:

> Another bonanza [for microbes] was the development of world trade routes, which by Roman times effectively joined Europe, Asia, and North Africa into one giant breeding ground for microbes. That's when smallpox finally reached Rome, as the Plague of Antoninus, which killed millions of Roman citizens between A.D. 165 and 180.
>
> (p. 205)

In 1980 the World Health Organization declared smallpox eradicated, although the report of the last case was sent to it two years earlier from Nairobi, Kenya. The road to eradication was long and began at some point in the 1600s in lands to the east of the Mediterranean Sea known as the Levant.[1]

The first western reports of a practice in the Levant of inoculating people with pus from the pustules of those with smallpox appeared in the *Philosophical Transactions* of the Royal Society in 1714. In two separate communications that year Emanuel Timoni and Jacob Pylarinius reported on the practice and its successes. Timoni's letter was reported by John Woodward who conveyed in English the main points of the letter (published in *Philosophical Transactions*; see Timoni and Woodward 1714):

> V. *An Account, or History, of the Procuring the* SMALL POX *by Incision, or Inoculation; as it Has for Some Time been practised at* Constantinople

> *Being the Extract of a Letter from* Emanuel Timonius, Oxon & Patav M.D. S.R.S. *dated at* Constantinople, December, 1713
>
> *Communicated to the* Royal Society *by* John Woodward, M.D. Profes. Med. Grefh. *And* S.R.S.

Woodward states that:

> The writer of this ingenious Discourse observes, in the first place, that the Circassians [peoples of the north Caucasus], Georgians, and other Asiaticks, have introduc'd this Practice of procuring the Small-pox by a sort of inoculation, for about the space of forty Years, among the Turks and others at Constantinople.

Woodward suggests that this places the origin of the practice at around the 1670s.

Pylarinius's communication appeared slightly later (published in Latin) (*Philosophical Transactions*; see Pylarinius 1716):

> A new and safe method of producing variola blisters by transplantation; recently developed and put into practice by Jacob Pylarino, M.D., of Venice, until recently the diplomatic representative of the Venetian Republic in Smyrna.
>
> (translation of the original Latin)

By the mid 1600s, two forms of smallpox had been identified: flux and distinct (today *variola major* – associated with a high mortality rate and morbidity/ disfigurement rate, and *variola minor* – a milder form). The pus from poxes was taken from those with *variola minor*, in effect transferring, by inoculation, an attenuated (weakened) form of the virus. This was found to be very successful:

> That altho' at first the more prudent were very cautious in the use of this Practice; yet the happy success it has been found to have in thousands of Subjects for these eight Years past, has now put it out of all suspicion and doubt; since the Operation having been perform'd on Persons of all Ages, Sexes, and different Temperaments, and even in the worst Constitution of the Air, yet none have been found to die of the Small-pox; when at the same time it was very mortal when it seized the Patient in the common way, of which half the affected dy'd.
>
> (p. 72)

The method is described concisely:

> The method of the Operation is thus. Choice being made of a proper Contagion, the Matter of the pustules is to be communicated to the Person proposed to take the Infection; whence it has, metaphorically, the name of

insition or inoculation. For this purpose they make choice of some boy, or young lad, of a sound healthy temperament, that is seized with the common Small-pox (of the distinct, not Flux sort) on the twelfth or thirteenth day from the beginning of his Sickness; they with a Needle prick the Tubercles (chiefly those on the Shins and Hams) and pres out the Matter coming from them into some convenient Vessel of Glas, or the like, to receive it; it is convenient to wash and clean the Vessel first with warm Water: A convenient quantity of this Matter being thus collected, is to be stop'd close, and kept warm in the Bosom of the Person that carries it, and, as soon as may be, brought to the place of the expecting future Patient.

The Patient therefore being in a warm Chamber, the needles Operator is made to make several little Wounds with a Needle, in one, two or more places of the Skin, till some drops of Blood follow and immediately drop out some of the matter in the Glas, and mix it well with the Blood issuing out. These punctures are made indifferently in any of the fleshy Parts, but succeed best in the muscles of the arm or *Radius* (p. 73).

Edward Jenner made the next major advance in the 1790s; he published his results in 1798.

As is now well known, Jenner happened upon a point of common knowledge among dairy farmers, that milkmaids who contracted from cows a mild form of pustule disease similar to smallpox were immune to smallpox. At the time, Jenner was a medical student; it was some years before he decided to experiment with *vaccinia* pus (cowpox). Jenner collected pus from Sarah Nelms who had *vaccinia*. He inoculated eight-year-old James Phipps with the pus; after six weeks, he inoculated him with smallpox pus. It is worth noting in passing that his experiment flies in the face of an array of ethical standards in place today. Fortunately, Phipps did not acquire smallpox. Jenner concluded that the cowpox pus made him immune to smallpox. The term *"vaccinia"* is derived from *Vacca* (Latin for cow). Since Jenner's process used *vaccinia* pus, he called the process *vaccination*.

Jenner's interpretation of the result of his experiment turned out to be correct but how confident should he and others have been about his interpretation in 1796? The Royal Society lacked sufficient confidence; they rejected his 1797 communication about the experiment. As mentioned before, sometimes a single experiment can be decisive. Philosophy of medicine examines just when that might be the case; it sets out the criteria that must be met (see Chapter 7). Jenner's experiment was lacking in many respects; for example, he had no way of knowing, and hence ruling out, whether Phipps had a natural immunity to smallpox.

When, in 1798, he self-published his monograph, he still had performed only this experiment but he had amassed numerous case studies, which he considers to be additional "experiments":

Had these experiments been conducted in a large city, or in a populous neighbourhood, some doubts might have been entertained; but here, where the population is thin, and where such an event as a person's having the Small Pox is always faithfully recorded, no risk of inaccuracy in this particular can arise.

Case studies can be useful; sometimes they are also decisive evidence. Again, this depends on criteria of validity being satisfied; developing and examining criteria of validity falls within the scope of philosophy of medicine. Jenner's case studies relied on anecdotal information; that is usually cause for suspicion about validity. There are many other matters that arise in Jenner's monograph that are within the scope of philosophy of medicine. For example, when Jenner uses the terms "cause" and "effect" in his treatise, to what do these refer and what does he, and presumably his readers, think they mean? Further, when the term "*vaccinia*" is used, is it just another term for cowpox or is it intended to designate a causative agent? If it designates a causative agent, what properties does it have apart from causing cowpox, and if that is its only property, how is that different from it just being a synonym for cowpox? Moreover, if, as in this case, the causal dynamics of a disease are unknown and all that is known is that some intervention results in a desired therapeutic or preventative outcome, does that suggest that knowledge of causes is not required for clinical medicine to advance? Or, does it entail that a cause has been identified but is not yet fully understood?

These historical examples illustrate the kinds of matters that fall within the scope of philosophy of medicine; there are others as well and these will emerge in the course of this book. For now, these two examples, drawn from the history of medicine, serve to illustrate a large number of philosophical issues that fall within the scope of philosophy of medicine: epistemological, metaphysical and logical issues. Before turning to another feature of philosophy of medicine, we should make it clear that many of the matters that fall within the scope of philosophy of medicine fall also within the scope of other disciplines, statistics and mathematics for example.

Contemporary medicine encompasses three different kinds of activities, although they are interconnected in complicated ways. Clinical practice – the activities of diagnosing, treating and preventing disease, as well as promoting health – is one kind. Clinical research is another. Clinical research investigates aspects of diagnoses, treatment and prevention of disease, as well as promotion of health, aspects such as the efficacy of a treatment or improvement of diagnosis. The historical cases set out above are examples of this kind of medicine.

A third kind is less clinical and involves research methods that are similar to those of biology, physics and chemistry – laboratory research and constructing physical and mathematical models, for example. Physiology, endocrinology, immunology, medical genetics, neurosciences and the like are examples; they are not principally focused on the clinical activities of diagnosis, treatment and prevention of disease, although they are usually motivated by a desire to enhance those clinical activities. The central difference between these research domains in medicine by contrast with biology is that they are principally interested in understanding features of humans; in biology the scope includes all organisms with the relevant systems. As this suggests, there is considerable similarity between biology and medicine and much cross-boundary activity, and exchange and use of knowledge. Understanding immunological features of dogs will have relevance to understanding immunological features of humans and vice versa, for example.

There is no unproblematic term for this third kind of medical activity. "Medical bench research" and "medical laboratory research" are cumbersome and inaccurate, placing an undue emphasis on laboratory work. "Medical science" is crisp and accurate but suggests that those doing clinical research are not doing science. "Basic medical science" – as opposed to "applied medical science" – is accurate but again a bit cumbersome. On balance, "bench medicine" seems to us best, with the clear understanding that this terminology does not prejudge the issue of whether clinical research is science. For the most part, philosophy of medicine focuses on clinical research and medical science; this follows from its focus on the nature and acquisition of knowledge, which is principally a function of research rather than applications of the fruits of research.

## Note

1 An area more or less bounded on the west by the Mediterranean Sea, on the north by Taurus mountains, on the east by the Zagros mountains and on the south by the Arabian desert. Today, it includes Israel, Lebanon, part of Jordan, the Sinai and a part of Syria.

# 2    Defining health and disease

There is a parable attributed to Francis Bacon (1561–1626). The attribution is widely held to be spurious. The earliest written source appears to be in a 1934 journal article (Mees). Mees does attribute it to Bacon but with no accompanying evidence or citation.

> In the year of our Lord 1432, there arose a grievous quarrel among the brethren over the number of teeth in the mouth of a horse. For thirteen days the disputation raged without ceasing. All the ancient books and chronicles were fetched out, and wonderful and ponderous erudition such as was never before heard of in this region was made manifest. At the beginning of the fourteenth day, a youthful friar of goodly bearing asked his learned superiors for permission to add a word, and straightway, to the wonderment of the disputants, whose deep wisdom he sore vexed, he beseeched them to unbend in a manner coarse and unheard-of and to look in the open mouth of a horse and find answer to their questionings. At this, their dignity being grievously hurt, they waxed exceeding wroth; and, joining in a mighty uproar, they flew upon him and smote him, hip and thigh, and cast him out forthwith. For, said they, surely Satan hath tempted this bold neophyte to declare unholy and unheard-of ways of finding truth, contrary to all the teachings of the fathers. After many days more of grievous strife, the dove of peace sat on the assembly, and they as one man declaring the problem to be an everlasting mystery because of a grievous dearth of historical and theological evidence thereof, so ordered the same writ down.

The lesson of the parable is clear; empirical evidence is the path to knowledge, not texts – secular or theological – as was often supposed by early mediaeval scholars. Today, it is not disputed that empirical evidence is at the heart of scientific inquiry; at least, it is not disputed within the scientific community and well beyond. Many literalist and fundamentalist Christians and Muslims disagree but their extreme religious views are not relevant to any discourse on scientific enquiry.

Nonetheless, while accepting the paramount importance of empirical evidence, seeking such evidence is not really as simple as opening a horse's mouth. The parable provides an apt basis for making this point. First and obviously, one must know what counts as a tooth. All horses have 12 premolars, 12 molars and 12 incisors. Most adult males have four canines that are found between the incisors and molars. Typically, females do not have canines. It seems reasonable to deem all these to be teeth. Some horses also have one or two – rarely more – vestigial teeth called wolf teeth. Although it is convenient to refer to them as teeth since the material is the same as the other teeth and they are positioned in the jaw, they do not function as teeth. If the designation "tooth" depends on material or location, these are teeth; if it depends on function, it's questionable that they are teeth. Of course, it is easy to resolve this issue by stipulating a definition that clarifies what a tooth is for this or that purpose. Nonetheless, until a definition is given, counting the number of teeth doesn't resolve the issue of the total number in a mouth. Defining a tooth is a first step but the complexities of empirical evidence do not end there.

The relevance of this to the topic of this chapter is that the meaning of a term (a concept) must be clear and that meaning must be common to all engaged in its use – at least, within a specific context. Sometimes defining the meaning of a term is reasonably simple, as in the case of a horse's tooth. Sometimes it is far more difficult, as it is with "health" and "disease" as we shall see.

Before leaving the parable, a further comment on evidence, to which we return, contrasts "crude" (or "short-sighted" – Bluhm 2017) empiricism with a "robust" empiricism. Suppose we all agree that wolf teeth are tooth-like but not really teeth (a common veterinary assumption), it remains that horses have between 36 to 44 teeth (since all have 12 premolars, 12 molars and 12 incisors, and males usually have four canines but there are deviations). Moreover, things are even more confusing than this; young horses have 24 temporary (deciduous) teeth and the norms (statistical means) for adult males and females differ, with males having 42 and females 40. Hence, how many teeth a horse has in its mouth *depends on the horse*. Looking in one or even ten mouths will not settle the question of number. One can determine a statistical norm but any given horse may not fit that norm. Moreover, determining what that norm is will require looking in the mouths of hundreds, if not thousands, of horses and along the way noticing patterns of differences based on age and gender. So really, there is no definitive answer, just a range of possibilities. These factors in no way undermine the parable's central message; "ancient books and chronicles" are not the bases for knowledge of the empirical world. Nonetheless, these factors do undermine the crude empiricism of the "youthful friar of goodly bearing". A sophisticated and defensible empiricism requires considerably more care, effort and methodological sophistication.

Three concepts that are common in medicine are "health", "disease" and "disability". On the surface, health might seem simply to be the absence of disease, and disease a departure from health. This, however, is not the way the use and definition of these terms have evolved. Disability seems neither to be a disease nor an absence of health. Let's begin with it.

## Disability

Myopia (near-sightedness: i.e. distant images are out of focus) is an interesting example of a disability. The most widely accepted characterisation of primary myopia is that it is due to the normal growth of the *healthy* eyeball.[1] This suggests that primary myopia is not a disease or illness, although it can be a disability. It is not a disease because it is due to "normal" growth of the "healthy" eyeball. Note the reference to "normal". Does that mean that an individual with primary myopia is healthy, even though, in some environments, she will find the condition an impediment – a disability (or put more weakly "a liability")? That, of course, depends on the meaning of "disability", about which there is a weak consensus. To the extent that there is a consensus it appears to be that a "disability" is a lack of the ability to function normally: physically or mentally.[2] Note again the reference to "normal". There are three other things worth noting about this definition. First, it is contextual; the employment success of someone with an intelligence quotient (IQ)[3] of more than one standard deviation below the mean will be significantly compromised in Anglo-European countries[4] but will fare much better in many rural villages of East Africa. Second, a disability can be primary and result from normal development, as in primary myopia, or it can be acquired, as in the case of an injury. Third, "disability" can be entirely value-laden as a result of social values at a particular time; that is, it is a disability because of certain social or moral values, as was the case with homosexuality until the later part of twentieth century in Anglo-European countries.

## Health

The World Health Organization (WHO) defines "health" as "a state of complete physical, mental and social well-being and not merely the absence of disease or infirmity" (World Health Organization 1946). This is an expansive definition and it might be that only rarely does anyone fulfil it. Defining "health" in terms of "well-being" seems only to push the definitional issue onto another also not well-defined term. The Merriam-Webster dictionary defines well-being as: the state of being happy, healthy or prosperous. That, of course, re-introduces "health", which is the term that we are trying to define. If the emphasis is on "happy", this will vary from person to person and occasion to occasion. Two individuals in identical circumstances may differ on whether they are happy in those circumstances. These judgements are based, in significant part, on an individual's values. The same is true of "prosperous". So, we have not made much progress in finding a medical standard of health. Indeed, a physician might think her patient healthy because under similar circumstances, she would feel healthy, even though the patient in front of her might feel very unhealthy. Hence, the WHO definition seems on the one hand circular – it defines health in terms of health – or entirely value-laden. One thing the WHO definition does underscore is that health, as the concept has evolved, is far more than an absence of disease. Many professions are involved in the promotion of health in addition to medicine. The spectrum includes social work, clinical psychology, pharmacology and sports. It is this broad spectrum of contributors that gives substance to the WHO definition.

## Disease

The pivotal concept in clinical medicine is disease. It is this that medicine strives to prevent, diagnose, treat and ameliorate. Any one of these activities promotes some aspect of health to some degree but the underlying goal focuses on disease. Moreover, on the surface disease seems more objective than disability and health. This, however, is illusory; disease is as value-laden as disability and health, although some philosophers have aspired to prove objectivity.

*Dorland's Medical Dictionary* defines "disease" as "any deviation from or interruption of the normal structure or function of a part, organ, or system of the body as manifested by characteristic symptoms and signs; the aetiology [causes], pathology, and prognosis may be known or unknown". It defines "illness" as "disease". Here again the word "normal" is invoked. In addition, there is a two-part test. Disease is a deviation from or interruption of the *normal* structure *or* a deviation from or interruption of the *normal* function. Recall the definition of primary myopia declares growth of the structure is normal but it is silent on the question of function. Hence, we now have another concept – "function". Since the concept "normal" is emerging as central to understanding the meaning of "disease", "illness" and "disability", a few initial observations are in order. Later we will expand these observations. Then we will examine the concept "function".

The definition of normal might seem obvious but, in fact, it is far from obvious. It could mean determined by genes or it could mean has long been present in humans or it could mean what is expected or it could mean a statistical average – the norm in a population; there are more candidates but these arise frequently and are sufficient to demonstrate the complexity. For each, counterexamples can be given. Consider "normal" = "unexpected". Cystic fibrosis is genetically based. Hence, both its likely occurrence and incidence rate can be predicted based on specific genetic knowledge. Moreover, its incidence rate in the EU is 1 in 2,500, making it reasonably prevalent. Consequently, it is not an unexpected phenomenon. Nonetheless, intuitively, cystic fibrosis seems to be a disease even though it is an expected phenomenon. Cleft palate also has a long history and is also not unexpected. One might be tempted to view cystic fibrosis as a deviation from the *normal* growth of a *healthy* lung, but this begs the question because "*normal*" has been smuggled in. So, an appeal to the concept "normal" has plunged us into epistemologically deep water.

Perhaps we can reach shallower water by defining normal as a statistical norm. That is, the average (mean) of the population with respect to some medical condition. If normal is the statistical mean, most people will be abnormal. Hence, we need to be more generous and consider as normal all those that are, say, one standard deviation $(\sigma)$[5] above or below the mean (average). As Figure 2.1 shows, in a large population that range will encompass 68% of the population. This seems promising; it is more mathematical and, hence, less subjective. Alas, this also is an illusion.

First, setting the range of "normal" is arbitrary and, hence, subjective. Why one standard deviation above and below the mean? Why not one-half a standard deviation or one-and-a-half? Second, using one standard deviation above and below the mean designates about 32% of the population as abnormal for any specific characteristic; that seems too high. But "seems" is also entirely subjective. Third, the value of using a statistical "norm" in setting an upper and lower boundary for some physiological characteristic, such as blood pressure, might provide a guideline about a potential for future disease (stroke, for example). It is, however, disease that we are trying define. Therefore, it is unhelpful if we need to know what is a disease (such as stroke) in order to know when something is a disease and set boundaries to guide decisions. Fourth, from an evolutionary biological perspective, the entire distribution of a characteristic is normal; it's just the way things are. Variability is essential to evolutionary dynamics. The statistical mean for a characteristic in one environment will differ from the statistical mean in another and it will change over time.

It turns out that a statistically based concept of normal presupposes knowledge of the definition of disease, which is the very concept it was supposed

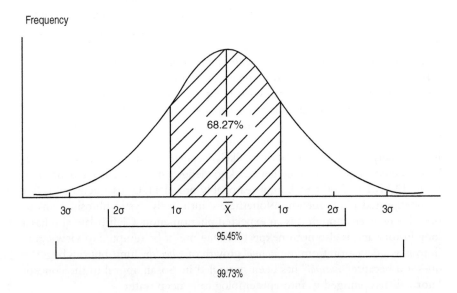

*Figure 2.1* A normal (Gaussian) distribution. The tails – above and below $3\sigma$ – are very rare traits (135 organisms per 100,000) ($\sigma$, known as a standard).

to be assisting us in defining. Moreover, it does not align well with what is biologically normal. Hence, the statistical concept of normal is an inadequate foundation for defining disease.

Perhaps a slightly different concept of normal might fare better. A prime candidate is "normal functioning". It cannot be completely separated from the statistically normal but it does change the focus. How things are supposed to function becomes the focus. Body temperature is a good way to ease into understanding this concept. If someone has a body temperature of 42°C (107.6°F), something is not functioning properly. Although the rise in temperature – to a dangerous level – might be a proper functioning of some of the systems of the body, it signals that something, somewhere is not functioning as it should. It might be that a virus or bacterium has interfered with the proper functioning of cells or that an organ is malfunctioning and so on. A normal functioning body should have a temperature between 36.1°C (97°F) to 37.2°C (99°F), with some minor variation outside that range. Age, activity and time of day affect temperature; also, where the reading is taken (mouth, anus, armpit or ear) will give different results even though the actual body temperature is, in each case, the same. Nonetheless, temperature seems about as objective as something gets. Looking more closely, however, it has a feature that is instructive. Temperature, unlike most physiological functions, is an indicator. In some rare cases, temperature regulation may be malfunctioning but in most cases of a temperature outside the "normal" range, the change is due to some other system malfunctioning. As a result, contrary to first impressions, it is not a robust example of normal functioning or abnormal functioning since it is just a symptom and not the malfunctioning itself.

Another example will illustrate how complicated "normal functioning" is. In iodine-deficient environments, the thyroid enlarges producing what is call goitre (goiter in the US). The thyroid produces a hormone called thyroxin. The production of thyroxin is regulated by thyroid-stimulating hormone (TSH) produced by the pituitary gland. When the level of thyroxin in the blood drops, the pituitary gland produces TSH. TSH signals the thyroid to produce more thyroxin. As the level of thyroxin rises, the TSH level declines. Iodine is a precursor element in the production of thyroxin. If it is absent the thyroid cannot manufacture thyroxin. The pituitary gland detects a low level of thyroxin and releases TSH. The thyroid is thwarted in its attempt to produce thyroxin even though it is constantly stimulated to do so. In response, the thyroid enlarges to attempt to meet the demand for thyroxin production. The result is a goitre. This illustrates a system that is functioning normally but its proper functioning leads to an undesirable outcome. There is no malfunctioning of the system. There is simply an insufficient supply of a needed element – iodine.

Notice that the most that can be said is that the outcome is undesirable. In most cases goitres produce only cosmetic disfigurement. Morbidity or mortality result from the impact of the enlargement on surrounding tissues (the trachea, larynx, superior and inferior laryngeal nerves and esophagus). They appear to increase the probability of thyroid cancer. Hyperthyroidism or hypothyroidism can also be a cause of morbidly and mortality. The system is working as it has evolved to work but in a specific environment it results in a goitre. From a biological point of view, there is no abnormality. From a personal and medical point of view, a goitre is a bad thing.

That is, almost everyone values a normal-size thyroid. That is a value judgement. Consequently, abnormal functioning is an unsatisfactory concept in defining disease and usually a value judgement lurks somewhere in the designation.

One of the most exhaustive and ingenious attempts to provide examples and analyses in pursuit of an objective definition of "health" and "disease" was undertaken by Christopher Boorse in 1977. He provided an update, and overview of the debates since that paper, in 2011.[6] Let's see where his analysis takes us. Boorse focuses on "function", specifically "normal function". He attempts to escape a purely statistical interpretation of normal function, where normal is the mean for the population or one standard deviation above and below the mean, by employing evolutionary thinking. Hence, the normal function of a cell, organ, physiological system or whole organism means functioning in the way it *evolved* to function. Disease is a deviation from this evolved normal function.

This does avoid a statistical interpretation of normal but it is less clear that it yields an objective definition of disease. Evolutionary theory and evolutionary dynamics are complex. Moreover, all biological concepts of evolution assume that it is purposeless. That is, evolutionary processes were not "aiming" at any specific "end-point", such as humans; humans are an accidental outcome of the process. A few changes at any point in the process – environmental differences, predator–prey interactions, for example – would very likely have led to a different present-day array of life. Humans are not the inevitable consequence of evolution. As a result, there is no evolutionary normal. Things are what they are, but could have been different. If the evolutionary process were started again, the probability of humans is reasonably low. Consequently, from an evolutionary point of view, the current normal function of human cells, organs, systems and whole organisms is an accident of nature, and not in any metaphysical or epistemological sense cosmically normal. Boorse's view, therefore, must rest solely on the actual evolved functions. Is this enough to provide objectivity?

The answer will depend on how faithful to evolutionary dynamics one wants to be. Consider a familiar example from biology and medicine. Alleles (Mendel's factors) occur in pairs at locations (loci) along chromosomes. Sometimes, there are many alleles that could form pairs at a particular locus; sometimes there are just one or two. When there is only one allele, the pair at that locus is always the same. Consider a locus with a single allele $A$. Then all organisms will have $AA$ at that locus. If there are two alleles, say $A$ and $S$, there are three unique combinations $AA$, $AS$ (same as $SA$) and $SS$.

There is a condition known as sickle-cell anaemia. The cause is now well understood. Haemoglobin is found in red blood cells and it absorbs oxygen when red blood cells circulate through the lungs; the oxygen is transported throughout the body and released into cells. When a person has a low red blood cell count, there is also a low haemoglobin count and insufficient oxygen reaches the cells. This is a classic instance of anaemia. In the case of sickle-cell anaemia, it is not a low red cell count *per se* that is the cause; it is abnormal red blood cells. Specifically, red blood cells with compromised haemoglobin. This, of course, means that "functioning" red blood cells are few in number. Hence, in a sense, the red cell count is low. The direct molecular cause at the cell-level is the haemoglobin protein. At the sixth position in the protein string of hae-moglobin, the amino acid valine occurs where glutamic acid would occur in normal haemoglobin. This is the result of a single mutation in the haemoglobin gene (nucleotide sequence that codes for haemoglobin). Where, in the normal nucleotide sequence, the nucleotide that codes for adenine occurs in the rel-evant codon (GAG), in the mutant form, thymine occurs (GTG). Although this is a small difference in the gene, and in the protein (haemoglobin) for which it is the code, it results in a different amino acid association that misshapes the molecule, which interferes with its oxygen-carrying ability. The complete molecular story is complicated and requires knowledge of biochemistry. This sketch is a sufficient characterisation for the purposes at hand.

The significant features of the story occur at the population genetic level. The gene for haemoglobin is on chromosome 11. There are over 100 alter-nate alleles for the specific locus but most are very rare, and essentially there are three common ones in West Africa: $Hb\beta^A$, $Hb\beta^C$ and $Hb\beta^S$. It is common to use the designation *A*, *C*, *S*, where *S* is the sickle-cell allele. A three-allele system yields six unique pairs: *AA*, *AC*, *AS*, *CC*, *CS* and *SS*. *AA* produces normal haemoglobin. *SS* produces sickled haemoglobin. Other things being equal, the mutant (*SS*) would be selected against and disappear from the population. But in certain parts of the world (Africa in particular), other things are not equal.

Malaria is caused by a parasite (*Plasmodium falciparum* is the most common of the five species of *Plasmodium* that cause malaria). Mild sickling of the red blood cells confers some immunity from malaria. The heterozygote *AS* gets mild sickling and is less susceptible to malaria and, if infected, the symptoms are mild. *CC* also has milder sickling than *AS*. *AC* has little to no sickling but is susceptible to malaria. The fitness of each pair can be estimated; these estimates can be compared with observed rates. The fit between estimates and observa-tion is robust. Table 2.1 gives the fitness of each pair.

*CC* has the highest fitness but if, as mutations usually do, it emerges as a low proportion of the three alleles, it will remain low because *A* and S dominate over it (*A* also dominates over *S*). Since *C* remains proportionally low, the major pairs are *AA*, *AS* and *SS*. In malaria-endemic areas of Africa, *AA* and *SS* are less fit than *AS*. Hence, in each generation, the *AS* will have higher reproduc-tive success than *AA* and *SS*. When *AS* breeds with *AS*, on average in a large randomly mating population, 25% of offspring will be *AA*, 25% will be *SS* and 50% will be *AS*. In that generation, selection will eliminate many *AA*s (malaria) and many *SS* (sickle-cell anaemia). Hence, the breeding population will be composed mostly of *AS* and this will continue in all subsequent generations. As

*Table 2.1* Fitness of each of the six genotypes. Since *CS* and *SS* lead to death from anaemia, susceptibility to malaria (as a cause of death) is not relevant.

| Genotype | Fitness | Susceptible to malaria | Sickling of red blood cells |
|---|---|---|---|
| AA | 0.9 | YES | NO |
| AC | 0.9 | YES | NO |
| AS | 1 | NO | MILD |
| CC | >1.2 | NO | MILD |
| CS | 0.7 | N.A. | MAJOR (anaemia) |
| SS | 0.2 | N.A. | SEVERE (severe anaemia) |

a result, *AS* will always be the highest proportion and that guarantees that *S* will be highly represented in each generation and *SS*, on average will be present in 25% of each generation.

Three things emerge from this example. First, normal functioning from an evolutionary perspective is context-dependent (mostly, environmentally dependent, as in this case). Second, some conditions that would normally be deemed "disease" – sickle-cell anaemia – are necessary for an evolutionary advantage. Because of the genetic dynamics, on average, 25% of the population will manifest sickle-cell anaemia. That is the price of 50% of the population having enhanced fitness. Without the sickle-cell allele, all the individuals would be susceptible to malaria and fewer would reach reproductive age or be able to rear what offspring they did produce. It would be somewhat incongruous, from an evolutionary perspective, to call a condition that is necessary for enhanced survival a disease. Third, evolution is a process. Boore's use of it to operationalise "normal function" seems to require a static (temporal slice) view of evolution. The way things have currently evolved to function to enhance survival is the norm. The whole point about an evolutionary perspective, however, is that things will change and there is no reason to believe that today's normal will persist into the future. The sickle-cell evolutionary process is a case in point. At some point 3,000 to 6,000 generations ago (70,000 to 150,000 years ago), the sickle-cell allele emerged separately in different geographic locations.[7] Hence, at one point in time this allele did not exist and "normal" would be non-sickled haemoglobin and susceptibility to malaria. At some point later, "normal" would be partially sickled haemoglobin, with the necessity of some individuals with sickle-cell anaemia and some with malaria. On average, 50% of the population would have neither. Normal usage would suggest malaria is a disease and that sickle-cell anaemia is a disease but from an evolutionary perspective these terms are inapplicable. They are a human imposition on the non-teleological (purposeless) and completely mechanistic process of evolution. This suggests that human values are still lurking in the background.

Whether Boorse and others can recast the evolutionary concept of normal functioning to address these points is yet to be seen. We are sceptical but it is not our goal in this chapter to resolve the controversy over disease as value-laden versus objective. Here we have pointed out some of the complexities and have made some observations about the various positions.

Drawing the threads of this issue together, superficially health and disease seem the inverse of each other. Health is the absence of disease and disease is the absence of health. The concept of health, however, has expanded in the last 60 or so years. It now encompasses physical, mental, emotional and social aspects. Disease has remained, more or less, specific to physical and mental challenges. Some emotional aspects have found a place but very few social aspects. Disease is a central concept in medicine. It is what medicine tries to prevent, what it diagnoses, what it treats, and for what it provides rehabilitation and palliation.

Challenges to mental, emotional and social aspects of a healthy state are nearly always value-laden. Whether the deviation from some concept of health requires intervention depends on personal and social evaluations. Physical disease seems, again superficially, to be value-free but, as we have seen, this is far from a settled question. Perhaps, at this point, the best we can do is to adopt a contextual and pragmatic definition of disease.

## Notes

1 See: *Dorland's Illustrated Medical Dictionary* – one of the most widely used medical dictionaries.
2 What counts as a disability has become exceptionally important, socially and legally, in many countries, especially Anglo-European countries. Hence, *Dorland's* also cites the United States' operational definition; inability to engage in any substantial gainful activity by reason of any medically determinable physical or mental impairment which can be expected to last or has lasted for a continuous period of not less than 12 months".
3 No particular view about what intelligence means is assumed. The claim relies only on the high correlation between scores on what are called IQ tests and ability to succeed in an Anglo-European school system (regardless of what is actually being measured). Those who score below one standard deviation below the mean have a high probability of not functioning *normally* in school and, hence, a high probability of not functioning *normally* in the technology-oriented Anglo-European workforce, where unskilled labour is less and less needed, except perhaps seasonally in agriculture.
4 Anglo-European = all the countries of Europe and most countries in which English is the principal language: United States, Canada (although officially bilingual – French and English – outside of Quebec, English is dominant), New Zealand, Australia and, of course, Great Britain. English is widely spoken in a number of sub-Saharan African countries but isn't the dominant language.
5 A standard deviation is a statistical measure of variation from the mean $\bar{x}$. The mean is calculated by adding together all the values (quantities) in a sample (height of females over 30 in Edinburgh, for example) and dividing that sum by the number of things in the sample (number of females over 30 in Edinburgh, for example). The standard deviation is calculated by subtracting each value from the mean, squaring the result, adding together those squared numbers and taking the square root of the sum.
6 Boorse 2011.
7 See Desai and Dhanani 2003.

# 3   Theories and models in medicine

As indicated in the introduction, medicine can be divided into two broad categories: bench medicine (genetics, immunology, haematology, biochemistry and physiology, for example) and clinical medicine (epidemiology, cardiology, urology and neurology, for example). This chapter focuses on a significant feature of bench medicine: the creation and use of models and theories. Here, we give an overview of the structure of models and theories and the roles they play in science generally and bench medicine specifically.

There are three different accounts of how scientific theories are structured and used: the syntactic account, the semantic account and, more recently, the pragmatic account. The pragmatic account is still evolving. The other two accounts have a longer history: the syntactic account about 100 years and the semantic account about 60 years. In this book, we adopt the semantic account, following the views of the one of the authors (Thompson 1986, 1987, 1989 and 2007). We describe each account beginning with a brief overview of the pragmatic account. Later in the chapter, we give some examples from bench medicine.

Early advocates of the pragmatic account concentrated on explicating the structure and role of models. Nancy Cartwright (1983) was an early and influential expounder of the pragmatic view of models. Her position emphasises model pluralism and model practices. In her view, the laws that theories encompass are frequently not true and are epistemically weak. Her emphasis was on models; these are the engine of science. Cartwright's model pluralism can be viewed as an external pluralism about how models are used. Others explored the internal pluralism of models – the pluralism of components of models. Morgan and Morrison (1999),[1] for example, claim that building a model requires "fitting together . . . bits which come from disparate sources" (p. 15). What is used is decided on pragmatic grounds. It could involve theoretical ideas, policy views, mathematisations, metaphors and empirical facts (see Boumans 1999).

In the last decade or so, there has been a growing interest in the pragmatic account of theories. Margaret Morrison (2007) and others have argued that a pragmatic view of theories is important and the emphasis on models has distracted attention from developing a pragmatic account of theories. She writes:

> Partly as a result of the semantic view of theories and responses to it, a good deal of attention has been paid to the role of models in scientific practice.

In fact, the semantic view of theories is, in most of its guises, not about theories at all, but about models, because the former are defined solely in terms of the latter.

...

However, I believe that the time has come to bring theory back into the picture and attempt a reconstruction of the relation between models and theories that emphasizes a distinct role for each.

This emerging interest in theories signals a maturing of the pragmatic account. Pluralistic and pragmatic stances nearly always stand as a corrective orientation to a more rigid stance and this appears to be a strength of this account of models and theories.[2] For the most part, the pragmatic account grew out of the emphasis on models embedded in the semantic account. Not surprisingly, therefore, pragmatic accounts and semantic accounts share a number of features and motivations.

Turning now to the other two accounts, we note the two accounts are connected. In principle, a specific scientific theory characterised on the syntactic account can be converted to a semantic account, and vice versa; the reasons for choosing one over the other are pragmatic. As Paul Thompson (1986, 1987, 1989 and 2007) and others (see Lloyd 1988, Suppe 1977 and 1989) have argued, the semantic account mirrors better actual theorising in biology and medicine. Hence, pragmatically, it is the preferable account of these two. The semantic account is the one assumed in the rest of this book. We start, however, with the syntactic account since it is older, was influential for more than half of the twentieth century and allows a number of features of theories to be explained, on a first pass, more easily. A key initial observation is that mature scientific theories are formalised mathematically.[3] Darwin's theory might appear to be an exception since there is not a single mathematical equation in *On the Origin of Species*. The modifier "mature" was chosen deliberately. Darwinian evolution was not mature in the requisite sense until around 1930, after a decade of work by J.B.S Haldane, Sewall Wright and Ronald A. Fisher. Their work mathematised the theory and, by so doing, resolved many post-*Origin* debates (see Thompson 2014 and 2015).

The syntactic account considers theories to be axiomatic-deductive structures. In that respect, it is structured in the same way as most of the domains of mathematics. The standard example of a scientific theory, for advocates of this view, is Newton's mechanics. Newton succeeded in formulating some very general regularities (laws) from which all other regularities could be derived. A regularity is a statement about the causal connections between (or among) events. Newton identified four very general regularities; these are the axioms of his theory:

1   All bodies remain in uniform rectilinear (straight-line) motion or rest unless acted upon by an external unbalanced force.
2   Force equals mass times acceleration: $f = ma$.

3  For every action, there is an equal and opposite reaction.
4  There is a force of gravitational attraction between bodies equal to the product of their masses divided by the distance between them squared: $f_g = (m_1 \times m_2)/(d_1 - d_2)^2$.

From these, every other regularity, in principle, can be deduced: Galileo's law of free fall[4] ($d = \frac{1}{2}gt^2$) and the movement of billiard balls on a billiard table are examples. Axioms are the most general statements about how things behave. Their only justification is that the less general statements that are deduced from them are consistent with the observed behaviour of things in the world. Theories, understood this way, integrate a large body of knowledge and, as a result, provide robust explanations and predictions of the behaviour of things.

As Figure 3.1 portrays, many generalisations (regularities) in a theory, including the axioms, are abstract; they do not refer to specific entities in the world.

A large number of abstract regularities can be deduced from the axioms. In turn, a large number of other abstract regularities can be deduced from these abstract regularities, other than the axioms. These regularities are interconnected creating a web in which all the regularities are connected – directly or indirectly to each other. (see Quine and Ullian 1978). Empirical regularities in this schema are not abstract; they refer to entities in the world and the behaviour of those entities. For example, if this billiard cue strikes the white ball with this force at this location on the ball, it will move in this direction with this speed. This states a regularity, which can be used to explain or predict the observed behaviour of things in the world. Explaining empirical regularities involves references to abstract regularities, sometimes including the axioms. Ultimately, all regularities are explained by reference to the axioms but most of the time abstract regularities far down the deductive chain from the axioms are sufficient to explain empirical regularities and, hence, empirical phenomena. Explanation involves citing an empirical regularity, asserting that the antecedent has occurred and concluding that the consequence, as observed, occurred.

1  If this billiard cue strikes the white ball with this force at this location on the ball, it will move in this direction with this speed (an empirical regularity).
2  This billiard cue struck the white ball with this force at this location on the ball (the causal action occurred).
3  Hence, the ball, as observed, moved in this direction with this speed (the effect occurred).

This explanatory pattern is known as the hypothetico-deductive (H-D) model of explanation[5] (see Hempel and Oppenheim 1948, Hempel 1965 and 1966). We will return to this pattern of reasoning in Chapter 6 on causality and induction.

This exposition is obviously a simplification; nonetheless, it will serve our purposes. On this view of theories, all phenomena, empirical regularities and

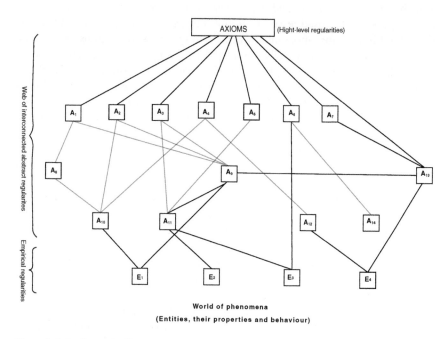

*Figure 3.1* A schematic-illustrative portrayal of the deductively interconnected web of regularities: from axioms to the world.

non-axiom abstract regularities can, in principle, be *deduced* from the *axioms*.
Hence, the label "axiomatic-deductive".

Three different mainstream views on how the axioms are discovered have
been articulated and defended. One view is firmly empiricist; the process begins
with experience. Simple regularities ($E_1, E_2, \ldots E_n$ in Figure 3.1) are discovered
from experience; if I release my wallet from my hand, it will fall to the ground,
for example. Examination of a large collection of these reveals that sets of them
can be deduced from more general regularities (a set of $A_i$ in Figure 3.1). That
is, a set of empirical regularities can be subsumed by a single abstract generalisation. Examination of these abstract generalisations reveals that sets of them
can be subsumed by more abstract generalisations (set of $A_j$ in Figure 3.1). This
continues all the way up to the most general statements of all – the axioms, at
which point the process of constructing the theory ends. The extreme opposite
of this is rationalism, which holds that one invents, using reason, the axioms and
then examines what can be deduced from them. This deductive exploration is
how the theory is constructed. The test of the validity of the theory is whether
the way things in the world behave matches what can be deduced from the theory. That is, whether they explain the behaviour of actual things. If not, reason
devises another set of axioms. The third view is a middle position; the axioms
come into focus, through reason, but only after a certain body of knowledge is

available from observation and experimentation. Newton is an example of the middle position. He used reason to figure out just why things behaved the way they did. He did not laboriously work his way up to the axioms. Instead, he took what had been empirically discovered and using reason constructed some general laws (axioms) that explained the behaviours of entities in the world.

The robustness of a theory, on all three accounts of theory structure (pragmatic, syntactical and semantic), comes from its integration of knowledge into a single interconnected framework and the accuracy of the deductions of regularities about the way things in the world behave. A single discovery obtained by observation or experimentation remains just that, single (and, hence, isolated), until it is integrated into a theory. Once there is a theory that includes it (i.e. has it as a deductive consequence of the axioms), it has the support of the entire system. Deductions from a theory about how things in the world behave can be empirically tested (by observation or experimentation). The more times a deduction from the theory corresponds to how things in the world behave, the more reasonable an acceptance of the theory becomes. Each successful empirical test further strengthens the theory, which, in turn, strengthens every component of it. This is because the additional successful tests make it more likely (more probable) that the axioms are correct. Since every other regularity encompassed by the theory is deduced from the axioms, each one of those regularities are made more probable. There is still no certainty but every already accepted regularity is nonetheless more probable. Schematically, this is:

1   New regularity is deduced from the axioms.
2   It is tested.
3   The test demonstrates that things in the world behave as predicted.
4   The probability that the axioms are true is increased.
5   Therefore, the probability of the truth of every other element of the theory is increased, since they are all deducible from axioms that are now more probable.

This point about theories is exceptionally important because confidence in a regularity that stands alone is vastly weaker than one embedded in a comprehensive well-confirmed theory, a point that will be important, and that we will emphasise, when we turn to an examination of methods and knowledge in clinical medicine.

On the syntactic account of theories, theories are formulated (expressed) using mathematical logic (specifically, first-order predicate logic with identity). This is the *grammar* of theories in the same way that English is the grammar in which we have expressed the ideas in this book. All languages have a *grammar* (a syntax) and *meaning structure* (a semantics). Mathematical logic provides the syntax (the grammar) for scientific theories on the syntactic account. For example:

$$(x)(W_x \supset H_x)$$

which is read: for anything $x$, if $x$ is a $W$ then $x$ is an $H$. This in mathematical logic is a well-formed expression,[6] just as "I walked to the store" is a well-formed sentence in English; "I stored to the walk" is ungrammatical and, hence, not well-formed. One difference is that the English sentence also has meaning because a reader knows what "I" is, what "walking" is and what a "store" is, as well as knowing what "to the" means. The mathematical logical formula doesn't "mean" anything. It doesn't specify what M means or what *H* means or what $\supset$ means. The mathematical formula can be given meaning; doing so consists in giving a semantics (an interpretation, a meaning structure) to the syntactical formulation. If $W$ = woman, $H$ = human and $\supset$ = if–then, the formula reads, "for anything (any object), if that object is a woman that object is human". Now, there is a syntax and a semantics. Hence, the syntactical account has two components: a set of mathematical formulas and an interpretation of those formulas. In the early years of the development of this view, logical empiricists – the designation of those who adopted the logical empiricist framework – thought that rules they called correspondence rules could be used to provide the interpretation.

Correspondence rules were bi-lateral reduction sentences. "Fragile", for example, could be interpreted as:

An object $X$ is fragile [*F*], if and only if when it is struck with force $S$ it breaks [*B*].

Symbolically:

$$(x)(y)(F_x \equiv H_y \cdot (S_{yx} \supset B_x)$$

For any $x$ and for any $y$, $x$ is fragile if and only if $y$ is a hammer and (if $x$ is struck by $y$ then $x$ breaks).

Many difficulties with this method of providing an interpretation were exposed. One significant problem was the open-ended number of correspondence rules that could be generated to interpret a single concept. For example:

An object $X$ is fragile [*F*], if and only if when it is dropped from three meters (or five meters or eight meters) above a tiled floor [*T*] it breaks [*B*].

Hence, any single correspondence rule only gives a partial interpretation. A complete interpretation, however, requires an almost inexhaustible number of correspondence rules.

Toward the end of the domination of this account, a method of providing the semantics was developed by Alfred Tarski. It involved using models; this became known as model-theoretic semantics. Once Tarski and others had developed ideas about models providing the semantics for the syntax of scientific theories, it occurred to some philosophers, and mathematicians, that all that was needed to express a scientific theory was its semantics; models were enough.

This was the point at which the semantic account of theories was developed. The semantics, and, hence, the theory was expressed using the specification of class of models that instantiated the theory; that is, that exemplified its application to phenomena. The essential elements of this account are the specification of the entities assumed to exist, the properties of those entities (the ontology) and how the collection of entities changes over time (the dynamics of the system); this is a model.

Gregor Mendel's model[7] of heredity (Mendel 1865) is an easy to describe, although profound, example. Mendel's experiments focused on hybridisation. Hybridisation occurs when two organisms, in most cases of the same species, with a different trait (characteristic) are interbred. Mendel had noticed that some of the offspring had one of the traits and others had the other trait. In some organisms, a modified trait emerged. Mendel correctly assumed that the best method for understanding hybridisation was a study of organisms where the traits were preserved but differently distributed in the offspring. He chose pea plants for his experiments. What he observed can be displayed graphically (see Figure 3.2).

He did the same experiments observing different traits of the pea plants:

1   Yellow vs. orange peas (seen through the transparent seed coats)
2   Seed coats white vs. grey, grey-brown, leather brown
3   Smooth or wrinkled ripe seed pods
4   Green vs. yellow unripe seed pods
5   Axial or terminal flowers
6   Long vs. short stems (he chose 6–7 feet and 0.75–1.5 feet).

In each case, he found the same pattern. Mendel then constructed a theory (a model) to explain these results. The core of the theory is elementary but far-reaching in its scope and implications. He assumed there were some entities he called "factors" (today we call them alleles, sometimes informally they are called genes). A key property of these factors was dominance. Some factors dominated over others; round dominated over wrinkled, for example. These factors occur in pairs in somatic cells of the organism. In the gametes (sperm and egg, for example) they occur alone.

Mendel did not know about chromosomes or about the two different processes of cell replication: mitosis and meiosis. Today, cells of the body are called somatic cells. They reproduce by mitosis. Gametes are the sex cells (germ cells). They are different in kind from somatic cells. They reproduce by meiosis. When somatic cells reproduce, the resulting cells have matched chromosomes. When gametes reproduce, the resulting cells have only one chromosome of each matched pair. Mendel knew that there are many matched pairs of factors in somatic cells. He experimented with seven different traits, each of which was the result of a distinct matched pair.[8]

Mendel claimed that the factors segregated when sex cells were produced (his law of segregation); this segregation was independent (his law of independent

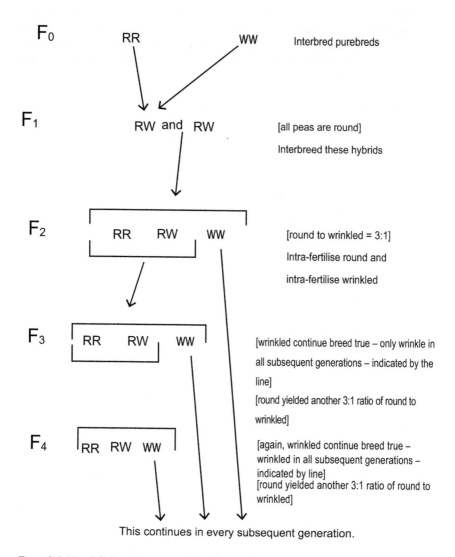

$F_0$   RR          WW          Interbred purebreds

$F_1$      RW and  RW          [all peas are round]

Interbreed these hybrids

$F_2$      RR    RW    WW       [round to wrinkled = 3:1]

Intra-fertilise round and

intra-fertilise wrinkled

$F_3$    RR    RW    WW        [wrinkled continue breed true – only wrinkle in

all subsequent generations – indicated by the

line]

[round yielded another 3:1 ratio of round to

wrinkled]

$F_4$   RR  RW  WW             [again, wrinkled continue breed true –
wrinkled in all subsequent generations –
indicated by line]
[round yielded another 3:1 ratio of round to
wrinkled]

This continues in every subsequent generation.

*Figure 3.2* Mendel's breeding pattern. Looking at the right-hand side illustrates that Mendel always observed the wrinkled pea characteristic when wrinkled pea-plants were bred with wrinkled pea-plants. Looking at the left-hand side illustrates that he observed the 3:1 ratio when round pea-plants were bred with round pea-plants.

assortment). That is, there was no pattern, mechanism or algorithm determining which factor ended up in which sex cell. During fertilisation, two sex cells combined and a new pair of factors was created. What trait an offspring inherited was a function of the pair of factors. Two Rs resulted in a round pea. Two Ws resulted in a wrinkled pea. The combination of one R and one W resulted in a round pea because R dominates over W. Hence, in a large population, one can expect that when two hybrids (WR or RW) are bred, the resulting combinations will be RR, RW, WR and WW. Since RW and WR will both produce round peas because of dominance, there will be three round pea plants for each wrinkled pea plant.

Mendel's model postulates entities: factors and cells. One property of his factors is dominance. A property of cells is that they come in two kinds: somatic cells and gametes. Another property of factors is that they are paired in somatic cells and single in gametes. What has become known as his two laws are transformation functions; they describe how a system will behave over time. A third transformation function is required: recombination in somatic cells. Mendel's theory was mathematical. He constructed an abstract mathematical model, which predicted the ratio of the factors in each generation after the first. This abstract mathematical model was based on his postulated entities, their properties and the dynamics of the system (see Table 3.1).

The absolutely important thing to note is that *what this mathematical description generates for each generation is exactly what Mendel observed*. It is this fact that validates his theory.

This might on first glance not seem to be a very complex theory. On first glance, however, Newton's theory, with only three laws of motion and a law of gravitation attraction, doesn't seem very complex; the implications of his axioms, however, are profound and far-reaching. They integrate a vast body of knowledge. The same is true of Mendel's theory. He has postulated entities with properties and provided a description of the dynamics of the system to which the entities belong – a description of the laws that govern their behaviour over time. This is all that is needed and the semantic account captures that point.

A few more details are in order. There are two different modelling approaches that philosophers have developed for characterising theories on the semantic

*Table 3.1* A display of the mathematically based generational sequence that an assumption of a 1:2:1 ratio (each plant is assumed to produce 4 seeds per generation). This is the mathematical model, which Mendel generated based on his postulated entities, their properties and the dynamics of the system. His experimental results confirmed his model. His experiments were carefully controlled; in nature, things are more messy and the observed outcomes, "on average", conform to what his model predicts."

| Generation | Seed outcome | | | Ratios | | |
|---|---|---|---|---|---|---|
| | $A$ | $Aa$ | $a$ | $A$ | $Aa$ | $a$ |
| 1 | 1 | 2 | 1 | 1 | 2 | 1 |
| 2 | 6 | 4 | 6 | 3 | 2 | 3 |
| 3 | 28 | 8 | 28 | 7 | 2 | 7 |
| 4 | 120 | 16 | 120 | 15 | 2 | 15 |
| 5 | 496 | 32 | 496 | 31 | 2 | 31 |
| $n$ | | | | $2^n - 1$ | 2 | $2^n - 1$ |

4 from A

2 from Aa :2 plants, 4 seeds from each, = 8 seeds in 1:2:1 ratio = 2 AA : 4 Aa : 2 aa

account. One account uses set theory; the other uses state spaces or phase spaces. The latter is easier to understand. This is in part because it does not require knowledge of set theory and in part because it can be represented graphically. Mendel's factors – today alleles, the term we will use henceforth – occur in pairs at specific locations (loci) on chromosomes. There can be more than two alleles capable of combining at any locus. If there are three alleles (*a, b, c*), the possible unique combinations will be *aa, ab, ac, bb, bc* and *cc*. There are actually nine combinations but *ab* is the same in effect as *ba*, and *bc* is the same as *cb*, and *ac* is the same as *ca*. Add a fourth allele and there are four more possible unique combinations at that locus. The important magnitude (metric or measure) is the proportion of each allele in each generation. For simplicity of exposition, explanations usually begin with a single locus, two-allele system, which is what we will do. The proportion of *a* to *b* might be 0.3 to 0.7. This can be graphed (see Figure 3.3).

Of course, things become more complicated when there are more alleles at the locus and even more complicated when more loci are added. Those complexities make an actual graphical representation difficult but the concept of a space within which the system at a specific time can be located is the same. Then laws of transformation must be specified. These specify how the system can change over time. In this case, there are two key classes of laws of transformation. The first specifies changes before reproduction, such as changes in the proportion of alleles due to one aspect of natural selection: deaths from predation, for example. The other specifies how the system changes through reproduction. The fitness of an organism determines reproductive success – another aspect of natural selection. Sexual selection – mate attraction and selection – belongs in this class of laws. We have constructed a theoretical model. If what the model predicts will happen over time matches observation and experimental results the theory is partially confirmed. Each successful prediction confers greater confirmation.

The set-theoretical account expresses the axioms of the theory, as the name suggests, set-theoretically. A glimpse of a theory formalised in this way will suffice. Staying with Mendel's theory and its descendent, population genetics, this is how the axioms can be formalised using set theory (see Thompson 1989):

*T*: A system $\beta$ = <*P, A, f, g*> is a Mendelian breeding system if and only if (iff) the following axioms are satisfied:

Axiom 1: The sets *P* and *A* are finite and non-empty.
Axiom 2: For any *a* ∈ *P* and *l, m* ∈ *A*, *f*(*a, l*) & *f*(*a, m*) iff *l* = *m*.
Axiom 3: For any *a, b,* ∈ *P* and *I* ∈ *A*, *g*(*a, I*) & *g*(*b, I*) iff *a* = *b*.
Axiom 4: For any *a, b* ∈ *P* and *l* ∈ *L* such that *f*(*a, l*) and *f*(*b, l*), *g*(*a, l*) is independent of *g*(*b, l*).
Axiom 5: For any *a, b* ∈ *P* and *l, m* ∈ *L* such that *f*(*a, l*) and *f*(*b, m*), *g*(*a, l*) is independent of *g*(*b, m*).

Where *T* = theory, *P* and *A* are sets, and *f* and *g* are functions. *P* is the set of all alleles *a* in the population, *A* is the set of all loci *l* in the population. If *a* ∈ *P* and *I* ∈ *A*, then *f*(*a, l*) is an assignment, in a diploid phase of a cell, of *a* to *I* (i.e. *f* is a

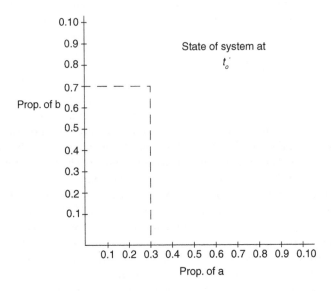

*Figure 3.3* A graphic display of a phase space for a two-allele, single-locus system.

function that assigns *a* as an alternative allele at locus *l*). If *a* ∈ *P*, and *I* ∈ *A*, then *g(a, I)* is the gamete formed, by meiosis, with *a* being at *I* in the gamete (the haploid phase of the cell). Although more sophistication could be introduced into this example (to take account, for example, of meiotic drive, selection, linkage, crossing over, etc.), the example as it stands illustrates adequately the nature of a set-theoretical approach to the formalisation of population genetic theory in its simple Mendelian system form.

An additional strength of the semantic account is its conception of the way a theory relates to the world. The theory, as we have seen in the Mendel example, is an abstract mathematical structure. Relating to the world requires a demonstration that the mathematical model is isomorphic to the world. That is, it has the same (iso) form (morphic) as the world. Mendel's model was somewhat easy to compare to his experimental results. In many cases, demonstrating an isomorphism requires other theories or conceptual tools. Sometimes, the data from experimentation has to be interpreted in order to render it comparable to the way it is formulated in the theory; a theory of data is required. Sometimes, reference to another scientific theory is required. To compare data obtained by microscopy with a model requires an appeal to a theory of optics (in the case of a light microscope) or atomic theory (for an electron microscope). Staining tissues for examination requires employment of the relevant part of chemistry, the part related to chemical changes that result from the chemical interaction of the stain and the chemicals of the cells. The strength of the semantic account is that it is explicit about the complexity of relating a theory to phenomena. Later we will discuss an observation made by the physicist Pierre Duhem and the philosopher/logician Willard van Orman Quine. They are both explicit about the complex nature of the relationship between theories and the world (something the semantic account captures well), and about how that complexity renders any simple confirmation or rejection of a theory, based on observations or experiments, impossible.

With this background, we can turn to medical examples, which we will formulate using the semantic account as our guide. The first example is a sub-theoretical one. That is, it is a component of a larger theory: endocrinology. The example is the menstrual cycle. Its compactness allows a clear exposition of this way of characterising theories. The second example is a full-fledged theory, immunology.

The menstrual cycle is not restricted to humans but medical science has provided the most in-depth and physiologically embedded advances in understanding the cycle in humans and other organisms – its hormonal, biochemical, physiological and evolutionary dynamics. Cycles that are more or less coincident with the day (circadian), the month (circalunar) and the year (circannual) began to be studied vigorously in the 1960s. Indeed, it is appropriate to date its inception at 1960, when the Cold Spring Harbor Symposium on circadian rhythms was held (published in 1961; see Cold Spring Harbor Laboratory 1961).

Any standard textbook on internal medicine, physiology or endocrinology will contain a description of the dynamics of the menstrual cycle. For those interested in a medical textbook account, Harrison's *Principles of Internal Medicine* (Braunwald et al. 2001) provides a clear and succinct account. The normal menstrual cycle is an activator–inhibitor system with a feedback complex. The cycle is divided into two phases: a follicular phase and a luteal phase. The cycle – the onset of one menstrual bleed to the onset of the next – is 28 days ± 3. A normal bleeding period is 4 days ± 2.

The entities of this system are chemicals (e.g. gonadotropins, ovarian steroids and many others as described below), cells (e.g. granulosa lutein cells, theca lutein cells) and organs (e.g. the hypothalamus, the pituitary, the ovaries). The key chemicals are:

- Progesterone: as its name suggests, it acts principally to prepare the uterus for a zygote (fertilised ovum), implantation and gestation. It is a 21-carbon steroid secreted by the corpus luteum.
- Androgens: a variety of 19-carbon steroids synthesised in the ovaries. The major one is androstenedione, of which some portion of the production is converted to oestrogen in the granulosa cells and testosterone in the interstitium.
- Oestrogen: a steroid produced by developing follicles in the ovaries as well as the corpus luteum, the placenta and, although of less importance in menstruating women, other organs. Both follicle-stimulating hormone (FSH) and luteinising hormone (LH) stimulate the production of oestrogen. Oestrogens are synthesised in the theca cells in the ovaries. Estradiol is the major oestrogen in humans.

- Follicle stimulating hormone (FSH) and lutenising hormone (LH): glycoprotein hormones synthesised in the gonadotropic cells of the anterior pituitary.
- Inhibin: a hormone secreted by the dominant (maturing) follicle. It inhibits the release of follicle stimulating hormone (FSH) by the hypothalamic-pituitary complex.
- Gonadotropin-releasing hormone (GnRH): a hormone that regulates the synthesis and secretion of FSH and LH.

These are the principal chemicals. Braunwald et al. (2001) describe the mechanism in this way:

> At the end of a cycle plasma levels of estrogen and progesterone fall, and circulating levels of FSH increase. Under the influence of FSH, follicular recruitment results in development of the follicle that will be dominant during the next cycle.
>
> After the onset of menses, follicular development continues, but FSH levels decrease. Approximately 8–10 days prior to the midcycle LH surge, plasma estradiol levels begin to rise as the result of estradiol formation in the granulosa cells of the dominant follicle. During the second half of the follicular phase, LH levels also begin to rise (owing to positive feedback). Just before ovulation, estradiol secretion reaches a peak and then falls. Immediately thereafter, a further rise in the plasma level of LH mediates the final maturation of the follicle, followed by a follicular rupture and ovulation 16–23 hours after the LH peak. The rise in LH is accompanied by a smaller increase in the level of plasma FSH, the physiological significance of which is unclear. The plasma progesterone level also begins to rise just prior to midcycle and facilitates the positive feedback action of estradiol on LH secretion.
>
> At the onset of the luteal phase, plasma gonadotropins decrease and plasma progesterone increases. A secondary rise in estrogen causes a further gonadotropine suppression. Near the end of the luteal phase, progesterone and estrogen levels fall, and FSH levels begin to rise to initiate the development of the next follicle. . . .
>
> (p. 2,157)

The process is a feedback and activation–inhibition cycle. Braunwald et al. (2001) also set it out this way:

> The secretion of FSH and LH is fundamentally under negative feedback control by ovarian steroids (particularly estradiol) and by inhibin (which selectively suppresses FSH), but the response of gonadotropins to different levels of estradiol varies. FSH secretion is inhibited progressively as estrogen levels increase – typical negative feedback. In contrast LH secretion is suppressed maximally by sustained low levels of estrogen and is enhanced by a rising level of estradiol – positive feedback. Feedback of estrogen involves both the hypothalamus and pituitary. Negative feedback suppresses GnRH and inhibits gonadotropin production. Positive feedback is associated with

an increased frequency of GnRH secretion and enhanced pituitary sensitivity to GNRH.

(p. 2,157)

The mathematics involved in modelling this system are complicated.[9] What follows is about as elementary an account as possible; those who find even this challenging – as many will – should just give the mathematical details a glance and concentrate on the focal point described after Figures 3.4 to 3.7; a strategy we recommend using in other places in the book where the technical details are designed to enhance understanding but for some are challenging. As already indicated earlier, the entities in this system (the ontology) are chemicals, cells and organs. Biochemistry, cell biology and physiology underpin the nature of these entities. Specifying the dynamics of the system involves rate equations:

$$dx/dt = f1(x, y)$$
$$dy/dt = f2(x, y)$$

where $x$ and $y$ are chemicals in interaction and the rate equations describe their continual rise and fall. In a two-dimensional phase plane $xy$, the nullclines[10] for $x$ and $y$ will be:

$$f1(x, y) = 0$$
$$f2(x, y) = 0$$

The steady state $(x, y)$ is the intersection point of the curves.

Differentiating these equations with respect to x yields the slope of the nullcline $f1 = 0$ at some point $P$, and the slope of the nullcline $f2 = 0$ at some point $P$. It is the point of intersection of these two nullclines that defines the steady state in the phase space. In a couple of deductive steps one can derive four partial derivatives evaluated at $(x, y)$. These can be arranged in a Jacobian[11] square matrix.[12] Since, in most cases in the menstrual cycle the chemicals have pairwise interactions, the interactions can be modelled as a two-chemical system. Hence, the sign patterns of the partial derivatives in the Jacobian can be specified as in Figure 3.4, 3.5 and 3.6.

$$+ \begin{pmatrix} - \\ - \end{pmatrix} \quad J1 = \quad + \quad -$$

*Figure 3.4* Activator–inhibitor system.

This pattern of signs indicates that chemical 1 has a positive effect (an activation effect) on its own synthesis and that of chemical 2; whereas, chemical 2 has a negative effect (an inhibitory effect) on its own synthesis and that of chemical 1. Using the same meaning of the matrix of signs:

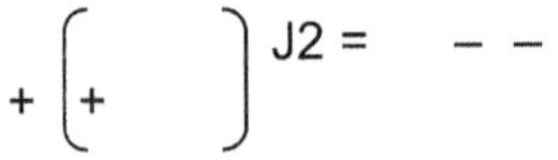

$$\left( \begin{matrix} & \\ + & + \end{matrix} \right) \; J2 = \quad - \; -$$

*Figure 3.5* Positive feedback system.

Graphically, the positive feedback system is represented in an *xy* phase plane as in Figure 3.7.

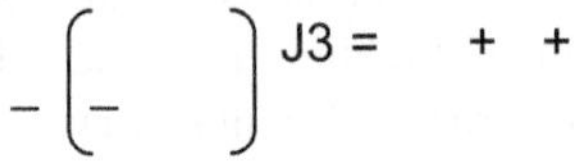

$$\left( \begin{matrix} & \\ - & - \end{matrix} \right) \; J3 = \quad + \; +$$

*Figure 3.6* Negative feedback system.

This modelling allows a clear understanding of the steady state of the system as well as the rates of change driven by the interaction of the chemicals. It also makes possible predictions about how external interventions will affect the behaviour of the system (for example, a prediction about what will happen if plasma levels of oestrogen and progesterone at specific points in the process are artificially increased by a human external intervention such as taking birth control pills). As a result, this mathematical model of the menstrual cycle has enabled a significant refinement of the dosage and timing of external interventions to alter oestrogen and progesterone levels during the menstrual cycle to achieve control of ovulation.

Now for an example from immunology. This is a fascinating field of study and advances in our knowledge have grown dramatically over the last 50 years, as did the integration of that knowledge using a theoretical model. Like Newtonian mechanics, immunology is complex and its explanatory and predictive power rich. Nonetheless, its core, again like Newtonian mechanics, is compact. Newton's theory has four axioms from which everything else, in principle, is deducible.

One basic set of entities of the immune system is cells. The fundamental cells are hematopoietic stem cells (also called progenitor or precursor cells). These are found in bone marrow. They give rise through transformation processes to an array of other entities. Red blood cells and platelets, the other major solid components found in blood, also arise in bone marrow but immunology focuses on the white blood cells that arise from hematopoietic stem cells in bone marrow. There are two kinds of hematopoietic stem cells: myeloid and common lymphoid. All the other cells of the immune system arise from these. Hence, the two fundamental entities of the immune system are myeloid and common lymphoid progenitor cells. Although a population-level formalisation can be constructed, it loses medical specificity. Hence, this theory is best characterised as person specific. The relevant metric is the number of progenitor cells of the two types that exist in the bone marrow of an individual. This will differ from person to person.

With these two basic entities, we can state the transformation laws. These specify the next state of the system. Common lymphoid progenitors give rise

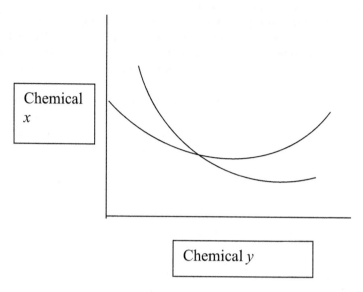

*Figure 3.7* An *xy* phase plane illustrating feedback.

to B–cells and T–cells. B–cells mature in the bone marrow. T–cells have an additional transformation. They migrate to the thymus and mature there. Myeloid progenitors give rise to a number of leukocytes: basophil, eosinophil, neutrophil and monocyte. There is another unknown precursor that, along with monocytes, gives rise to mast cells and macrophages but that is a second transformation step. At this point we have a system with progenitor entities and some laws of transformation that lead to the creation of other entities. This is the beginning of the dynamics. The cells to which the two progenitors give rise circulate in the blood stream and the lymphatic system and circulate between them.

There is another class of entities: antigens. An antigen is any material foreign to the system (the individual's body). Antigens can be cells, proteins, organisms (bacteria and parasites) or viruses. At this point, we can lump them together under the label "foreign material", even though the response of the immune system does depend, as we will see, on the features of the antigen. In a fully functioning immune-response system, abnormal cells produced by one's own body (cancer cells, for example) are an antigen. The metric is the number of antigens.

The system as described so far is in a holding pattern. The state space has a determinable (measurable) number of the entities identified above. This holding pattern is essentially an equilibrium state of the system. Most theories have an equilibrium state. For Newton's mechanics, it is expressed by his first law: every body remains in a state of rest of uniform rectilinear (straight-line) motion unless acted upon by an external unbalanced force. For game theory, it is a Nash equilibrium. For evolution, it is the Hardy–Weinberg law. The latter states that the proportion of alleles in the population will remain constant unless something happens, such as natural selection. Natural selection changes the trajectory of the system and alters the proportion of alleles. Antigens change the dynamics of the immune system and move it out of its equilibrium.

The introduction of an antigen causes the system to change over time in a number of new ways. These changes can be formalized as additional transformation laws. These laws are different from those that specify how the system will change in a more-or-less steady state. That is, where the relevant cells are created and die in a cyclical pattern. These additional laws specify how the system will change when an immune response is activated by the presence of an antigen. Let's look at trajectories in the state space, one when the antigen is a bacterium. Other immune responses to the variety of other antigens (viruses and proteins, for example, that mosquitoes, bees and wasps inject) are variations on these two themes.

Antigens are ingested by macrophages and B-cells (both are kinds of white blood cell, also known as leukocytes). These in the equilibrium state have been circulating in the blood and lymphatic system. They can be considered as patrolling the body for foreign material. This ingesting process is triggered by helper T-cells (another leukocyte), which bind to the sites on the antigen known as epitotes and start secreting lymphokines. Lymphokines (interleukins) cause B-cells to do two things: (1) create antibodies against the antigen (up to 2,000 antibody molecules per second!) and (2) create memory B-cells, which last for ages and will start making antibodies *en masse* next time they encounter the same antigen. This is the basis for immunity against the antigen. There are also two kinds of T-cells: helper T-cells and cytotoxic T-cells (the latter make proteins that are toxic to specific antigen cells). Memory T-cells (both helper T and cytotoxic T) are also generated. Again, this an immunity mechanism; the next time the antigen appears, many active helper T and cytotoxic T-cells will be generated quickly. Lymphokines also signal cytotoxic T-cells to attack any cells, protein and so on that display the antigen.

There are many more processes but this is sufficient to illustrate the transformation laws that describe the changes in the system over time when its equilibrium state is disturbed by the presence of an antigen. There is a quantity of antigen factor, sometimes referred to as the titre (the amount of a substance needed to produce a reaction). The immune system will deal with low titre levels of an antigen without any indication of infection. Above a certain titre level, clinical systems will appear (minor or severe). The symptoms will abate once the immune system has cleared the blood and lymphatic system of the antigen. This is the norm. There are, of course, cases where the immune system is overwhelmed. This may be because the quantity of the antigen is too large or the system is fooled, such as autoimmune responses where the immune system begins to attack its own host system because normal cells of the body are seen as antigens.

With some simplifications, we have characterised immunological theory as having three fundamental entities: cells, proteins and antigens. There are two different kinds of transformation laws – laws that describe how the system changes over time. The first are transformations that hold the system in an equilibrium. Hematopoietic stem cells duplicate and die in the bone marrow and they give rise to a number of other cells that circulate in the blood stream and lymphatic system. These die and are replaced. The other set of transformation laws specify how the system behaves (changes over time) when the system is disturbed by the presence of antigens. This is a rich and robust theory with incredible explanatory and predictive power.

The above examples indicate the important role that theories and models have in bench medicine. This it shares with most other domains of the natural sciences. Studying and explicating the structure and roles of theories and models in science are a fundamental part of philosophy of science and of the, now long-standing, applications of the analysis to specific disciplines such as physics and biology. Hence, it is not surprising to find that this is a feature of philosophy of medicine. For clarity, it is worth restating that bench medicine differs in this and other respects from clinical medicine, despite the interconnection of the two domains. Bench medicine seldom refers to or uses randomised controlled trials; clinical medicine makes extensive use of them. Bench medicine is a thoroughly theoretical domain, using models and theories extensively; theories and models are used sparsely in clinical medicine. In Chapter 7, we will indicate the root difference that underpins these differences. Essentially, bench medicine seeks to develop an integrated understanding of systems (interacting entities in a causal network), as the example above illustrates; clinical medicine, by contrast, is largely focused on discovering associations of individual events isolated from a system (that is, its focus is on a specific intervention and its outcome). Sometimes an association is causal and that can be demonstrated but determining causality without a model or theory is elusive. Research is on this intervention in this context; it is particulate. Meta-studies examine multiple individual researches on the same intervention and the same range of outcomes. This is still particulate in that meta-studies are focused on an intervention and its outcomes.

As explained in this chapter, theories integrate a large number of particulate pieces of knowledge, strengthening each through their interconnections. The absence of this in clinical medicine makes that domain more like a social science in methods. Whether or not it is a social science is an interesting philosophical question. Chapters 7 and 8, and to some extent 9, suggest that its methods and applications of knowledge are more akin to a social science. A more interesting question, we think, is whether this is its most appropriate modus operandi? Again, Chapters 7 and 8, by highlighting the conceptual challenges that clinical research and practice face, suggest that some parts of clinical medicine are not well served by the social science model. Chapter 10, on the other hand, highlights aspects of clinical practice that benefit enormously from being deeply social and interpersonal.

## Notes

1   See also Chang 2011.
2   Those interested in a more comprehensive exposition and defence of this account will find Morrison (2000) and Winther (2016) useful entry points.
3   Technically, the syntactic account is meta-mathematical but it is formalised using mathematical logic and, hence, employs mathematics.
4   That is, the distance an object, in a vacuum, has fallen is equal to one half the force of gravitational attraction times the time it has been falling squared.
5   There are many variants of this model of explanation. Most prominently is a probabilistic variant. The empirical regularity cited is a probabilistic one. For a historically significant critique see Bromberger (1966).
6   Called a well-formed formula (wwf).
7   As with many technical terms, "model" is used differently in different contexts. Here, we consider a comprehensive model to be the same as a theory. Smaller models of simple processes – as in the case of Bolie's glucose–insulin model – are very useful but do not have the scope of theory. "Model" as used in the semantic account of theories considers theories to be complex models. On that account theories are model-theoretic entities. For simplicity, we consider a theory to be a positing of entities and a set of equations that describe the behaviour of those entities. The more comprehensive the framework of equations and the scope of the phenomena they cover, the more it is appropriate to call it a theory.
8   He did separate and combined experiments on seven traits: form of seed (pea), colour of seed, colour of seed coat, form of pod, colour of unripe pod, flower position and stem length.
9   Those with a strong mathematical background should consult Edelstein-Keshet 1988 or Murray 2002.
10  The x-nullcline is a set of points in the phase plane such that $dx/dt = 0$, and the y-nullcline is a set of points in the phase plane such that $dy/dt = 0$.
11  A Jacobian determinant (or Jacobian for short) is named after the Prussian mathematician Carl Gustav Jacobi (1804–1851). A Jacobian is a matrix of partial derivatives.
12  The signs for the partial derivatives in this Jacobian are determined by the mutual effects that interacting chemicals have on each other.

# 4  Materialism and reductionism in science and medicine

Materialism is the view that all that exists is matter. Hence, all explanations of the characteristics and behaviour of things must only cite other matter and its behaviour. All scientists must adopt a materialist stance – even if in their personal lives they have religious views. Science is the quest for materialist explanations. The moment one says, "it's a mystery" or "the hand of God explains this", the scientific quest is over. One thing we have learned from history is that many of the explanations of phenomena that assumed something beyond the material world have turned out to be wrong. Hence, the quest within science must be to keep seeking a materialist explanation. Perhaps there are some phenomena for which the explanation is beyond the material world but science must always assume that the quest for a material explanation is its goal.

That is a heuristic acceptance of materialism; an acceptance of it as a *tool or principle* serving to aid learning, discovery or problem-solving by observation and experiments. There need be no commitment to it beyond the scientific domain. A complete materialist, on the other hand, accepts materialism as a reality and not as a necessary heuristic for doing science. For her, there is only matter and its properties. No mystical, spiritual or other immaterial realm exists and nor do any mystical, spiritual or other immaterial entities exist.

All that really matters in a scientific context is that a materialist stance is essential. Just what does that stance entail? Until the turn of the twentieth century, materialism and determinism went hand in hand. Determinism is usually captured in the expression, "same cause, same effect". If *exactly* the same causal factors are duplicated, the exact same effect will occur. Quantum mechanics, which is entirely materialistic but, on the most widely held interpretation, is not deterministic, ruptured the connection between materialism and determinism.[1] That case aside, for most of science, a commitment to materialism is also a commitment to determinism.

There are two connected but different kinds of reductionism. One is ontological (or entity) reductionism; the other is theory reductionism. Ontological reductionism is the view that every level of phenomena has its causal explanation at a lower level. All the properties of a dining room table are explainable in terms of its molecular structure. Its molecular structure is explainable in terms of the properties of elementary chemicals and the interaction of those chemicals. In turn, the molecules that make up the table and their interaction are explainable in terms of fundamental elements that constitute the molecules. Wood, for example, is mainly composed of cellulose, several hemicelluloses and lignin. The percentages vary slightly depending on the species. By far the highest percentage is cellulose (around 40–45%). Cellulose is composed of the fundamental elements hydrogen, oxygen and carbon (see Figure 4.1).

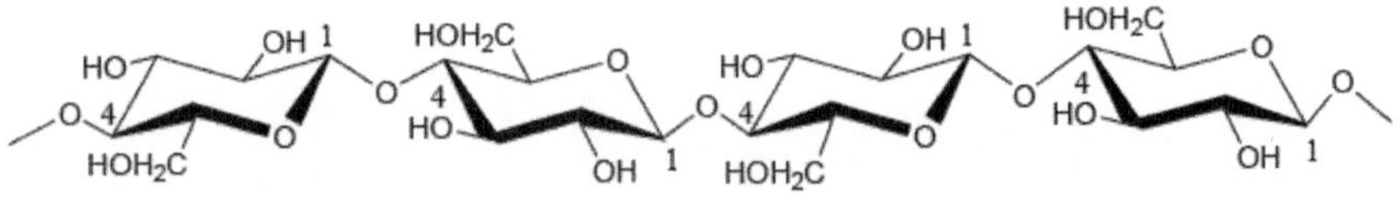

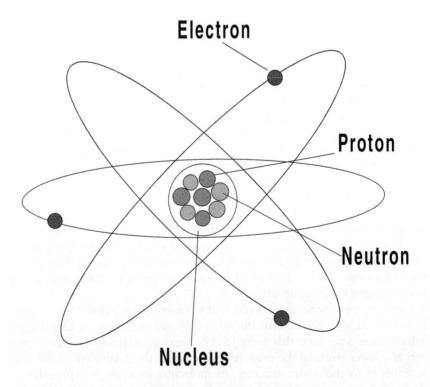

*Figure 4.1* An illustration of a molecular structure – cellulose – with repeating configurations of atoms.

The chemical formula is $(C_6H_{10}O_5)_n$, where $n$ designates repeating chains. These fundamental elements (atoms) are composed of electrons, neutrons and protons. The nucleus of an atom is composed of protons and neutrons. The electrons orbit the nucleus (see Figure 4.2).

*Figure 4.2* A diagram of an atom, composed of electrons, protons and neutrons. Different atoms will have a different number and combination of these particles.

There are additional fundamental particles that are the building blocks of the universe. According to the standard model, the most fundamental particles are fermions and bosons. Electrons, protons and neutrons are fermions, as are quarks and a few others. Gluons and photons are bosons, as is the famous Higgs boson. What we have described is the reduction of a wooden table – its composition and properties – to lower and lower levels. Ultimately, the composition and properties of a wooden table are explained in terms of fermions and bosons.

This is an example of entity reduction (or ontological reduction). Most of science is deeply reductionist in this sense and much of the success of science has resulted from a commitment to this kind of reductionism. From time to time philosophers and scientists have argued for an anti-reductionist view known as *holism*. Many attempts have involved appeal to non-material causes or processes. But there are physicalist-materialistic examples of the explanatory and heuristic value of holism. One such example is Barbara McClintock's work on maize.

By the 1930s, reductionist science had led to the view that genes were fundamental and that the phenotype (adult whole organism) was the result of genes. Hence, the phenotype was explainable in terms of a lower level – genes. McClintock was awarded her PhD in Botany from Cornell University in 1927. She worked on *Zea mays* (maize in most of the world, corn in North America). She viewed the whole organism and the various parts as equal partners and not as levels underlying other levels, as in a reductionist view. Her research led to transposable genes (so-called jumping genes). The mechanism requires that each part of the whole – the lower-level parts making up the whole – function in part autonomously and in part as an element in the whole. That is, the whole has a determining role in the functioning of the part and the part has a role in determining the functioning of the whole. There are no parts (as in the case of atoms) that determine the whole (as in the case of molecules). Wholes and parts are in a feedback system. Her work has spawned more than a half-century of philosophical and theoretical research on ideas like self-organising systems and self-regulating systems. Her work also had a transformative effect on cytogenetics – a field whose origin she helped establish. In 1983, she was awarded the Nobel Prize in Physiology or Medicine for her work on cytogenetics and transposable genes.

In biology today, it is recognised that sometimes a reductionist approach yields important results and sometimes a holistic approach yields important results. Medicine's close relationship with biology might lead one to expect that medicine would embrace the same pluralism. Superficially, this seems to be the case. The importance of negative and positive feedback systems is an example but this is more appearance than reality.

We have already discussed two such systems, one in Chapter 2 and another in Chapter 3. Both are reductionist. There are a number of hormones and a number of ways one or more of them increase or decrease the presence of others. The processes and hormones all occur at a specific level of analysis. In one of these cases, the resulting physiological condition is a goitre. In the other, the physiological outcome is ovulation. In the first case, the goitre has no effect on the hormonal cycle; it is a consequence and in no sense a cause. Similarly, in the second, ovulation, the maturation of an ovum and its release and travel down a fallopian tube has no effect on the hormonal cascade; it is a consequence and in no sense a cause. A truly holistic explanation requires that the whole affects the behaviour of the parts and vice versa.

One case that comes close is the effect that a mental process has on a physical process. Once the physical process occurs – raising one's arm for example – there will be feedback to the mental. This, however, is complicated. First, simplistically, there are two different entities that are interacting. Moreover, whether these have a parts-and-wholes relationship is not at all clear. As we will see in Chapter 11, mental processes may not have a separate reality. They in some way are completely dependent on brain processes. In that case, the feedback is not between parts and wholes (or consequences and causes) but between parts – brain and muscles, in our example. This is, in effect, another instance of the kind of feedback in the hormonal systems we have explored.

It appears that medicine explains the structure and properties of entities in terms of microstructures. The explanations are not as straightforward as the wooden table example of reductionism. Nonetheless, reductionism is widespread. Properties of the brain, for example, are explained in terms of neurons, synapses, neurotransmitters and so on – the micro-components of the brain – and the ways these behave. The behaviour of the components at this level is explained in terms of the cellular structure of neurons and the electrical and chemical transfer from cell to cell. Although this is very complex, it is still a multi-level framework. Each level is explained in terms of the components and their properties at a lower level.

What makes thinking about reduction in medicine difficult is that keeping wholes and their parts separate is challenging. At one point, the brain is a whole but at the next level of analysis a neuron becomes a whole, and then nerve cells are the whole, and so on. Then proteins (structural and functional), which were parts at the level of nerve cells, become the wholes and they are explained in terms of amino acids and the specific folding conformation of specific proteins. Amino acids are chemicals. Now we are at the level reached in the wooden table example when we arrived at its molecular structure.

There, of course, are other reduction pathways from the brain. The genetic pathway is another important one. Once at the level of nerve cells, this pathway looks at the DNA and chromosomal determinants of structural and functional proteins. That takes us to the level of protein transcription and translation. This occurs at the DNA molecular level. This does, ultimately, take us to the chemical level – the chemical structure and behaviour of nucleotides and phosphate sugar chains. Below this are again atoms and then sub-atomic particles. A different narrative of reduction but it is entity (ontological) reduction all the same.

The other kind of reduction is theory reduction. In this case, one theory is reduced to a more comprehensive theory. One example is the relationship between population genetics (Mendel's genetics), which focuses on chromosomes and entities (alleles) which are combined at locations on a chromosome, and molecular genetics, which focuses on DNA. There is still an element of a higher level of analysis being reduced to a lower level of analysis. Chromosome-level analysis is being reduced to molecules. That is why it is appropriate to call it reduction. But this is different in a number of ways.

First, this attempts a reduction of one explanatory framework to another explanatory framework, again at a micro-level. Second, all the laws of the reduced theory have to be deducible from the laws of the reducing theory. Third, all the entities in the reduced theory have to be related to entities in the reducing theory. That is, all the entities in the reduced theory must be definable in terms of one or more entities in the reducing theory. For example, genes in the population/chromosome theory (population genetics and quantitative genetics) must be related to entities in the molecular theory – sequences of nucleotides, for instance. These are exceptionally onerous requirements and there are no clear examples of this kind of reduction. There is a presumption (or intuition) that population genetics is underpinned by molecular genetics but establishing the required links has proved elusive. Moreover, population genetics does explanatory work that cannot be provided by molecular genetics.

Consider larvae of the boll weevil and the corn borer. These are pests that can ruin a cotton crop or a corn crop. Since the 1950s, farmers have used a variety of pesticides. One that has the lowest environmental impact is a toxin produced by *Bacillus thuringiensis* (*Bt*). It is a bacterium that occurs naturally. Farmers – including organic farmers – have been spraying crops with either the bacterium or the toxin it produces for more than 60 years. For almost 20 years, a biotechnological solution has been developed. The segment of DNA that codes for the toxin produced by *Bt* has been inserted into the chromosomal DNA of cotton, corn and a number of other plants. Hence, each cell of the plant produces the toxin. As a result, the current exposure level of larvae pests to the toxin is exceptionally high. The concern, from the first regulatory approval of the genetically modified crops, has been the development of resistance to the toxin.

To avoid the development of resistance, several techniques have been employed. One involves more genetic modification. The crops produce other compounds toxic to the larvae. If *Bt* doesn't kill some small portion of the larvae – those with some natural resistance – the other compounds likely will kill them. This technique is known as "stacking". The other very important technique is to require all farmers using *Bt* crops to plant a "refuge" plot. The refuge plot is a non-genetically modified crop. This is where population genet-ics becomes involved. Population genetics predicts that the moths emerging from the very small number of naturally resistant larvae will breed with moths emerging from the very large number of larvae that have been in the refuge part of the field and, hence, not exposed to the *Bt* toxin. The resistance genes will, therefore, be swamped. All that needs to be determined is how large the refuge portion has to be. Again, population genetic models demonstrate that something around 10% is adequate. To have a margin of safety, farmers are required to plant a 20% regular crop. Modelling these factors cannot be done at the molecular level. Hence, population genetics provides predictions and explanations that cannot be provided – at least not currently and likely never – at the molecular level.

Medicine encompasses both population-level research and interventions, as well as molecular-level research and intervention. As with the *Bt* resistance example, in many cases both levels are involved. For example, in dealing with an infectious disease (e.g. Ebola), there are numerous population-level activities that are undertaken, from quarantine to issuing protective masks or clothing. There are also numerous models employed, such as the Reed–Frost model of the spread of the disease and population genetic models. There are also molecular activities. Attempts, for example, are made to identify the molecular structure of the infectious agent, and where possible develop methods for killing it or interrupting its lifecycle. This often involves the use of pharmaceuticals but can also involve changes in lifestyle – hand washing, avoiding known sites of contamination, for instance. Again, as in the case of the *Bt* example, there are explanations and predictions that can be made at the population level that cannot be made at the molecular level and vice versa.

We have indicated that entity reductionism is the default view in medicine. There are a number of philosophers and physicians who have challenged this commitment to reductionism – in medicine and in other sciences, especially biology. A leading advocate of holism (and rejection of reductionism) is Stuart Kauffman, who holds a BA in philosophy and an MD.. He, along with many of his colleagues at the Santa Fe Institute in California, maintains that living things are autocatalytic and self-organising. An organism is autocatalytic if it catalyses its own process. In effect, it controls its own activities. The processing speed of many chemical processes is enhanced by other chemicals called catalysts. Cells that are autocatalytic regulate their own catalysing of chemical processes. As a result, the processes of the cells, and also autocatalytic aggregations of cells, are self-regulating and must be studied as wholes. The whole is greater than the sum of its parts, and that additional "greater than" can only be understood by studying the whole.

Self-organisation is a bit more complicated. Living cells are capable of organising themselves and changing that organisation. Ilya Prigogine, a chemical physicist (1917–2003), was awarded the Francqui Prize in 1955, the Rumford Medal in 1976 and the Nobel Prize in Chemistry in 1977 for his work on far-from-equilibrium thermodynamic systems. Thermodynamic systems can be closed, which means external energy does not affect the system. These systems are in thermodynamic equilibrium and obey the second law of thermodynamics. That is, over time, the energy in the system equalises: the energy differential reduces to zero. A classic, although simplistic, example of the second law of thermodynamics is a piano. It has the structure it does because someone built it – putting energy into the system (the piano). If left for a few hundred years, it will fall apart. The energy differentials that held its structure in place will have diminished. There are also open thermodynamic systems. These systems capture energy. The earth is an example. The energy from the sun sustains life and other processes on the earth by providing energy that is absorbed by open systems.

A far-from-equilibrium system is one that absorbs a lot of energy and gives up a lot of energy. Hence, its energy state is always in flux. Cells, and many aggregations of cells, are far-from-equilibrium systems. Energy is always flowing in and out of them. What Prigogine discovered is that these systems organise themselves, which also means they can re-organise. This feature means that they have to be studied as wholes since how the parts interact depends on the organisation of the whole, which is independent of the parts. The research of Barbara McClintock's, described above, and her model of the molecular genetics of maize are a specific example of this.

This holistic view is a direct challenge to a reductionist position in medicine and biology. It has a significant impact in biology. Whether it will find a place within medicine and whether it will prove to be useful is yet to be seen. At this point, medicine seems deeply reductionist.

## Note

1 For an influential account of quantum mechanics as probabilistic but deterministic, see Nagel 1961 (Chapter 10).

# 5    Probability and randomness

Probability is an important element in clinical medicine, especially when research employs randomised clinical trials. Hence, some familiarity with it and the statistical techniques that are derived from it are important. For some, this will be a challenging chapter. The material, however, is central to understanding the methods of clinical research in medicine, decision-making in clinical settings and much of the material in this book, and philosophy of medicine generally. Hence, the investment of mental energy will be rewarded. The material, however, is reasonably elementary.

Probability theory is philosophically rich. Ian Hacking sets the stage in his book *The Emergence of Probability* (2006):

> We do not need to ask how some concept of probability became possible. Rather we need to understand a quite specific event that occurred around 1660: the emergence of our concept of probability. If there were Indian concepts of probability 200 years ago, they doubtless arose from a transformation quite different from the one we witness in European history. From a purely historical point of view, both transformations may be of equal interest. But for me the search for preconditions is more than an attempt at historical explanation. I am inclined to think that the preconditions for the emergence of our concept of probability determined the very nature of this intellectual object, 'probability', that we still recognise and employ and which, as philosophers, we still argue about. The preconditions for the emergence of probability determine the space of possible theories about probability. That means that they determine, in part, the space of possible interpretations of quantum mechanics, of statistical inference, and of inductive logic.
>
> (p. 9)

Four broad interpretations of the probability calculus[1] have been explicated over the last century: logical, frequency, subjective and propensity. Most of the writings on the interpretation of probability have focused on the difference between frequency and subjectivist interpretations. Since this is a critical mathematical underpinning of clinical research, we will look at all four.

## Logical interpretation

The logical interpretation is the least well understood outside mathematics and philosophy. Its fundamental tenet is that probability is a logical (mathematical) relation among propositions – nothing more. That is, it is a purely mathematical calculus – the same as linear algebra and various mathematical axiomatic geometries, a comparison to which we will return. The key observation is that on this interpretation the mathematical calculus does not contain any specification of its connection to the empirical world. This is one thing that distinguishes it from the other three.

The famous economist John Maynard Keynes, who was also an excellent mathematician, held this view and set it out in his 1921 book, *A Treatise on Probability*.[2] This interpretation considers probabilities to be expressions of degrees of rational belief. That is, given the same evidence, any rational person will have the same degree of belief in the conclusion. This is so because given the same evidence, the probability calculus will lead to the same conclusions and, hence, the same degree of belief.

Because this interpretation is the least familiar and the one towards which we lean, it is worth a slightly longer exposition. First, let's look at some of the claims John Maynard Keynes made. Then, we draw an analogy with geometry, using the history of geometry to draw out what is meant by, "The key observation is that on this interpretation the mathematical calculus does not contain any specification of its connection to the empirical world."

Keynes signals at the beginning that he is looking for a system with propositions and rules of inference, just like formal logic (mathematical logic) as developed by Russell and Whitehead in *Principia Mathematica*.

> Inasmuch as it is always assumed that we can sometimes judge directly that a conclusion follows from a premise, it is no great extension of this assumption to suppose that we can sometimes recognise that a conclusion *partially follows from*, or stands in a relation of probability to, a premise.
>
> (p. 52)

And again

> The Theory of Probability deals with the *relation* between two sets of propositions, such that, if the first set is known to be true, the second can be known with appropriate degree probability by argument from the first.
>
> (p. 123, emphasis added)

The link with formal logic is made even more explicit in this passage.

> In the development of my own thought, the following chapters have been of great importance [the chapters in his *Treatise* in which he sets out formal logic]. For it was through trying to prove the fundamental theorems of the subject on the hypothesis that probability was a *relation* that I first worked my way into the subject; and the rest of this Treatise has arisen out

of attempts to solve the successive questions to which the ambition to treat Probability as a branch of Formal Logic first gave rise.

(p. 115)

Although he recognises that frequencies play a role in probability, he quite explicitly rejects any theory of probability based on *statistical* frequency. That is, he rejects the frequency theories (discussed below) of John Venn, Karl Pearson, Jerzy Neyman, Fisher and others.

> In the meantime it is only possible to raise general objections to any theory of probability which seeks to found itself upon the conception of *statistical* frequency.
>
> The generalized frequency theory which I propose to put forward, as perhaps representative of what adherents of this doctrine have in mind, differs from Venn's in several important respects. In the first place, it does not regard probability as being *identical* with *statistical* frequency . . . It accepts the theory that *propositions* rather than *events* should be taken as the objects of probability.
>
> (pp. 100–101, emphasis on "statistical" added)

And again, in the following passage, he is clear that he is seeking an inferential and axiomatic theory (a term that will appear again when we examine the analogy with geometry), not a statistical theory.

> The object of this and the chapters immediately following is to show that all the usually assumed conclusions in the fundamental logic of inference and probability follow rigorously from a few axioms, in accordance with the fundamental conceptions expounded in Part I. This body of axioms and theorems corresponds, I think, to what logicians have termed the *Laws of Thought*, when they have meant by this something narrower than the whole system of formal truth. But it goes beyond what has been usual, in dealing at the same time with the laws of probable, as well as of necessary, inference.
>
> (p. 133)

These passages make it clear that Keynes thinks that probability is a logical relation – an inferential relation – among propositions.

Now for the analogy with geometry and lessons we can learn. Let's start with Euclid. The mathematician David Hilbert provided the currently widely accepted axiomatisation of Euclidean geometry. He specifies its axioms. All the other theorems of Euclidean geometry must, in principle, be deducible from these axioms. A few familiar axioms, both of his formalisation and of standard accounts of Euclid's axioms, are:

- Two distinct points *A* and *B* always completely define a straight line *a*.
- If *A*, *B* and *C* are points of a straight line and *B* lies between *A* and *C*, then *B* also lies between *C* and *A*.

- If $A$ and $C$ are two points of a straight line, then there exists at least one point $B$ lying between $A$ and $C$ and at least one point $D$ so situated that $C$ lies between $A$ and $D$.
- Of any of three points situated on a straight line, there is always one and only one that lies between the other two.
- The axiom of parallels: in a plane, there can be drawn through any point $A$, lying outside of a straight line $a$, one and only one straight line that does not intersect line $a$. This straight line is called parallel to $a$ through the given point $A$.

The last axiom had been part of Euclidean geometry ever since Euclid formulated his geometry but it was always contentious. There were attempts to show that it could be derived from the other axioms. In which case, it would not itself be an axiom. Those attempts failed but not because there was any proof that it was an axiom or that it was needed to deduce fundamental theorems. Rather, it was a difficult mathematical problem. It was not until the nineteenth century that a proof was found but it was not what mathematicians expected.

The technique that solved the puzzle was indirect proof (similar to *reductio ad absurdum* in philosophical logic). It is a powerful technique. One assumes the negation of an axiom or theorem and tries to deduce a contradiction. If the axiom of parallels (since it is now under dispute as an axiom, it is best to call it a postulate or theorem) is replaced by its negation and a contradiction can be derived, then the other axioms are sufficient for the geometry. That a contradiction can be deduced indicates that the other axioms allow the parallel line theorem to be deduced even if no actual deduction has been produced. The only way the negation of the parallel postulate could lead to a contradiction is if the parallel postulate itself is deducible from the other axioms. This is where things get interesting.

The more familiar statement of the parallel postulate is: given a line and point not lying on that line, one and only one new line can be drawn through the given point such that the two lines never cross when extended infinitely in both directions (i.e. they are parallel). This makes clear that there are two possible negations. If there is "one and only one new line", then one negation is that there are NO new lines that are parallel to the given line. The other negation is that there are *more lines than one* that can be parallel to the given line. Using the technique of indirect proof, a contradiction could not be deduced using either of these negations of the parallel postulate. Consequently, two new non-Euclidean geometries emerged. Nikolai Lobachevski and James Bolyai discovered the first of these independently in the 1820s. They assumed that more than one new line could be parallel to the given line. Stunningly, in 1902 Eugenio Beltrami proved that if Euclidean geometry is consistent then this non-Euclidean geometry is also consistent.

In the 1850s, Bernhard Riemann proved that a consistent geometry could be formulated that assumes that no new line parallel to a given line can be drawn. This is again a non-Euclidean geometry. Both of these non-Euclidean geometries can be given an interpretation in terms of a physical model. Euclidean geometry is the geometry of the surface of a two-dimensional plane (a flat sheet of paper is an example), which can be extended to three dimensions (two intersecting planes). The Lobachevski and Bolyai non-Euclidean geometry is the geometry of the surface of a hyperbola. Riemann's non-Euclidean geometry is the geometry of the surface of a sphere. On the surface of a sphere every line crosses every other line. Remember, a line (mathematically) is the shortest distance between two points. None of the lines of latitude on a globe of the earth, except the equator, is a line in this sense; all the lines of longitude are and they all meet at the north and south poles.

With the discovery of non-Euclidean geometries, it was possible to ask which geometry best characterised the space of the physical world. It was assumed until 1910–1914 that physical space was Euclidean, even though other geometries now existed. From 1910 to 1914, Einstein published his general theory of relativity. That physical theory, now orthodoxy in physics, holds that space is Riemannian. One point of this discourse on geometry is to explicate the distinction between a mathematical calculus and its application to the world. Hilbert, along with the vast majority of mathematicians and philosophers, was clear on this distinction.

> It [Hilbert's development of geometry] emphasized that the undefined terms in geometry should not be assumed to have any properties beyond those indicated in the axioms. The intuitive-empirical level of the older geometric views must be disregarded, and points, lines, and planes are to be understood merely as elements of certain given sets. . . . Similarly, the undefined relations are to be treated as abstractions indicating nothing more than a correspondence or mapping.
>
> (Boyer 1991, p. 609)

This is precisely the view of those advocating the logical interpretation of probability. The mathematical calculus is just that – a mathematical calculus. How, and in what ways, it applies to physical reality is a completely separate enterprise. Other interpretations of probability collapse this distinction, just as physicists did with geometry and physical space until the twentieth century. Post-Einstein, we should know better.

## Frequency interpretation

The most common interpretation of probability is the frequency interpretation. This is the interpretation that Ronald A. Fisher, Karl Pearson, Egon Pearson and Jerzy Neyman adopted. *This is the dominant interpretation in clinical medicine* (both research and practice). According to this interpretation, probability is the limiting frequency of similar events in the long run. Unlike the logical interpretation, probability is not an expression of relations among propositions but rather the likelihood of an outcome or a relation between events. The common example is the tossing of a fair coin (one with equal weighting of heads and tails). The claim is that *in the long run* heads will equal tails. In any short run (small number of tosses), all heads or all tails might occur. The probable outcome of tosses can be described using the binomial theorem. A thousand tosses is far from a long run. Nonetheless, at that point the binomial distribution converges on a Gaussian (normal) distribution. The mean of that distribution (500 heads and 500 tails) is the most probable. An outcome of all heads or conversely all tails is improbable but the probability is not 0.0. If a coin did turn up heads 1,000 times in a row, we would have to keep tossing it since it is the long-run frequency that is being claimed. Even after 10,000 heads, the only way, empirically, to be sure of the assumption is to keep tossing. John Maynard Keynes wrote in his 1923 *The Tract on Monetary Reform*:

> The long run is a misleading guide to current affairs. In the long run we are all dead. Economists set themselves too easy, too useless a task if in tempestuous seasons they can only tell us that when the storm is past the ocean is flat again.
>
> (p. 80)

He made this claim in the context of economics. It is worth noting that it has been frequently quoted out of context and in ways inconsistent with Keynes' own economic thinking. Recall that Keynes was also a mathematician who wrote a treatise on probability. His view about the long run in that treatise is the same, although he never uses this phrase. The long run is an ill-defined term and is too tidy an escape valve in the face of failure in a humanly meaningful time-frame.

The frequency interpretation does not separate the probability calculus from its application to the world. The calculus simply describes the way things behave in the world, or at least that is the assumption. This is similar to assuming that Euclidean geometry is simply a description of the way things are in the world. We now know that assumption is problematic. If, as was the case with Euclidean geometry prior to the nineteenth century, the frequency interpretation was the only interpretation, little would hang on the assumption. But, as we have already seen, there is a logical interpretation and, as we will describe soon, there is a subjectivist interpretation.

The best general formulation of the standard frequency theory is that of Richard Von Mises (*Probability, Statistics and Truth*, 1928). Von Mises formulated his theory using the concept of 'collectives': "A collective denotes a sequence of uniform events or processes which differ by certain observable attributes, say colours, numbers, or anything else" (p. 12[3]). For von Mises, there are two very different kinds of collectives: empirical collectives, which are finite, and mathematical collectives, which are infinite. Von Mises has two empirical laws of probability:

1   Law of increasing stability of statistical frequencies:

> It is essential for the theory of probability that experience has shown that in the game of dice, as in all other mass phenomena which we have

mentioned, the relative frequencies of certain attributes become more and more stable as the number of observations is increased.

(p. 12)

2    Law of randomness:

Genuine empirical collectives are disordered. Whatever sequence of outcomes of die rolling has occurred, the next one is indeterminate.

Randomness, for Von Mises (and for Fisher), is understood in terms of the failure of gambling systems:

> The authors of such systems [gambling systems] have all, sooner or later, had the sad experience of finding out that no such system is able to improve their chances of winning in the long run, i.e., to affect the relative frequencies with which different colours or numbers appear in a sequence selected from the total sequence of the game.

(p. 25)

Von Mises derives, by abstraction from these laws, three axioms to underpin his theory of probability. For example:

1)    The axiom of convergence:

Let A be an arbitrary attribute of a collective C, then $\lim n \rightarrow \infty m(A)/n$ exists.

The important axiom, in connection with randomised controlled trials, is the axiom of randomness. Von Mises was successful in generating appropriate axioms – including an axiom of randomness – but a problem arose post-Kolmogorov (post-1933). It can be shown that Kolmogorov's axioms are deducible in Von Mises mathematical theory (which underpins his *empirical* theory of probability). Importantly, however, they can be deduced without reference to the axiom of randomness. But the axiom of randomness, and the law of randomness that rests on it, is a key element in Von Mises' (and Fisher's) frequency theory. The upshot is that the universally accepted axioms of probability do not require an axiom of randomness. The remarkable character of this is well put by Donald Gillies:

> there is nothing in the Kolmogorov axioms corresponding to the axiom of randomness. This is certainly a strange situation. The axiom on which Von Mises [and Fisher] laid such stress does not seem to appear at all in the standard mathematical axiomatisation.

(p. 112)

For those who follow Fisherian reasoning with respect to justifying and grounding randomised controlled trials, this is a puzzle. Kolmogorov's axioms, and the probability calculus that flows from them, are best understood on the logical interpretation.

## Subjectivist interpretation

On the subjectivist interpretation, probability is an expression of an individual's degree of belief (strength of belief) in a proposition (a claim) about events, such as the likelihood of an event occurring under certain circumstances or of a causal connection between events. Different *rational* individuals will have different degrees of belief in a proposition even when it is based on the same body of evidence. This interpretation captures the intuition that different people will have different thresholds of evidence for belief in a proposition. Consider the case of the prostate-specific antigen test (PSA test).

Many physicians continue to use the test because they believe it provides an early warning of prostate cancer. It needs to be noted that only a subset of these physicians has studied the evidence; most base their confidence on medical digests and medical organisations' bulletins and recommendations. Most reviews of the evidence by experts suggest that the test does not decrease the likelihood of death from prostate cancer and the harms associated with the test exceed any benefit (more details are provided in Chapter 9).

Later in Chapter 8, we will look in some detail at the different ways data is expressed statistically. The one that is relevant here is "number to treat": that is, how many people need to be treated to have a desired outcome. A European study found that to prevent one case of prostate cancer 1,400 men would need to be screened, which would result in 48 men undergoing surgical and/or radiation treatment. Clearly, 47 men had unnecessary surgery and many experienced the harms just mentioned. For some time, the controversy continued despite this evidence. By 2011, considerable new evidence was available. A research team led by Dr. Roger Chou reviewed it. The team's review was published in December 2011 in *Annals of Internal Medicine*. The finding was that a PSA test is a blunt instrument and it produces more harm that benefit. The comments previously made are drawn from that review. The American Urological Association, with the same body of knowledge, responded quickly and negatively to the findings and recommendations of the review.

The subjectivist interpretation captures the dynamics of these differences. Probability expresses the degree of one's acceptance of a proposition based on a body of evidence. The frequency interpretation does not capture the dynamics of these differences. Probability is a function of frequency, not strength of belief. Only one set of propositions follows from the evidence. Hence, in the case of PSA testing, there is only one correct set of propositions expressing probabilities. Both the subjectivist and frequency interpretations, however, in contrast to the logical interpretation, hold that probability describes the way the world behaves.

## Propensity interpretation

The fourth interpretation is a variation on the frequency interpretation. The propensity interpretation treats propositions as expressing an inherent propensity for an outcome to occur under the same conditions. Contrary to the logical interpretation, it holds that probability does not express a relation among propositions; it expresses the propensity for an outcome (an event) to occur.

Let's return to Keynes and the logical interpretation. According to Keynes and others, probability is an axiomatic theory. That means, in technical terms, that the theory is based on a set of propositions that cannot be derived from any other proposition but from which all the theorems of the theory can be derived. The axioms, and all the theorems, are well-formed formulas (WFFs). That is, they are constructed in accordance with rules of the mathematical system, just as an English sentence is well-formed if it follows the rules of English grammar. These are powerful theoretical frameworks. An important observation, however, diminishes slightly the power of axiomatic systems. All axiomatic-deductive systems are incomplete. That means that one or more of the theorems of the system that are taken to be true cannot be deduced from the axioms. Kurt Gödel proved this feature in 1931. His two incompleteness theorems and proofs are referred to as Gödel's theorems. This was refined to embrace consistency, such that a formal system cannot be complete *and* consistent. Completeness can be bought at the price of consistency. That said, as we have seen in the geometry example, and have seen again in the chapter on scientific theories, axiomatic deductive systems are exceptionally powerful. As a historical side note, the earliest axioms for probability theory were given in 1657 by the Dutch physicist Christiaan Huygens (1629–1695).

Understanding clinical medical research requires a modest understanding of the probability calculus, the most important part being conditional probability. Hence, we provide a brief primer at this point. Probability is expressed as a number from 0 to 1.

Some easy-to-master symbolisation is required to understand material in subsequent chapters. Many students will have encountered most of these in secondary school; others will need to work through the next few pages carefully.

The probability of something is expressed as $\Pr(x)$ – probability of $x$.

> $\geq$ means greater than or equal to
> $5 \geq 4$ means 5 is greater than or equal to 4, and $0 \geq x$ means 0 is greater than or equal to $x$
> $\leq$ means less than or equal to
> $4 \leq 5$ means 4 is less than or equal to 5, and $0 \leq x$ means 0 is less than or equal to $x$

With these symbols, we can symbolise that probability is expressed as a number from 0 to 1 as:

$0 \leq \Pr(x) \leq 1$
When $\Pr(x) = 1$, A necessarily will happen; A is certain

When $Pr(x) = 0$, the occurrence of A is impossible (alternatively, the non-occurrence of $x$ (not $x$) is necessary)

An exhaustive set of possible outcomes (the addition of all possible outcomes) is 1. Hence, obviously:

$Pr(x) + Pr(\sim x) = 1$
["not" – negation – is symbolised as $\sim$, so this expression is read as probability of $x$ plus probability of not $x$ equals 1]

Less obviously, if $x$, $y$ and $z$ exhaust all the possible outcomes, then:

$Pr(x) + Pr(y) + Pr(z) = 1$

Consider a metal tub filled with 100 billiard balls from which you blindly pick one ball.

Suppose the tub contains only black balls, then:

$Pr(b) = 1$

Suppose it contains 40 black balls and 60 white balls, then:

$Pr(b) = .4$ and $Pr(w) = .6$, moreover
$Pr(b \text{ or } w) = 1$

because black and white exhaust the possible outcomes.

Now suppose it contains 20 black balls, 40 white balls and 40 red balls, then:

$Pr(b) = .2 \quad Pr(w) = .4 \qquad Pr(r) = .4$

Moreover, $Pr(b \text{ or } w \text{ or } r) = 1$, that is, $Pr(b) + Pr(w) + Pr(r) = 1$ because black, white and red exhaust the possible outcomes.

Two important laws of probability are the additivity laws and the product law. These require probabilistic independence. This is a simple concept in which $Pr(x/y) = Pr(x)$ and $Pr(y/x) = Pr(y)$. This requires understanding conditional probability, which will be discussed immediately after the statement of the two laws.

Additivity laws:

1   If $x$ and $y$ are probabilistically independent, then:
    $Pr(x \text{ or } y) = Pr(x) + Pr(y)$
2   If $x$ and $y$ are *not* probabilistically independent, then:
    $Pr(x \text{ or } y) = Pr(x) + Pr(y) - Pr(x \text{ and } y)$ [the minus deducts the times they are true together or occur together]

Product law:

> If $x$ and $y$ are probabilistically independent, then:
> $\Pr(x \text{ and } y) = \Pr(x) \times \Pr(y)$

This leads us to a central concept, conditional probability. Conditional probability is the probability of one proposition or event, given the truth of another proposition or the known occurrence of another event. The propositions or events in conditional probabilities are not probabilistically independent. The probability of one can be linked to the other.

For a meteorologist, the probability of rain tomorrow depends on cloud formations, wind patterns, temperatures, temperature inversion, dry adiabatic rates, etc. When you hear a forecast that states there is a 40% chance of rain tomorrow, it means that 40% of the time that events have been like today and also have been like what is expected for the next day, it has rained the next day. In probability theory, this means that the $\Pr(r)$ given the collection of conditions ($c$) is 0.4 and is written:

> $\Pr(r \text{ given } c) = .4$

Then symbolising the "given" as "/", it becomes $\Pr(r/c)$.

Using this notation, conditional probability is defined as:

> If $\Pr(y) > 0$, then:
> $\Pr(x/y) = \Pr(x \mathbin{\&} y)/\Pr(y)$[4] (the symbol for "and" is &, so this expression is read "probability of $x$ given $y$ equals probability of $x$ and $y$ divided by probability of $y$")

There are a few other important features flowing from conditional probability. First, multiplication:

From the definition of conditional probability.

Multiplication:

> If $\Pr(B) > 0$, then:

> $\Pr(A \mathbin{\&} B) = \Pr(A/B)\Pr(B)$

Total probability

> If $0 < \Pr(B) < 1$, then:

> $\Pr(A) = \Pr(B)\Pr(A/B) + \Pr(\sim B)\Pr(A/\sim B)$

With this background, we can explore an exceptionally important theorem for the subjective interpretation, Bayes' theorem (sometimes referred to as "rule"; we will call it "theorem")[5]. It is named after the English minister and mathematician Thomas Bayes (1702–1761). The essay containing this theorem and his larger theoretical framework was not published until after his death (1763).

Using H for hypothesis and E for evidence, the theorem is:[6]

$$Pr(H/E) = Pr(H)Pr(E/H)/Pr(H)Pr(E/H) + Pr(\sim H)Pr(E/\sim H)[7]$$

One great advantage of Bayes' theorem is it provides a method for giving a quantitative account of the incorporation of new evidence. What makes it a theorem within the subjective interpretation of probability is the requirement that one have what is called a "prior probability" H (or more generally x). That is, it requires a statement of the subjective strength of belief with which someone begins. Here is an example; assume you believe – maybe on your assessment of current evidence, maybe by intuition, maybe as an educated guess – that the $Pr(H) = .6$ [this is the prior probability]. Assume also that some piece of evidence is probable with $Pr(E) = 0.7$ if H is true. That is:

$$Pr(E/H) = 0.7$$

Assume that the evidence occurs.
  Information:

  Prior probability $Pr(H) = 0.6$
  $Pr(E/H) = 0.7$
  $Pr(E/\sim H) = 0.3$

The last two need not sum to 1, since if H is false, $Pr(E)$ will rest on factors other than H.
  Let's plug this information into Bayes' rule:

  $Pr(H/E) = Pr(H)Pr(E/H)/Pr(H)Pr(E/H) + Pr(\sim H)Pr(E/\sim H)$
  If $Pr(H) = 0.6$, then $Pr(\sim H) = 0.4$

Hence:

  $Pr(H/E) = (0.6 \times 0.7)/((0.6 \times 0.7) + (0.4 \times 0.3))$
  $= 0.778$

Hence, the new evidence has raised the $Pr(H)$ to 0.778 from 0.6.
  Ian Hacking in his excellent textbook, *An Introduction to Probability and Inductive Logic* (2001, pp. 75–76), has a wonderful, although unrealistic, example, since seldom would more than one swab be taken.
  An individual arrives in a physician's office with complaints of a sore throat. Based on the symptoms, a physician suspects her patient has strep throat. Her strength of belief in this diagnosis can be determined. The standard diagnostic test for strep throat is a nasal-pharyngeal swab. The physician takes five swabs. Like all lab tests, this lab test is not perfect. Sometimes the test indicates strep throat when it is not strep throat (this is known as a false positive. Sometimes

the test indicates no strep throat when in fact the individual has strep throat (this is known as a false negative). The probability of a false positive is 0.3 ($Pr(FN) = 0.3$)). The probability of a false positive is 0.1 ($Pr(FP) = 0.1$). The lab results come back: Yes, No, Yes, No, Yes. What should one conclude? Has this actually helped with the diagnosis? Bayes' theorem can help us out.

Let $S$ = the patient has strep throat
Let $\sim S$ = the patient does not have strep throat
Let $Y$ = a positive test result
Let $N$ = a negative test result

Known information:

$Pr(Y/S) = 0.7$ (accurate positive)
$Pr(N/S) = 0.3$ (false negative)
$Pr(Y/\sim S) = 0.1$ (false positive)
$Pr(N/\sim S) = 0.9$ (accurate negative)

Hence, the probability of the sequence results when strep throat is the correct diagnosis and when it is not, are:

$Pr(YNYNY/S) = 0.7 \times 0.3 \times 0.7 \times 0.3 \times 0.7 = .03087$
$Pr(YNYNY/\sim S) = 0.1 \times 0.9 \times 0.1 \times 0.9 \times 0.1 = .00081$

Based on the symptoms, the physician is reasonably confident the individual has strep throat. She accepts that $Pr(S) = .9$ [this is her prior probability]. Using this information and Bayes' theorem:

$Pr(S/YNYNY) = Pr(S)Pr(YNYNY/S)/Pr(S)Pr(YNYNY/S) + Pr(\sim S)$
$Pr(YNYNY/\sim S)$

Plugging in the numbers yields:

$Pr(S/YNYNY) = (0.9 \times 0.03087)/((0.9 \times 0.03087) + (0.1 \times 0.00081)) = 0.997$

Hence, the evidence has raised the strength of belief in strep throat to 0.997 from 0.9.

Assume the physician was overly confident in her initial assessment and a $Pr(S) = 0.5$ is more reasonable.

Then, again using Bayes' theorem:

$Pr(S/YNYNY) = Pr(S)Pr(YNYNY/S)/Pr(S)Pr(YNYNY/S) + Pr(\sim S)$
$Pr(YNYNY/\sim S)$

yields:

$$\Pr(S/YNYNY) = (.5 \times .03087)/((.5 \times .03087) + (.5 \times .00081)) = 0.974$$

Hence, the evidence has still raised the probability of strep throat from 0.5 to 0.974. If the prior probability is assumed to be 0.1, the evidence still raises it to 0.884. Consequently, this is important evidence and makes the diagnosis of strep throat more likely.

Two additional things about the subjective interpretation are important. First, probability statements express a claimed relationship. Consider, the following two statements:

1   If you are suffering from depression, it is probable that the SSRI (selective serotonin reuptake inhibitor) Celexa (Citalopram HBr) will alleviate the condition.
2   It is probable that, if you are suffering from depression, then the SSRI (selective serotonin reuptake inhibitor) Celexa will alleviate the condition.

In the first, the probability claim is attached to the outcome. In the second, the probability claim connects the condition and the outcome. This might seem a minor distinction but it is not. Claims made assuming the frequency interpretation are most naturally stated as in (1). Claims made assuming the subjective interpretation are most naturally stated as (2). That is because (1) is stating the frequency of an event when it provides a probability claim. (2), on the other hand, is stating a measure of the likelihood of the truth of the claim. That is, it states how confident one can be that the claim is true. It is not a statement about the frequency of an event.

The second important thing about the subjective interpretation is that personal probabilities (prior probabilities) must be coherent – they must be consistent. The best illustration of this is a descendant from Frank P. Ramsey ("*Truth and Probability*", 1926) known as a Dutch book. Ramsey used it to demonstrate that violating any of the rules of probability leads to irrationality.

Consider a betting context in which a bookmaker declares on fifteen days before a game that he will accept a bet on the number of runs the Toronto Blue Jays (a baseball team) will achieve (the Blue Jays play against the Yankees that day). The bet is simple. Will the Blue Jays get more than 10 runs, or fewer than, or equal to, 10 runs? The terms of the bet are that the bookmaker will accept your odds but he determines the bets. You set your odds on R > (greater than) 10 at ½ (2:1); your odds on R ≤ (less than or equal to) 10 are ¾ (3:4). The bookmaker chooses a \$10 bet for you on R > 10. Hence, the bookkeeper's exposure is \$20. The bookmaker chooses a \$12 bet for you on R ≤ 10. Hence, the bookkeeper's exposure is \$4.

*Table 5.1* An example of a "Dutch book". The betting structure violates the probability calculus; in that sense, it is not rational. No matter what the outcome, the better will lose.

| | | Bets | | |
|---|---|---|---|---|
| | | R > 10 | R ≤ 10 | Cumulative win/loss |
| Outcome | R > 10 | Bet $10; Take $20; Win $10 | Bet $12; Lose $12 | ($2) |
| | R ≤ 10 | Bet $ 10; Lose $10 | Bet $12; Take $16; Win $4 | ($6) |

As Table 5.1 shows, no matter how many runs the Blue Jays achieve, you always lose. What has gone wrong? Consider the odds again:

R > 10: ½    R ≤ 10: ¾

If R ≤ 10 is ¾ then ~(R ≤ 10) must be ¼ but ~(R ≤ 10) is the same as R > 10, which you have set at ½. Hence, you have set odds that are inconsistent. If R ≤ 10 is ¾, then R > 10 must be ¼ but you have set it at ½. Hence, your betting is not rational; it is incoherent. Since personal probabilities (degrees of belief) can be quantitatively represented as betting rates, personal probabilities must be coherent to avoid irrational behaviour and outcomes. It can be proved that betting rates are coherent (rational) if and only if they conform to the basic rules of probability. Hence, probability theory, in the case of strength of belief, is interpreted as a theory of rational thought (decision, choice).

## Randomness

Randomisation has become enshrined as a fundamental component of a specific research methodology: randomised controlled trials (RCTs). RCTs pervade clinical medicine. Indeed, it is widely regarded as the gold standard of evidence in clinical research. It is mostly used to demonstrate efficacy of a medical intervention (pharmaceutical, dietary regime, life style and so on). Because of its importance in clinical medicine, this methodology will be explored in detail in a later chapter. Here, because of its connection to probability, we look briefly at the concept of randomness. Simply stated, an event is random if its occurrence cannot be predicted based on complete knowledge of the state of the universe. That is, even an omniscient being (one that knows all that can be known at time $t_1$) cannot predict whether the event will or will not occur at $t_2$. This definition of "random" is an axiom of the standard interpretation of quantum mechanics.

RCTs employ a slightly different sense of random. That methodology uses random in the sense of random sample rather than the predictability of the occurrence of an event. A population of experimental subjects is divided into two (sometimes more) groups. The assignment to a group is random. This, in principle, ensures that each group has the same array of characteristics as the original population and as each other. Hence, it will not be the case that one group has more individuals that eat a high-fibre diet than the other group. The two groups are assumed to have been made homogeneous (made the same). This removes, in principle, any confounding elements – elements that might be part of, or the whole of, the cause of any differences in outcome between the two groups. The goal is to ensure that it is the intervention being studied that accounts for any difference. Since the two groups are assumed to be homogenous, any differences must be due to the intervention.

The concept of a random sample is a mathematical concept. It is defined as:

> A sample of *n* individuals from a population chosen in such a way that all possible sets of *n* individuals are equally likely to occur.

When *n* is sufficiently large, genuine random samples are sets of individuals "equally likely to occur" and confounding factors are, therefore, equally likely to occur in the same proportions in each random sample.

In the context of a mathematical proof or the derivation of a mathematical theorem, this requirement is made true by fiat – by stipulation within the context of the proof or derivation. This is not possible when dealing with empirical populations and empirical random samples. An experimental population, for example, is divided into two groups by using some mechanism that is at best quasi-random. Using a table of random numbers is one such mechanism. Each individual is assigned a number. Working through a table of random numbers, when an assigned number occurs, that person is put into group A. When the next number occurs, that person is put into group B, and so on. Random number tables are not truly random; they are as random as a computer can generate.

A mathematical system is a completely abstract deductive system. Claims that are made need not be "shown" to be correct. They will either yield useful results or not. As a set of claims, they can be shown to be consistent or not. Recall the geometry analogy given above. Demonstrating whether or not a mathematical system is isomorphic (same form and structure) with the empirical world is an extra-mathematical enterprise. Hence, exporting the mathematical definition of a random sample to empirical studies needs separate, and extra-mathematical, justification. The importance of this will be clearer when RCTs are explored in Chapter 7.

## Notes

1 It has become common to shorten the mathematical designation "infinitesimal calculus" to "the calculus". In fact, all well-formulated domains of mathematics are expressed as a calculus.

2 Republished in 2004 by Dover Publications, Inc. All page references are to the Dover publication.

3 All page numbers are from the English 1961 edition.

4  The rational for this definition is:

> There are four possible cases: $x$ and not $y$, $x$ and $y$, not $x$ and $y$, not $x$ and not $y$. Since we are looking for the Pr that $x$ will occur when $y$ occurs, the two cases where $y$ does not occur are uninteresting. Hence, the two relevant cases are the occurrence of both $x$ and $y$, and the occurrence of $y$ without the occurrence of $x$. If $x$ and $y$ always occurred together, the $\Pr(x/y) = 1$. The occurrence of $y$ without $x$ lowers the $\Pr(\Pr(x/y))$. How much it lowers it depends on the frequency with which $y$ occurs without $x$. That is why the $\Pr(y)$ is divided into the $\Pr(x \,\&\, y)$.

5  There are non-subjectivist accounts of Bayes' theorum but Baysians are today overwhelmingly subjectivists.

6  Sometimes, the notation for conditional probability is $\mathbf{Pr}_H(E)$ (the probability of $H$ conditional on $E$) rather than $\Pr(H/E)$. Hence, Bayes' theorem is written:

$$\mathbf{P}_E(H) = \mathbf{P}(H)\mathbf{P}_H(E) \,/\, [\mathbf{P}(H)\mathbf{P}_H(E) + \mathbf{P}(\sim H)\mathbf{P}_{\sim H}(E)]$$

7  Proof of Bayes' theorem:

1. $\Pr(H \,\&\, E) = \Pr(E \,\&\, H)$ [the order of the $H$ and $E$ is irrelevant because "and" is commutable: this is just a statement of the equivalence]
Adding probabilities that $= 1$ (e.g. $\Pr(E)/\Pr(E)$) does not change the equivalence expressed in (1), hence
2. $\Pr(H \,\&\, E)\Pr(E)/\,\Pr(E) = \Pr(E \,\&\, H)\Pr(H)/\Pr(H)$
the definition of conditional probability is: $\Pr(x/y) = \Pr(x$ and $y)/\Pr(y)$ – in this case $\Pr(H/E) = \Pr(H \,\&\, E)/\Pr(E)$: it is easier to see the next step if we restate the equivalence as $\Pr(H \,\&\, E)/\Pr(E) = \Pr(H/E)$: hence, we can substitute $\Pr(H/E)$ for any occurrence of $\Pr(H \,\&\, E)/\Pr(E)$: if we do that in (2), it yields:
3. $\Pr(H/E)\Pr(E) = \Pr(E/H)\Pr(H)$
Dividing both sides of an equation by the same thing does not change the equivalence, hence
5. $\Pr(H/E) = \Pr(E/H)\Pr(H)/\Pr(E)$
$(H)$ and $(\sim H)$ are exhaustive and probabilistically independent: hence, by the definition of total probability
$\Pr(E) = \Pr(H)\Pr(E/H) + \Pr(\sim H)\Pr(E/\sim H)$
That is, the probability of $E$ equals its probability under the two relevant conditions $H$ and $\sim H$: the first right-hand expression deals with the probability of $E$ given $H$ times the probability that $H$ occurs; the second deals with the probability of $E$ given not $H$ times the probability that $H$ does not occur.
Using this equivalence, substitute $\Pr(H)\Pr(E/H) + \Pr(\sim H)\Pr(E/\sim H)$ for $\Pr(E)$ in (5): this yields
6. $\Pr(H/E) = \Pr(H)\Pr(E/H)/\Pr(H)\Pr(E/H) + \Pr(\sim H)\Pr(E/\sim H)$
(6) is Bayes' theorem.

# 6 Causality and induction

The importance of this chapter and the previous one will become clear in Chapter 7 on randomised controlled trials. Probability, causality and induction are central to clinical research. After all, the supposed goal of research is to uncover causal relationships and induction lies at the core of generalisations to causes. Most clinical researchers rely on probability theory and statistical techniques derived from it to validate inductive inference to causes. We will see that things are not that simple; there are significant and deep philosophical issues.

Science aims to discover causes of phenomena (things that occur in the world). Sometimes a cause is simple; one event is the cause of another. Sometime a cause is complex; many events together cause one or some conjunction of events; sometimes an event has more than one cause. Although for simplicity, as in the explanation just given, causes and their effects are cast as events causing events, things are much more complicated. A "complete" cause is the entire collection of relevant things existing at one time, including all the environmental factors. Hence, it is more accurate to claim that this event *in these circumstances* caused another event. One defining feature of a deterministic world is that the same cause will always lead to the effect. Establishing that the world is deterministic is challenging because the complete cause of an event is exceptionally complex. Hence, recreating a cause exactly is nearly always impossible.

Fortunately, there are strategies for taming, at least partially and usefully, this complexity. The most common in scientific research involves identifying some important elements of a cause. These are manipulated while all the other elements – background conditions – are held constant or assumed to be constant enough that any variation is unimportant. A refinement is to analyse the background conditions to identify elements that are important and those that are considerably less important.

Consider the firing of a handgun. A typical effect is called recoil and it is manifested by the movement of the gun and the shooter's arm in the opposite direction to that of the bullet. Among the crucial elements are the size of the gun, the type of bullet and the gunpowder load. Change any of these and the effect will be different. By contrast, the shirt that the shooter is wearing is unlikely to be important. One might hypothesise that a shirt with tight-fitting sleeves rather than loose-fitting will change the effect but this is unlikely to result in a significantly different effect. The difference might not even be measurable and, hence, for almost all investigations and experiments it will be irrelevant.

This provides an initial sketch of the concept of cause. The complications, however, have only just begun. The cause–effect relationship is an inferred one. That is, one only observes an event (C) – the cause – in a context and another event (E) – the effect – in its context. One does not observe the relationship between the two; one assumes (infers) the relationship based on temporal order and what the Scottish philosopher David Hume called constant conjunction. If every time we have observed C, we observe that it is *followed* by E, we infer C causes E. This can be represented in logic as, if C, then E. This logical relationship is known as material implication; C materially, not logically, entails E. Based on a body of evidence, an inductive inference is made to the general claim, if C, then E. Looking a little closer at generalising from a specific body of evidence requires distinguishing two kinds of inference: deductive and inductive.

Deductive inferences are the kind one finds in mathematics and symbolic logic. These inferences involve "necessity". If the premises, theorems or axioms are true, the conclusion(s) cannot be false; it is necessarily true. Some examples will make this point clearly. First consider a well-known syllogistic example. In logic, an "argument" has premises and a conclusion.

A.   All men are mortal
B.   Socrates is a man
C.   Therefore (symbolised hereafter by ∴) Socrates is mortal

If (A) is true and (B) is true (known as the premises), (C) (known as the conclusion) MUST be true. Of course, sometimes the premises are not true.

D.   If the moon is made of green cheese, cows can jump over it
E.   The moon is made of green cheese
F.   ∴ Cows can jump over it

*If* (D) and (E) were true, (F) would necessarily be true. In this case, we can safely assume that neither (D) nor (E) are true. Nonetheless, the argument (D) + (E) entails (symbolically →) (F) is deductively valid because the conclusion *cannot* be false *If* the premises are true. Logicians distinguish between valid arguments and sound arguments. A valid argument only requires that the conclusion is necessarily true, if the premises are true. When an argument is valid but the premises are known to be, or suspected to be, false, the argument is unsound. Arguments that are valid and whose premises are known to be, or assumed to be, true are sound arguments. It is validity that is the cornerstone of deductive inference.

Two examples from mathematics will further illustrate this essential feature of deduction and allow a stark contract to be made with induction. Consider an example from set theory – the axiom of choice (AC). This axiom is fascinating but a detailed discussion goes beyond what is necessary to make the point about deductive inference; some simplification is warranted. Sets are collections of things (physical things, numbers, journal articles and so on). Mathematically, the most common entities in sets are numbers or algebraic symbols. Some sets are infinite like the natural numbers $\{1, 2, 3, \ldots\}$, where the brace brackets $\{\}$ signify a set of the entities they enclose. Some sets are finite such as the set of coloured pencils on Peter's desk – {coloured pencils on Peter's desk} – or the set of numbers that can be divided into 30 and yield a natural number – whole number. Some sets are collections of other sets. One special set is empty – the null set. It contains no entities. Given this framework, a common formulation of the axiom of choice is:

> Let $A$ be a collection of non-empty sets. Then we can choose a member from each set in that collection.

More precisely and using, as is now common, a choice function, this means that there exists a function $f$ defined on $A$ which has the property that, for each set $S$ in the collection, $f(S)$ is a member of $S$.

$f$ is the choice function. Note the requirement that the sets in $A$ be non-empty. One feature that makes AC interesting is that during the century after Ernst Zermelo (1904) formulated the axiom,[1] a number of theorems that were derived from it were later shown mathematically equivalent to it; hence not really derivations at all. A classic example is Löwenheim–Skolem–Tarski theorem (Löwenheim 1915, Skolem 1920, Tarski and Vaught 1957),[2] which Tarski later proved was equivalent to AC.

Another interesting feature is that, like the parallel postulation in Euclidean geometry (discussed in Chapter 5), when conjoined to the other axioms of set theory, neither assuming the axiom nor negating it leads to a contradiction. Hence two consistent set theories are available. Nonetheless, for a variety of reasons, the axiom has been embraced by most mathematicians because it allows the *deduction* of many significant theorems. As John L. Bell (2015) puts it:

> As the debate concerning the Axiom of Choice rumbled on, it became apparent that the proofs of a number of significant mathematical theorems made essential use of it, thereby leading many mathematicians to treat it as an indispensable tool of their trade. Hilbert, for example, came to regard *AC* as an essential principle of mathematics and employed it in his defence of classical mathematical reasoning against the attacks of the intuitionists. Indeed, his ε-operators are essentially just choice functions.

The central point here is that because mathematics employs deduction (deductive inference) the theorems that are deduced from the axiom of choice are as certain as the axiom. Of course, reject the axiom and those theorems whose proof requires it fail to be supported.

Now consider another mathematical example (not specific to set theory and much briefer in exposition): finding the domain and range of a real-number function $f$ where:

$$f(x) = \sqrt{x} - 4$$

*Solution*

$$x - 4 \geq 0, \text{ that is } x \geq 4$$

When $x < 4$, $f(x)$ is not a real number since $\sqrt{x} - 4$ is a negative number.

Hence, the domain of $f(x)$ is always positive for all values of $x$, where $x \geq 4$, and the range is the set of all positive real numbers. This solution is deductive since the conclusion about the range and domain cannot be false if the function is well-formed, which it is, and the function is a real number.

The above discussion and examples are designed to underscore that the key feature of deduction (deductive inference) is that it is truth-preserving; deductive inference guarantees *necessarily* the truth of conclusions deduced from true premises. By contrast, inductive inference – the central logical inference pattern in science – is not truth-preserving. It is possible for the premises to be true but the conclusion false. The kind of inductive inference to which Hume's constant conjunction applies is enumerative induction. We observe that $(C)$ is always followed by $(E)$. After a certain number of observations, we conclude that $(C)$ will always be followed by $(E)$. That is, we inductively infer (rather than deductively) that $(C)$ will always be followed by $(E)$. Hume's correct contention was that we have no guarantee that the next instance of $(C)$ will be followed by $(E)$. We "expect" that to be the case but we cannot know it. Consider a case where we know a sequence is a fluke. The tossing of a "fair" coin by a machine could result in 3,000 heads in a row. As noted earlier, we know this is highly improbable (essential impossible[3]), because we can mathematically calculate the probability that the first 3,000 outcomes will all be heads. We also know that "in the long run" an outcome will be a tail; probabilistically, the long run in this case is not much "longer" than 1,000 tosses. In this case, we know, by design, that the outcome of tossing the coin is quasi-random and that a tail is as likely as a head. Hume was drawing attention to the fact that for *all* events, we cannot know that the association of events is not a fluke. Although it is highly improbable that $(C)$ is followed by $(E)$ 3,000 times if $(C)$ is not the true cause of $(E)$, it is nonetheless possible. The more times $(C)$ is followed by $(E)$, the more probable it becomes that there is a causal relation, but there is never certainty. Unlike the coin case, for almost all associations in medicine (and other contexts) we have no knowledge of the wide array of contextual factors lying behind the observed association.

An important consequence of this uncertainty, in clinical medicine and some other fields, centres on the challenge of distinguishing between *C* causing *E*, and *C* and *E* being merely correlated; merely just happening to occur together. In the epidemiological literature, the term "association" is used frequently and signals a significant relationship between *C* and *E* but one that has not been established as causal. Temporal order is important for cause and effect relationships but it is far from decisive. One may observe constant conjunction and a consistent temporal order. This may embolden the observer to infer, by induction, that *C* causes *E*, but the two events (or collection event) may still only be correlated and not causally related. That is, even if (*E*) were observed to follow (*C*) on a million occasions, inferring, with a very high probability, a causal relationship between them is a fallacy. It still might be that they are merely correlated. Consider two events that *always* occur together, and hence have a correlation coefficient of 1. This might be because they are causally connected but it might be that there is a common cause; that is, both events are caused by some third factor. That is why they always occur together and in the same temporal order (see Figure 6.1).

Consequently, in order to conclude that two events that always occur together are *causally* connected and not just *correlated*, the existence of any third factor(s) (often called confounding factors) has to be eliminated. Conceptually and abstractly, randomised controlled trials are supposed to eliminate the possibility of a common cause, a topic to which we return later.

Causality has been given a lot of attention by philosophers and some statisticians in the last 100 years. Bertrand Russell threw down the gauntlet (mediaeval: glove, the throwing down of which signified a challenge) in 1913 by claiming:

> The law of causality, I believe, like much that passes muster among philosophers, is a relic of a bygone age, surviving, like the monarchy, only because it is erroneously supposed to do no harm.
>
> (p. 1)

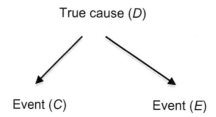

*Figure 6.1* *C* and *E* have always been observed to occur together and in a specific temporal order because both are caused by a third, undetected, event *D*. Temporal order is a function of the delayed effect of *D* when causing *E* compared with its causing *C*.

Russell was not the first to question the coherence and utility of the concept of causality. Karl Pearson in his *Grammar of Science* (1900) argued that causality has no place in modern science. These are lone voices. Most have continued to attempt to explicate the nature and utility of causality. Four accounts have dominated the philosophical literature in the last five decades: probabilistic, mechanistic, counterfactual and interventionist (sometime called manipulationist).

Patrick Suppes (1970) developed an impressive probabilistic theory causality. The thrust of this account is that a cause must raise the probability of its effect. Wesley Salmon (1984, 1998) provides an interesting exposition of the mechanistic account. The thrust of this account is to ground causality in the physical interaction of things during which some property of things is exchanged, sometimes in only one direction, sometimes both. The causal structure of the movement of billiard balls during a billiard match is a classic case. David Lewis (1973a, 1973b, 1979) has articulated a counterfactual account. The thrust of this account is that a causal relationship exists between $E$ and $C$ when, were $E$ not to occur, $C$ would not occur either. In Chapter 7, we will examine Bradford Hill's consideration on causality. Michael Höfler (2005) has argued that Hill's conception of causality is best understood on a counterfactual account. Jim Woodward (2000) has championed an interventionist account. The thrust of this account is that the central reason we are interested in causes is to manipulate things; to intervene to eliminate an illness, to slow, or perhaps reverse, climate change, for example. Each of these accounts has other supporters and expositors; the ones cited are among the important advocates. The philosophical debate about each of them continues to be engaged. Each has its defenders and critics.

Recently, another account has been crafted and defended. Judea Pearl and his book *Causality: Models, Reasoning and Inference* (2nd edition 2009) sets out this view in a comprehensive way. Pearl examines causal modelling, central to which is his directed acyclic graphs (DAGs). DAGs are Bayesian networks (recall the discussion of Bayes' theorem in the previous chapter). The meaning of "graph" in this account is the one employed in the field of mathematics called graph theory. The graphs consist of edges and nodes. In the case of DAGs, the edges are lines with arrow heads; the nodes are causes or effects. In moderately complex cases, they are usually letters of the alphabet enclosed in a box.

The graphs are directed because each edge has only one arrowhead; they are acyclic because even the most complex graph will not allow a path from a node back to that node. These graphs allow "common causes" of various kinds to be represented such as the simple case in Figure 6.2 but also in more complicated cases, where $(F)$ causes $(C)$ and also causes $(G)$ which, in turn, causes $(E)$. Here the reason that there is temporal ordering of $(C)$ and $(E)$ is clearer (see Figure 6.3).

There are also "collider causes", where one effect has two or more different causes (see Figure 6.4).

There are a number of conditions on the structure of DAGs. The most important is the *parental Markov condition*. Luc Bovens and Stephen Hartmann,

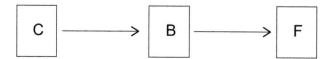

*Figure 6.2* A simple edges and nodes directed acyclic graph.

in an excellent paper on the application of Bayesian networks to the problem of unreliable instruments, express this condition as:

(PMC) A variable represented by a node in the Bayesian Network is independent of all variables represented by its non-descendant nodes in the

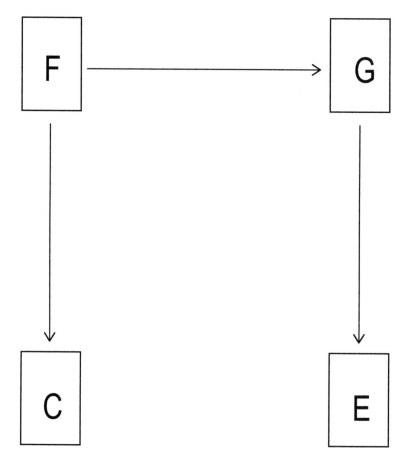

*Figure 6.3* E is observed to always follow C; G and F are not observed but are, in fact, causal mechanisms that explain the association of C and E.

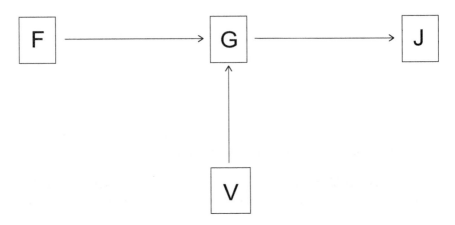

*Figure 6.4* Colliders: many causes for a single event.

Bayesian Network, conditional on all variables represented by its parent nodes.

(p. 33)

Those interested in the details of the conditions should read Luc Bovens and Stephen Hartmann's (2002) paper and a chapter by Daniel Steel (2011). A central feature of DAGs that make them Bayesian networks is that a probability distribution is specified for the variables in the root (initiating) nodes of the graph (prior probabilities) and a conditional probability distribution for the variables (posterior probabilities). The conditional probabilities are the same as those encountered in Bayes' theorem (i.e. $\Pr(H/E) = \phi$) in the previous chapter.[4] Abstract mathematical graph theory has no commitment to particular applications. We will revisit Bayesian networks again briefly in the next chapter.

At this point, this sketch of the elements and challenges associated with understanding and revealing causes is all that is required. Refinements will be added later in this chapter and the next.

Thus far, inductive inference to causes has been cast as enumerative; observation of many instances of two events occurring together justifies, additively, inferring a causal connection. The pitfalls of this method of inductive inference should now be clear. Inductive inference, however, has another formulation in science. It is known as the hypothetico-deductive method. One forms a hypothesis about a potential cause. An experiment is devised to test the hypothesis; the experiment is conducted and the result noted. If the result is what is expected, the hypothesis is "confirmed". Confirmed is in quotes because, as will shall see, it is a hasty inference.

First, do not be fooled by the use of "deductive" in this label. The deduction is real but it is from the hypothesis to the experiment. One deduces that if the hypothesis is true, then a certain empirical consequence will occur under certain conditions. Once this deduction from the hypothesis is made, the rest of the inferences are inductive. The structure of the hypothetico–deductive method is:

A)   *If* the hypothesis is true, *then* empirical consequence ϑ will be found under Ψ conditions
B)   Empirical consequence ϑ has been found
C)   Therefore, the hypothesis is true.

This is, however, fallacious reasoning; that is, it can lead to false conclusions even though the premises are true. The fallacy is called as "the fallacy of affirming the consequent". Consider a simple example,

A')   If it is raining and there is no protective covering, the sidewalk will be wet
B')   The sidewalk is wet
C')   Therefore it is raining

The sidewalk, however, might be wet because I had my sprinkler on and it over-sprayed onto the sidewalk or I might have deliberately hosed down the sidewalk to clean it. In such circumstances, (A') is true (*If* it were raining, *then* the sidewalk would be wet unless there is a protective covering) and (B') is true (the sidewalk is indeed observed to be wet). But (C') is false; it is not a *necessary* consequence of the truth of (A') and (B'). There are other ways in which the sidewalk could be wet, which means (C') could be false even though (A) and (B) are true.

To address this logical problem, the philosopher Karl Popper (1963) suggested a different method for science; he inverted the reasoning. He claimed that the appropriate method for science is to generate bold conjectures (hypotheses) and attempt to disprove them. The logical structure in this case is:

A')   If it is raining and there is no protective covering, the sidewalk will be wet
B")   The sidewalk is *not* wet
C")   Therefore it is *not* raining.

This is a valid deductive inference called modus tollens. The more times attempts to falsify a hypothesis fail, the stronger the grounds for accepting it. This, of course, assumes that there are a finite number of possible tests of the hypothesis. As each one fails, there is one fewer possible falsifying possibility. As the probability of falsifying the hypothesis decreases, the probability of its truth increases. There is another benefit of Popper's method. It can be used to determine whether a hypothesis is a scientific hypothesis or a pseudoscientific one. Hypotheses that cannot, in principle, be falsified are pseudoscientific. Although a true scientific hypothesis cannot, in fact be falsified (because it is true), it nonetheless gives rise to tests, which in principle would falsify it. A pseudoscientific hypothesis does not allow any tests to be constructed that would falsify it. In short, there is no way to test it – no rational method to reject it.

This method avoids the fallacy of affirming the consequent but it fails to capture actual scientific practice. A hypothesis inferred from a well-confirmed and well-accepted theory (which virtually all are) will not be rejected on the basis of one, or even a number, of failed tests. There are a host of reasons why the test might have failed even if the hypothesis is true. The inference of the hypothesis from the theory may be invalid. The construction of the test(s) may be inadequate. The data collection might be flawed. The analysis of the data may be impoverished. Moreover, there are always auxiliary assumptions. This is highlighted in what has become known as the Quine–Duhem thesis (after Willard van Orman Quine (1953) and Pierre Duhem (1906)).

It states that any apparent disconfirming evidence can always be accommodated by any theory. Hypotheses inferred from theories always involve a host of auxiliary assumptions. Consider the case of the mass (simplified, weight) of different-size ball bearings being irrelevant to the velocity of their fall to the ground (Galileo law of free fall). A test of this will have to assume they are falling in a vacuum, that there are no electromagnetic forces involved, and that they are falling in the same frame of reference (one falling on a moving boat, the other on the shore complicates the situation). For a failed experiment, any one of these conditions might be the culprit rather than the theory. Add to that the fact that there may be many other possible perturbing factors that are not known when the experiment is constructed and Popper's solution loses its force.

In short, any one of the assumptions used to generate a hypothesis and experiment to test it might be the culprit in a failed test. They are numerous and many are often not made fully explicit – perhaps not known. In essence, the Quine–Duhem thesis asserts that there are always auxiliary assumptions that will rescue a theory from refutation. The real modus tollens argument is

$$\text{If (T and A), then O}$$
$$\underline{\text{O was not found or did not occur}}$$
$$\therefore \text{ not (T and A)}$$

The central epistemic problem this reveals is that theories: (a) are "whole" integrated structures, and (b) are applied using many auxiliary assumptions. A single failure of a prediction, or inferred hypothesis (or even a collection of failures), might suggest the need for some adjustment to the theory (a tweaking) but almost never that the entire edifice should be rejected. Moreover, there will be resistance to jettisoning a theory that in almost all respects is successful at explaining and predicting phenomena – the one, or even a few, failures, notwithstanding. There are two reasons for this resistance. First, the level of confirmation of the theory and its overall success make rejection based on only a single failed test – or even a few failed tests – seem precipitous. Second, in the absence of a more successful alternative theory, a slightly flawed theory is better than no theory. By the turn of the twentieth century, Newton's theory had many failed predictions but it was not until special relativity, general relativity and quantum mechanics were formulated that it was replaced – or, as some have argued, shown to be a special case within general relativity.

These are classic problems with induction, which undermine science's claim to certainty. There is no way to escape this but there is a way to yield scientific knowledge that is robust and credible. The heart of this method is uncovering mechanisms and also unifying knowledge into a powerful explanatory framework. This does not change the fact that science cannot provide certainty but it does allow robust explanations, predictions and manipulations of phenomena. Sometimes a unification begins to falter, as Newtonian mechanics did at the end of the nineteenth century and into the early part of the twentieth century. Nonetheless, it served as a powerful unification of knowledge, which had remarkable explanatory, predictive and manipulatory success. Even today, it explains well the movement and interaction of objects moving at human observable speeds and over human comprehendible distances. That is, it explains and predicts well the world as humans experience it. Such unifying frameworks – Darwin's theory of evolution is another example – are often called theories but sometimes models.

Given the significant challenges posed by causality and induction in science generally, numerous attempts have been made to provide a useful account of causality and induction. Increasingly, these have become complex – mathematically and conceptually. Most invoke some account of probability. One account that has special resonance in clinical medicine is more than 70 years old. It originated with Ronald A. Fisher and we will look closely at it in Chapter 7.

A move out from the trees to get a view of the landscape is useful here. Why are we interested in causality in science and, in particular, in medicine? There are three fundamental reasons: explanation, prediction and manipulation. Different domains of medicine will place greater emphasis on each of these. Clinical medicine has a greater interest in explanation and manipulation. Diagnosis is obviously connected to the explanation of health and disease from a collection of symptoms and investigations. If these suggest that the person is healthy, no further action is required. If these suggest that there is a "deviation" from a healthy condition, then a diagnosis (tentative explanation of what is likely the cause) is made. This leads both to a prognosis (prediction) and options for intervention (manipulation).

Theoretical domains of medicine (immunology, genetics, endocrinology, for example) focus more on explanation and prediction than manipulation. Manipulation is tied to experimentation, where the situation is structured (manipulated) to control variables that would otherwise confound the experiment. Nonetheless, the goal is to uncover causes that will explain the behaviour of entities or a system of entities. This difference between clinical medicine and theoretical medicine has been compared to the difference between physics and chemistry, and engineering. This is a useful comparison in highlighting the different goals. Physics and chemistry seek to uncover the features of entities and the web of causal connections among them. Engineering seeks to apply the knowledge uncovered by physics and chemistry. Theoretical domains of medicine seek to uncover the features of entities and the web of causal connections among them. Clinical medicine seeks to apply that knowledge in diagnosing and treating individuals. These lines of demarcation were sharper 100 years ago than they are today. Engineering isn't confined to the application of physics and chemistry. There are synergies among these areas. Similarly, clinical medicine is not simply an application of the knowledge generated by theoretical domains of medicine. There are synergies across all the domains of medicine. Hence, a more sophisticated characterisation of differences is needed.

With attention on the purposes of seeking and employing causes in medicine (explanation, prediction and intervention), the complexity and variability of causes comes into sharper focus. The specification of a cause runs the gambit from all antecedent factors to a single factor. The "complete" specification of a cause always requires a statement of every condition of the world at the moment before the effect but this requirement would be debilitating – indeed, unachievable. Ideally, a single event can be isolated as the "relevant" cause. The pneumococcal bacterium as the cause of bacterial pneumonia is an example. The assumption is that all the other "background" factors are either non-significant or remain constant. Hence, if this causal factor can be eliminated, the disease can be cured.

Things are usually a bit more complex. Consider a classic example. A person walks into his house and strikes a match to light a cigarette. His house explodes and several adjacent houses are destroyed. A single-cause explanation would focus on the striking of the match. But more is required in this case. There was a natural gas leak in the house. The gas was confined because there was no ventilation and the density of the gas had reached a critical point. There was still sufficient oxygen in the house to support combustion. The volume of gas was not only great enough for an explosion but had sufficient density to create an explosive force sufficient to destroy that building and others. Although, in this example, more than one factor is involved, identifying the relevant causal factors is still manageable. A forensic investigator would be able to narrow the scope of the specification of the cause to a small number of factors. An important component in this "ability to narrow" is the use of relevant portions of theories – the role of oxygen in combustion, for example.

In medicine, we are occasionally fortunate enough to find a single relevant cause (the presence of pneumococcal bacterium, *Plasmodium falciparum* (malaria parasite) or arsenic, for example). Identifying these causes allows an uncluttered explanation of the symptoms of the disease. In the case of pneumococcal bacterium, the symptoms include fever, fluid in the lungs, painful breathing and coughing. In the case of *Plasmodium falciparum*, the symptoms include anaemia (low blood oxygen resulting in weakness, dizziness, headaches and spots before the eyes), jaundice (yellowing of the skin) and fever. In the case of arsenic poisoning, symptoms include constriction of the throat, burning gastro-intestinal pain, vomiting, diarrhoea and dysphagia. The cause explains these symptoms in relevant cases. Since many of these collections of symptoms are also found in other diseases, differential diagnosis is still required. Once, however, a diagnosis is made (today often with the aid of blood tests, x-rays and so on), the cause of the symptoms, or test results, is claimed to be known. If available, an intervention can be employed. In each of these three examples, successful interventions are available. "Successful" requires qualification because not all those with a disease respond well to the standard intervention and for a few the intervention has unwanted side-effects that undermine further the health of the patient.

These are reasonably simple causal structures. Many causes in medicine are more multifaceted. Malignant tumours are examples (tumours that if left will continue to grow but most importantly will metastasise (spread) to other parts of the body). First, different kinds have to be distinguished since different tumours have different characteristics, different developmental patterns and different causes. Within each type causes can be different: genetic, environmentally induced or spontaneous. In some cases, the causes will be multiple: a genetic disposition plus an environmental trigger plus an ineffective early immune response and so on. Obviously, this clouds the explanatory waters, compromises prediction and complicates intervention (therapy).

Some specifications of causes border on, or cross over into, the unmanageable. Alzheimer's is an example. It is also an instructive example of how causes can move from unmanageable to greater understanding. The cause(s) of Alzheimer's seems to be part genetic, part inflammatory, part protein abnormality among many other potential factors – some researchers have recently suggested a viral component. Our knowledge is still partial but over the last twenty years, brain biopsies have revealed amyloid plaque deposits similar, but with important differences, to the plaques found in prion disease (diseases caused by abnormally folded protein: bovine spongiform encephalopathy is considered to be an example). This, along with work on the negative effects of inflammation, is narrowing the causal space. This illustrates a method of taming the complexity of some causes: experiments or investigations designed to control some potential factors in the causal array, to allow the role of those that remain uncontrolled to be observed.

To this point, causes and effects have been described as individual events, albeit in some cases multifaceted. There are methodological advantages to this approach; it is often easier to probe nature in constrained contexts. The danger is that the forest gets lost due to a focus on the trees. This takes us back to the points made in Chapter 3 about the crucial role of theories and models in unification of knowledge, explanation, prediction and manipulation. Much of medicine uses theories or models as a unification of current knowledge and the mechanisms underlying the behaviour of things: immunology, haematology, medical genetics and physiology, for example. Clinical medicine (diagnosis, treatment, prevention) draws on these areas of medicine, as well as other sciences (physics and chemistry for diagnostic imaging and other tests, for example). It also draws on clinical research, which, currently, is not itself a theory-based or theory-driven domain of medicine. Some argue that is because of the complexity of clinical medicine; some argue that the experimental methods of other sciences are not applicable to clinical research; yet others argue that clinical research is focused on safety and efficacy of diagnostic tools, therapies and prevention of disease. This latter entails that clinical research requires special methods. Randomised controlled trials, case controlled studies, cohort studies and the like are examples of those special methods of investigating safety and efficacy. These research methods (discussed in detail later) focus on causes and effects individually, without much attention to the forest (the appropriate theories and models needed to integrate the isolated causal accounts). There is a growing chorus of clinical researchers, philosophers of science and scientific researchers in other fields who are challenging the lack of emphasis on theory in clinical medicine.

We now step back from these details to examine some more general issues. Induction is essential to clinical research and practice. First, any inference from research data to a causal claim will be inductive. As will any inference that the probability is low that an observed association is due to chance. Second, in most cases, an inference from the research data that is based on a sample of the population to the entire population is required. Both these inferences assume that a successful inductive logic exists. That a deductive logic exists was established by Whitehead and Russell in 1910–1913 (3 volumes). Their codification of symbolic (mathematical) logic is the basis for modern computer programmes. By 1931, Gödel had improved on Whitehead and Russell. He had developed two formal systems which encompassed all known mathematics, as well as the Zermelo–Fraenkel axiom system (see Gödel 1930 and 1931). A successful inductive logic remains elusive. Harold Kincaid has noted, accurately:

> The argument ad Carnapium given by Quine: if Carnap could not find a successful inductive logic, then there is not one or, more seriously, informative general inductive logics have not been forthcoming
>
> (2011, p. 71)

The flight to statistics presumes to substitute for an informative inductive logic. The cornerstone of this for more than 50 years has been randomised controlled trials (RCTs) (discussed in detail in Chapter 7). The discussion of causality in this chapter can be linked to RCTs by a comment on "Fisher's mantra". The majority of researchers in clinical medicine have accepted the view of Ronald A. Fisher, even though most do not know its Fisherian origins and also do not know the differences of view between Fisher, and Pearson and Neyman. Fisher claimed that if a cause and effect relationship exists, satisfying three experimental conditions will reveal it. Randomisation, control and replication are the three conditions. Fisher developed this experimental method in the context of agriculture. In that context, a field is divided into numerous identically sized "blocks"; a process he called blocking. Adjacent blocks are matched and one of each pair is chosen for the intervention – addition of fertiliser, for example. The assignment of intervention blocks is done randomly. Because there are numerous paired blocks in a field, the intervention-control pattern is simultaneously replicated. Fisher claimed that if the intervention blocks had a different outcome from the control blocks, then a cause can with certainty be proclaimed; that is, the intervention can be asserted as the cause of the different outcome. This claim is, as we will see, contentious and complex.

## Notes

1 Zermelo's first formulation is not expressed as a choice function (in the way the current common formulation is). Zermelo's original formulation is:

> Imagine that with every subset $M$ there is associated an arbitrary element $m'_1$, that occurs in $M$ itself; let $m'_1$ be called the "distinguished" element of $M$. This yields a "covering" $g$ of the set $M$ by certain elements of the set $M$. The number of these coverings is equal to the product [of the cardinalities of all the subsets $M$] and is certainly different from 0.

2 A first-order sentence having a model of infinite cardinality $\kappa$ also has a model of any infinite cardinality $\mu$ such that $\mu \leq \kappa$.

3 In the case of 100 tosses, a fair coin will fall within the range 40–60 heads 95% of the time. In the case of a 1,000 tosses, it will fall within the range 469–531 heads 95% of the time. Each increase in tosses narrows the range. With 3,000 tosses, the range is very small. Hence, "in the long run", tosses of a fair coin will converge on 50/50.

4 For critical examination of DAGs, see Cartwright 2001.

# 7 Randomised controlled trials, other study designs and meta-studies

This chapter is the first to draw extensively on the material in Chapters 1–6 and to relate those discussions and the complexities they highlight to medical research, knowledge and practice. Here we see the import of the distinction between frequentist and subjectivist interpretations of probability and the importance of the vagaries of inductive inference and of causal claims. The value of theories emerges as well. It also deals with highly contentious material. We have chosen not to shy away from presenting our view, and arguments, that randomisation has at most a benefit in avoiding experimenter bias (sometimes called selection bias). Moreover, we are explicit about our scepticism regarding the claims made about the knowledge that randomised controlled trials (RCTs) yield, which is mostly about the efficacy of interventions. Additionally, we dispute that randomisation, control and replication entail causal connection – a central claim of R.A. Fisher.

Although RCTs have been dubbed by many as the gold standard of evidence for therapeutic efficacy in clinical medicine, there are other study designs that are frequently used. These have yielded important knowledge and need to be an important part of the arsenal of clinical research methodologies.

One increasingly important set of methods are Bayesian methods, which is why our earlier discussion of Bayes' theorem is important. We discuss Bayesian methods somewhat superficially, because, we suspect, most readers will not have the mathematical background required to follow a more detailed account; some obviously will and can turn to the material we cite. In the spirit of full disclosure, we declare our endorsement of Bayesian methods over conventional methods and analytical tools historically using RCTs. We recognise that there is no strict either–or involved but the current resistance to Bayesian methods and entrenched support for RCTs require a strong stance in favour of Bayesian methods.

We close this chapter by returning to the quest for causality in clinical research. This leads us immediately to a ground-breaking contribution by Bradford Hill. His contribution has in some respects been overstated – treating his considerations as criteria for determining causality, for example – and in others underappreciated – his observation on significance tests and the context dependence of an evidential base, for example. We explore whether he has added clarity to the determination of causality. It emerges that he has added some clarity but he leaves us great distance still from the goal. At the end of the chapter, we are left with a significant question. We conclude that RCTs fall short of the goal of revealing causal connections, as do other study designs, and Hill's considerations, although helpful, also leave us far from the goal. In light of this, it is reasonable to ask, "how significant is causality to the practice of medicine?"

In the final chapter of *On the Origin of Species*, Charles Darwin wrote:

> Although I am fully convinced of the truth of the views given in this volume under the form of an abstract, I by no means expect to convince experienced naturalists whose minds are stocked with a multitude of facts all viewed during a long course of years, from a point of view directly opposite to mine.
>
> . . .
>
> I look with confidence to the future, to young and rising naturalists, *who will be able to view both sides of the question with impartiality*. Whoever is led to believe that species are mutable will do good service by conscientiously expressing his conviction; for thus only can the load of prejudice by which this subject is overwhelmed be removed.
>
> (1859, pp. 481–482, emphasis added)

This crisply captures the problem of entrenchment. Entrenchment occurs when individuals, in fact usually a community of individuals, are committed to a framework that is used to explain, predict and codify phenomena such that they are unwilling or reluctant to examine different and new frameworks. Sometimes the new is complicated to understand; sometimes careers have too much invested in the old framework and change is threatening; sometimes there are other commitments that the old framework supports and the new one challenges, such as, in Darwin's time, religious commitments.

As mentioned, randomised controlled trials (RCTs) have been dubbed the "gold standard" of evidence in clinical medicine. Notwithstanding that lofty assessment by many researchers and regulatory agencies, RCTs have come under heavy criticisms in the last three decades. Some critics are statisticians or epidemiologists (e.g. Salsburg 1993 and Upshur 2003, for example); some are philosophers of science (e.g. Ashcroft 2004, Bluhm 2009, 2010, Cartwright 1989, 2007, Howson and Urbach 2005, Kravitz et al. 2004, Worrall 2002, 2007, 2010a, 2010b, 2010c and 2011 and Thompson 2010, 2011a, 2011b). These have had little impact on clinical researchers and regulatory agencies. Indeed, the vast majority of clinical researchers, regulatory agencies and clinical practitioners either reject, ignore or are oblivious to these criticisms. We attribute this to entrenchment but there are obviously other elements. Moments such as this often signal the beginning of a conceptual revolution.

Although experimental designs similar to RCTs occurred prior to Ronald A. Fisher's *Design of Experiments*, it is reasonable to date the rise in popularity of

RCTs to that publication. In it, he set out what has become "Fisher's mantra": randomisation, control and replication reveal *causal* relations. Fisher's research was mainly in agriculture. His application of RCTs in agriculture involved dividing a field into numerous equal blocks. He assigned one of two adjacent blocks to the intervention (adding fertilizer, for example) and the other as a control (no intervention). The assumption was that two adjacent blocks would be homogeneous with respect to many causally relevant features related to plant growth (same hours of sunlight, same amount of rainfall, same natural nutrients, same soil structure and so on). Since the plants were bred to have the same agriculturally important traits, they were known to be genetically homogeneous for the traits being studied. Hence any differences between the intervention blocks and the control must be due to the intervention. Since there were numerous paired blocks, there was also built-in replication. The key features are the very high probability that adjacent blocks are homogeneous, that the plants are genetically homogeneous in relevant respects, that assignment of intervention and control is truly random and that multiple paired-blocks constitute replication. The same reasoning and method was used to explore plants with known genetic differences. In this case, all other factors are controlled and assumed to be homogeneous across blocks. As in experiments on adding nutrients or irrigation, randomisation eliminates bias and makes statistical analysis possible.

Since the end of the Second World War, clinical research in medicine has increasingly embraced this experimental design and accepted that randomisation, control and replication reveal *causal* relations. Importing this experimental design into clinical medicine, however, is not straightforward. The assumption of genetic homogeneity, the assumption of context homogeneity and the assumption of random assignment are all vastly more complicated.

The goal of clinical research is to determine the safety and causal efficacy of an intervention (pharmaceutical, dietary regime, surgery, for example). There are obvious reasons why this is the correct goal; unsafe interventions exacerbate existing conditions and create negative conditions where nothing was previously problematic. Inefficacious ones will fail to ameliorate or cure a condition and waste scarce resources. Safety is obviously paramount but, as Bradford Hill (1965) noted, the importance of establishing efficacy is context-sensitive – more on this later. In general, an intervention that is deemed safe (will do minimal harm) but is demonstrably not efficacious (will do no good) should be avoided. Its use may be harmless *per se* but might lead to tragedy where there is some urgency to intervening effectively to ameliorate or cure the condition; time wasted can be a very real harm.

There are several approaches to determining safety and efficacy. Determining the safety and efficacy of new pharmaceuticals provides a window onto a standard method. The process may begin with animal studies. If there are no reasons to question its safety based on these studies, research on humans is undertaken. Typically, there are four phases but phase IV sometimes does not occur, and in some cases a pre-phase I investigation can occur (called phase 0). This involves a very small number of individuals. The goal is usually not efficacy of the pharmaceutical but its behaviour: the metabolic pathway or decay rate, for example. The dosage is often sub-clinical.

The four phases are:

- **Phase I:** A small group of people are involved. Even if there have been successful animal studies, this is the first determination of the safety in humans. This is the phase in which dosage for clinical effectiveness is determined and side effects are monitored.
- **Phase II:** The size of the group is larger, which, it is assumed, increases the probability of correctly determining true efficacy and amplifies the detection of side-effects. There is still a reasonably small sample (100–200). An RCT might be used in this phase.
- **Phase III:** The size of the group is significantly expanded. Determining the appropriate size is known as determining the power needed – discussed later. This phase involves RCTs.
- **Phase IV:** The pharmaceutical has been approved and marketed by this phase. Information is collected on the efficacy and side-effects in large and diverse populations. Information is also collected on long-term use.

The trial can be stopped at the end of, or during, any phase. Sometimes it is stopped because safety concerns have emerged, sometimes because the expected efficacy is not manifested, and sometimes because the efficacy is so apparent and the condition it is designed to ameliorate so debilitating or life-threatening that it would be unethical to delay skipping to phase IV.

As part of the phases of the trial, an RCT is considered the optimal study design to eliminate confounding, hence revealing genuine causes rather than spurious causes and mere correlations. This is largely achieved by the function of randomisation. That is, randomly sampling the relevant population and randomly assigning those in the sample to an intervention group or control group, ideally, eliminate confounding factors. The latter (random assignment) also eliminates experimenter bias (selection bias). An experimenter might consciously or unconsciously assign individuals suspected to be least likely to benefit from a treatment to the control group and those suspected to be most likely to benefit to the intervention group. Random assignment eliminates this bias. Random sampling from a relevant population, in Fisher's method, provides the basis for generalising results found in a random sample to the larger population and allows statistical analysis of experimental results. We turn now to an examination of each of these features of RCTs.

First consider confounding; confounding occurs when A and B vary together – are correlated – but they do so not because A causes B but because a third factor, or concatenation of factors, C, causes them both. We discussed this in Chapter 6 and provided a diagram (see Figure 6.1). Because an RCT requires that participants in an experiment (a clinical trial) be *randomly* assigned to either an intervention group or a control group, it is reasonable to assume that differences among individuals will be equally represented in the intervention group and control group. This justifies an assumption that the groups are effectively homogeneous, just as Fisher assumed his adjacent blocks in a field were homogeneous (same rainfall, hours of sunlight, soil composition and the like). In agriculture, Fisher did not need to rely on randomisation for this assumption; only in extremely rare cases would two adjacent blocks (say of one hectare) be meaningfully different with respect to the relevant variable. Moreover, there are other ways to determine homogeneity – moisture meters in several locations in each of the two blocks as well as sunlight intensity and duration sensors, and so on. Randomisation of assignment of intervention and control blocks over a large number of adjacent blocks could be considered strengthening the homogeneity assumption but replication (yielding similar results from many paired blocks) is what underpins this. The main value of randomisation in agricultural research is the elimination of experimenter bias and underpinning the employment of statistical analysis, especially significance tests.

Fisher's insistence on RCTs to avoid confounding is exemplified in a now classic disagreement between Ronald A. Fisher (1958), and Richard Doll and Bradford Hill (1954) on smoking and lung cancer. Fisher challenged the causal connection that Doll and Hill were making, arguing that there might be – he thought likely was – a confounding factor. Here are the key parts of his paper:

> Seven or eight years ago, those of us interested in such things in England heard of a rather remarkable piece of research carried out by Bradford Hill and his colleagues of the London School of Hygiene
>
> (Fisher 1958, p. 151)

> The key words which emerged in the course of these inquiries – *replication, randomisation and control* – are now widely understood.
>
> (Fisher 1958, p. 153, emphasis added)

> The subject is complicated, and I mentioned at an early stage that the logical distinction was between A causing B, B causing A, something else causing both. Is it possible, then, that lung cancer – that is to say, the precancerous condition which must exist and is known to exist for years in those who are going to show overt lung cancer – is one of the causes of smoking cigarettes? I don't think it can be excluded. I don't think we know enough to say it is such a cause.
>
> (Fisher 1958, p. 162)

> For my part, I think it is more likely that a common cause supplies an explanation. Again, we do not know. I do not put forth any explanation as proved, but as requiring investigation. The obvious common cause to think of is the genotype.
>
> (Fisher 1958, p. 163, emphasis added)

Fisher's mantra is captured in the second sentence: "The key words which emerged in the course of these inquiries – replication, randomisation and control – are now widely understood" (Fisher). That they "are now widely understood" was, at the time, a somewhat bold assertion. Today, however, in clinical research they are very well understood and dominate clinical methodology.

As this debate illustrates well, randomisation is believed essential because it reduces – ideally eliminates – confounding. It ensures that each experimental group is equally representative of the larger population from which a random sample is drawn. As a result, the only factor that could be responsible for a difference between a group receiving an intervention and the group that is not is the intervention. If there is a third factor, or concatenation of factors, $C$, its effect will be distributed evenly in both groups and the intervention and control groups will manifest no difference; the intervention will be neutral (i.e. not efficacious). One potential factor believed to be an important confounder is the placebo effect. This describes a situation where experimental subjects seem to benefit from an intervention but the benefit actually derives from psychological expectations; that is, from one's mind affecting physiological status (including the mind itself). The change in status is what the subject expects and his mind produces the expected physiological effect. Randomisation ensures that the propensity to manifest this effect is distributed equally in the two groups and blinding removes knowledge of which group is the intervention group. Blinding means that the subjects do not know whether they are receiving the intervention or not. Double-blinding means that the experimenter is also blind to which group is the intervention group.

Moving to experimenter bias; consciously or unconsciously an experimenter could assign individuals more likely to benefit from an intervention to the intervention group. There are a number of techniques used to avoid this potential bias. Randomised assignment of individuals to the two groups is one. If the assignment is truly random, the experimenter is not making the choice; it is made by following a random process. As with the placebo effect being a confounder, blinding is a technique that can be used to avoid experimenter bias. The random assignment is not done by the experimenter; it is done by someone (a technician perhaps) who, ideally, does not know the nature of the experiment and uses a random number generator to make the assignments.

The two other benefits of randomisation are grounding the application of statistical analysis to the results of an experiment and allowing the results to be generalised to the entire population from which the sample of experimental subjects was drawn. In the frequentist conception of probability, randomisation is crucial to both. Ronald Fisher, Karl Pearson and Jerzy Neyman were all committed to a frequentist interpretation of probability and their edifice of statistical techniques requires that interpretation.

The reason randomisation grounds any generalisation to the larger population is easy to understand. If the sample is "truly" random, it is highly likely that the characteristics of those in the sample represent the range and frequency of those characteristics in the population. There is, of course, another factor – size.

A small random sample is unlikely to include the range and frequency of diversity in the larger population. We will revisit the determination of how large a sample needs to be when we discuss the power of a study.

The ways in which randomisation grounds the validity of the application of statistics to the analysis of results is more complicated. Statistics is an application of the probability calculus. Recall that the most widely accepted axiomatisation of probability is that of Kolmogorov but that axiomatisation does not include or require randomness. Hence, it is the interpretation of probability, and its application to statistical analysis that introduces it, and is deemed to require it.

Although actual clinical applications are complicated, a simple example will provide a glimpse into the reasoning that deems randomisation essential to the application of statistics. Consider, yet again, a coin toss. The expected outcome of a fair coin tossed 10,000 times is that it will yield 50% tails and 50% heads more than 99% of the time.[1]

The outcome of any toss is random; the cumulative outcome is not. Suppose you suspect that the coin is not a fair coin (weighted, let's say, to produce 60% heads). How could you detect this? We begin with a null hypothesis; that is, we hypothesize that the coin is a fair coin. We know that a fair coin will yield heads in the range 40–60 times on 100 tosses 95% of the time. A biased coin has to fall outside that range to be declared biased. That means that there is only a 50% chance of detecting a coin biased for 60% heads. This trial is "underpowered". Increasing the tosses to 1,000 increases the power of the investigation. A fair coin will fall heads in the range 469–531 heads 95% of the time. Consequently, if in 1,000 tosses, the coin being tested lands heads 540 or more times, the probability that it landed that way by chance is less than 5%. Although it is arbitrary, this is usually deemed sufficient to reject the null hypothesis (i.e. reject that the coin is fair). Obviously, increasing the tosses beyond 1,000 will decrease the probability that a deviation from 50/50 is due to chance.

The concept of "the power of a study" is important to the statistical tools of Neyman and Pearson, so a brief discussion, at this point, is appropriate. The power of a study relates to the size of the study population that is needed to detect an effect. If a drug is remarkably effective, such as amoxicillin in resolving inner-ear infections, a small number of subjects in each comparison group (antibiotic group and control) is sufficient to reveal an effect. If the effectiveness of a drug is real but small, a very large number of subjects will be needed to detect a difference. If a small effect requires 20,000 subjects in a study to be able to detect it, a study with only 10,000 will be underpowered. Determining how much power is needed is complicated. Simply put, the power of a study is the probability that it will distinguish a real effect from a chance occurrence. As Alex Reinhart (2015) explains it in the context of a fair coin and a biased coin:

The power is affected by three factors:

- *The size of the bias (or other effect) you're looking for.* A huge bias is much easier to detect than a tiny one.

- *The sample size.* By collecting more data (more coin flips), you can more easily detect small biases.
- *Measurement error.* It's easy to count coin flips, but many experiments deal with values that are harder to measure, such as medical studies investigating symptoms of fatigue or depression.

Power is obviously important. An underpowered study might conclude there is no effect when there is one. A standard threshold is 80%. If a study is powered to detect a real effect 80% of the time, this is reasonable, although arbitrary as is so much in this domain. With this in mind, it is chilling that:

> In the prestigious journals *Science* and *Nature*, fewer than 3% of articles calculate statistical power before starting their study [Tressoldi et al. 2013].
>
> . . .
>
> In one sample of studies published in prestigious medical journals between 1975 and 1990, more than four-fifths of randomized controlled trials that reported negative results didn't collect enough data to detect a 25% *difference* in primary outcome between treatment groups. That is, even if one medication reduced symptoms by 25% more than another, there was insufficient data to make that conclusion.
>
> . . .
>
> A more recent study of trials in cancer research found similar results: only half of published studies with negative results had enough statistical power to detect even a large difference in their primary output variable [Bedard et al. 2007].
>
> (Reinhart 2015)

Returning to the Neyman–Pearson statistical methods, the biased coin toss example illustrates the value of using their methods of a known distribution (e.g. the distribution of outcome for a fair coin tossed a specific number of times) for which probability calculations can be generated. The data allows the calculation of a test statistic; in this case very elementary but in most clinical trials the calculation of a test statistic is more complicated and follows a formula devised by Neyman and Pearson, to which we return below. If the experiment is designed to be random in relevant respects, the results of the tosses can be compared with the known distribution *of a fair coin, as is typical in binary outcomes.* If the deviation of the distribution of the experimental result (e.g. the tossing of a biased coin 1,000 times) is such that the deviation is attributable to chance only 5% or less of the time (i.e. $P(0.6 \text{ heads}) < 0.05$), the null hypothesis can be rejected. This reasoning and analysis from the coin toss example can be applied to pharmaceutical testing. If the null hypothesis is the hypothesis that drug A is not efficacious and we have a probability distribution describing the expected outcome, a deviation of experimental results from the known distribution can be examined. If that deviation could occur by chance less than 5% of the time, the experimenter is justified in rejecting chance and with it the null hypothesis. Hence, drug A is deemed efficacious, otherwise not.

An important epistemological point to note here is that the coin toss yields frequencies and the probability analysis of the experimental data assumes a frequentist interpretation of probability. This is important to note because a subjectivist interpretation of probability employs a different set of assumptions and methods. Until recently, the ability to apply what is now known as a Bayesian probabilistic experimental design and probabilistic analysis was limited. The increasing computing capacity over the last three decades has changed that. We look later at Bayesian methods.

There are conceptual and practical problems with randomisation and statistical analysis on a frequentist account. First, we look at the conceptual issues, then at the practical.

Although Fisher's *Design of Experiments* was influential in orienting clinical research to RCTs and the use of significance tests, it was the work of Jerzy Neyman and Egon Pearson that had the greatest influence on the employment of statistics. They worked during the late 1920s and into the 1930s on goodness of fit; that is, how to determine how statistically well the fit of experimental data is to a postulated distribution. Fisher, it should be noted, did not agree with Neyman and Pearson's methods; their methods are not those of Fisher's *Design of Experiments*. He specifically criticised Neyman–Pearson's methods, arguing that their use of their statistical theory in analysing scientific data is invalid.

The result of the collaboration between Neyman and Pearson was a method of hypothesis testing involving two descriptions: a null hypothesis and an alternative. The data is used to make a decision about which to accept. The null hypothesis states that there is no effect of $A$ on $B$. The alternative hypothesis is that there is an effect. The central task is to determine the probability of obtaining the experimental data when the null hypothesis is true; that is, there is no effect of $A$ on $B$, even though the data suggests there is. That the data suggests an effect is a "mere" chance occurrence and not an accurate reflection of the nature of reality. Using the experimental data and assuming the null hypothesis is true, we can calculate the value of a test statistic; we will not explore the specific details of this calculation but instead provide a very brief description of the process. To test the hypothesis for the population-mean $\mu$, we use the test statistic, which is a distribution.[2] We are interested in how probable it is that the association found in the data is a result of chance and the null hypothesis (no association) is true. Put another way, if the null hypothesis is true, what is the probability that we would have experimental data that yields a more extreme test statistic in the direction of the alternative hypothesis than we did? This yields a $p$-value. Arbitrarily, we set the relevant probability for a decision based on a $p$-value at 0.05. If the probability that experimental data occurred by chance is less than 0.05 (or some other accepted, arbitrary $p$-value probability), then the null hypothesis is rejected. The probability that the alternate hypothesis occurred by chance is very low; low enough that chance can be rejected.

It is worth underscoring that the *p*-value is arbitrary but there are other concerns. As award-winning statistician David Salsburg (1993) points out:

> The problem he [Neyman] faced was that the *p*-value we calculate from the test statistic is a random variable whose value depends upon the random fall of the data in the study. A slight change in a few patients leads to a different *p*-value. This *p*-value has no frequentist interpretation, since there is no way of constructing a sequence of future trials which will have the same *p*-values. However, if we use a fixed cutoff (say 0.05) and reject the null whenever the *p*-value is less than that cutoff, the event of rejecting the null becomes one with the frequentist interpretation.
>
> This means among other things, that there is no difference between a *p*-value of 0.049 and one of 0.00001. Both provide the same degree of evidence against the null. It means nothing, within the framework of the Neyman-Pearson formulation, to talk about "very" significant or "highly" significant. A result is either significant ($p \geq 0.05$) or not. Keifer and Arrow [see Berger 1983] have shown that it is impossible to make any other distinction, as long as we use the frequentist definition of probability.
>
> If we do not use the Neyman-Pearson formulation, there is no reason to consider a predetermined cutoff value as important. We protect the alpha-level of a study only because the purely arbitrary formulation is based on fixing $\alpha$ [the probability of rejecting the null when the null is true] and minimizing $\beta$ [the probability of rejecting the alternative when the alternative is true].
>
> And so, the Neyman-Pearson formulation lays in rubble at our feet. *It is an arbitrary construction with no apparent relationship to the needs of clinical research. It rests on the rotten beam of frequentist probability. The basic optimization that it attempts is impossible in most clinical studies. And, it does not allow us to make relative judgments about two studies, one of which shows a major difference and one of which shows a barely "significant" difference.*
>
> (p. 24, original emphasis)

Of course, there are many statisticians who will disagree with his analysis, although, in our view, no one has provided a successful mathematical or philosophical rebuttal. Moreover, Fisher himself levelled the same criticism against the Neyman–Pearson formulation. For Fisher, significance tests are more or less exploratory techniques; he even recognizes the arbitrary nature of fixing the critical value at a particular value like 0.05. Fisher thought that scientists should use the null hypothesis ('no effect') *only if* they were *completely* ignorant of the underlying phenomena in such a way that they could not formulate a working statistical model of the phenomena. Once they had appropriate statistical models, Fisher thought that the import of statistical data on the hypotheses was given by the likelihoods, not by acceptance and rejection error characteristics, thereby clearly rejecting the Neyman–Pearson methods. We contend that Fisher's and Salsburg's analysis is correct and that it provides grounds for suspecting that no successful mathematical or philosophical rebuttal will be forthcoming. All this being said, surprisingly in our view, the Neyman–Pearson methods pervade the use of statistics in clinical medicine. Fisher's critique is seldom noticed, or Salsburg's for that matter.

Turning now to the practical problems, we discuss why the empirical application of random sampling in clinical research is less robust than advertised, making inferences based on the probabilistic and statistical analysis of data problematic. One challenge is that the mathematical definition of a random sample is abstract. From a mathematical perspective, it is clean, clear and precise but from an empirical perspective its demands are too stringent to enable it to be applied *simpliciter*. A clear mathematical definition of a random sample is:

> A sample of *n* individuals from a population chosen in such a way that all possible sets of *n* individuals are equally likely to occur.

When *n* is sufficiently large, genuine random samples are sets of individuals "equally likely to occur" and confounding factors are, therefore, equally likely to occur in the same proportions in each random sample.

This is an abstract mathematical concept. The challenge is relating this mathematical concept to empirical phenomena. There are more methodological and pragmatic issues with RCTs. The first step in creating random samples from a population is to define the population. Let's assume we are researching the efficacy of a new pharmaceutical for the prevention of ischemic stroke. Since, once approved, the pharmaceutical can be prescribed to anyone in the population, the population encompasses everyone; let's, however, restrict it to individuals in high-income countries (that is, for the most part, European and English-speaking countries). Even with this restriction, it is an unrealistic population from which to sample. For one thing, the cost of sampling, say, two groups of 30,000 each from the complete spectrum of those countries is challenging. Moreover, the logistics of managing the research trial are complex. Despite the challenges and complexity, there are today more international trials than a decade ago but most trials still focus on a small geographic area or a few hospitals or some similar constriction of the total population that will be treated.

This population will be further reduced because some individuals will be "unsuitable": for example, the very young (under five years old), the very old (over 70 years old), those with other known morbidities – high blood pressure, high LDL to HDL ratios and so on – and those on medications that might interact with the one being tested or the effectiveness of the current medication might be compromised by the one being tested. At this point, the population that will be sampled is very small compared with the population of individuals eligible to receive the medication, if it is approved. In fact, although it is a sample of the "target" population, it is not even close to a random sample. That is, it is not a sample of *n* individuals from a population chosen in such a way that all possible sets of *n* individuals are equally likely to occur. Hence, no assumption about this sample being representative of the target population can be made. Moreover, there will also be individuals who were selected by "pure" randomisation who will decline to consent to be part of the trial.

All of this highlights that there is a general tension between creating groups in a clinical trial that are as alike as possible in all relevant respects and for the most part absent of known confounding factors. The more tightly and comprehensively the inclusion and exclusion criteria are applied in a clinical trial, the stronger the inferences that can be drawn from them. Inclusion and exclusion criteria are applied in order to strengthen the internal validity of the trial. However, the more an investigator strives for a fair comparison between intervention and control by using such criteria, the less externally valid (applicable to populations outside the trial) the results become. There is no easy way around this paradox. Strict interpretations of randomised trials would hold that the results of the trial are applicable only to the participants in the trial or to members of the population who are identical in all relevant respects to those in the trial. In practice, once a therapy has been assessed in a clinical trial and entered into practice, it is often used in populations completely unlike the study population, casting significant doubt on whether the effects in the trial can be extrapolated to this population (Fuller 2013).

Once a sample is established, two groups are created from the sample yielding the participants. Individuals are assigned to these groups randomly – avoiding selection bias. Usually, there are only two groups and everyone in the assembled population is assigned to one of the two groups. Because these are random assignments – or at least as close as randomising techniques in any empirical context allow – we can assume that confounding factors are equally likely to occur in the same proportions in each group. Moreover, selection bias will be avoided.

Once we have the two groups, there are known factors that "unbalance" groups: gender, age, lifestyle (smoker/non-smoker, exerciser/non-exerciser, diet and so on), ethnicity and so on. Depending on the study, smokers may have already been eliminated from the population being sampled. If the two groups have an imbalance with respect to these known relevant characteristics, they will need to be re-balanced, compromising, yet again, the randomisation. It should be clear, at this point, that randomisation, in the required mathematical sense, will rarely be achieved.

As stated already, randomisation is supposed to do at least three critical things: eliminate the importance of confounding factors (the assumption is that they are equally distributed in all large truly random samples), allow a determination of the probability that a result is a chance occurrence and eliminate selection bias. The fact that the original sampling was far from random compromises the first of these three goals.

That the original sampling was far from an ideal sampling also compromises the assessment of the probability that the result occurred by chance. Let's look at this one more carefully.

A result in any given experiment could be due to chance. For example, by chance one could get 150 heads from 200 tosses of a fair coin. The probability of that is, of course, very low but not 0.0. As we have seen, what statistical analysis – based on probability theory – allows is an estimate of the likelihood that an outcome is due to chance rather than the intervention. Again, as we have seen, random sampling *is essential* to this statistical determination because it enables us to compare an observed outcome distribution with a reference set – distributions of other outcomes that are just as likely to occur. Regrettably, for quite understandable reasons that have been outlined, neither the original sampling of *the target population* in RCTs is random nor is the assignment of individuals to the two groups (experimental and control), although the latter comes much closer than the former.

A key element of any experimental methodology is validation. Application of probability is often assumed to validate the RCT methodology but as we have seen there are complexities. Hence, the ultimate validation for RCTs is use after approval: how close the predicted efficacy is based on RCTs to the experience in the years after it has been in widespread use. That method of validation does not distinguish RCT-based determinations of efficacy from other clinical methodologies – case-controlled studies, for example. These other methodologies also can be validated by post-use outcomes. To see this in a different context, consider election polling.

A target population is sampled in a quasi-random way and the preferences of individuals in the sample are obtained, usually by a series of questions. A prediction is made. The closer to the election, the more settled people's views and preferences are and, hence, the more robust the predictions. On, or shortly after, election day, there is an outcome that is known. The predictions and the outcome are analysed. Using a database of such analyses from past elections an inductive inference is made; such as this polling methodology is accurate within 5%, 19 times out of 20. This validates the methodology within known margins of error. This validation rests on two things, the quasi-random sampling and the analysis after the results are known. Both are necessary for a robust validation. In the case of RCTs, there is no database equivalent to pre-election predictions and actual outcome. It is not that such a database could not be assembled; it is the logistics and cost that make it very complicated. This is compounded by privacy concerns about personal medical data.

There is a further complication. Even if there were a relevant post-approval database, its relevance for inductive inference would be invalid because the randomisation condition isn't satisfied. That is, only a small portion of the relevant population was randomly sampled for the experiment. Hence, with all the complications already noted taken into account, the only valid inference is to the small portion of the relevant population. The issue centres on how to compare the phase IV knowledge (the analogue of post-election knowledge) with the result of the trial on a sample (analogous to the polling sample). If the experimental subjects were in fact selected randomly from the target population (or those polled were randomly selected), a comparison would be possible. If there is a deviation from random selection, any inference to the larger population will be compromised. This is exacerbated by, as we have seen earlier, the fact that no substantive inductive logic has been created, making inductive inference shaky, at best. Consequently, generalising from a small sample – selected in a questionably random way – to the relevant target population is fraught with logical and practical challenges.

Returning to election polling, let us draw one last point. Even a cursory examination of election polling illustrates that if one wants to know how Canadians will vote in a federal election two days hence, even a truly random sample of Torontonians will give invalid results. No inference exists that validates a generalisation from Torontonians to Canadians as a whole. That's why polls draw conclusions *only* for the population polled: all Canadians, Albertans, Calgarians and the like. RCTs are conducted using a selected subset of the target population, which is then randomly assigned to groups. Judea Pearl terms these "imperfect experiments".[3]

Robyn Bluhm (2009, 2010) has pointed out that evidence-based medicine and its commitment to RCTs are an example of "shortsighted" empiricism. Recall from Chapter 2 the discussion of crude empiricism; "short-sighted" is a more gentle adjective than "crude" but it amounts to the same critique. In Chapter 2 it was illustrated by a parable attributed to Francis Bacon (1561–1626). To explore Bluhm's claim, let's assume RCTs satisfy completely the requirements of random sampling from a target population. RCTs will then have achieved two things: elimination of confounding factors and a reasonable basis for determining that the results are not the result of chance.[4] Nonetheless, at best, RCTs demonstrate a connection between events: this intervention leads to this outcome (in a statistically significant number of cases); that is, it establishes an association. The claim to have established a causal connection is weak, a point we now examine in more detail since, logically and philosophically it is a more important challenge to RCTs than what has gone before.

Recall, Fisher's reasoning was that three situations can give rise to an association of $A$ and $B$:

1   $A$ causes $B$

2   $B$ causes $A$

3   $C$ causes ($A$ and $B$) – $C$ can be one or more events or factors.

Often, temporal order allows a judgement of whether it is (1) or (2). It is generally assumed that a cause precedes its effect. It is separating (3) from (1) and (2) that is critical to justifying an assertion of a causal connection between events found to be associated. RCTs are supposed to support the conclusion: not (3). Since temporal order is almost always known in the case of RCTs, a decision between (1) and (2) is straightforward. At best, RCTs establish that "this intervention" is accompanied by "this outcome": an association. A more interesting question, at this juncture is, "would a mathematically ideal RCT support the claim of not (3) (i.e. not (C causes A and B)), as Fisher and others have asserted?"

What the past 300 years of physics and 150 years of biology have taught us is that there is an entangled network of causal relations in nature. Moreover, any population can be partitioned in a multitude of ways, all consistent with the characteristics of the population. This means that making causal claims requires that "causal partitions" of populations must be separable from "non-causal partitions" (mere correlations) – background conditions being held fixed. Advocates of RCTs, following Fisher's methods, assume a specific partition is causal; they do not demonstrate it. Simpson's paradox illustrates the challenge of demonstrating it.

Simpson published his influential paper in 1951. Earlier (in 1934), based on actual death data, Morris Cohen and Ernest Nagel posed this paradox:

1   The death rate from tuberculosis for African Americans in 1910 was *lower* in Richmond than in New York.
2   The death rate for Caucasians in 1910 was *lower* in Richmond than in New York.
3   The death rate for the total combined population of African Americans and Caucasians was *higher* in Richmond than in New York.

Cohen and Nagel posed two questions: does it follow that tuberculosis caused a greater mortality in Richmond than in New York, and are the two geographic populations really comparable – are they homogeneous?

The generalized mathematical form of the paradox is:

$$a/b < x/y$$
$$c/d < m/n$$
$$(a + c)/(b + d) > (x + m)/(y + n)$$

In the aggregated data, the inequalities are reversed; hence the paradox.

For example:

$$1/5 \ (.2) < 2/8$$
$$6/8 \ (.75) < 4/5$$
$$7/13 > 6/13$$

There have been a flood of attempts to resolve the paradox. Some advocate resolving the arithmetic paradox through normalization. This seems successful but it fails to address the causal question that Cohen and Nagel posed. Most of those who have tackled the causal question rely on ways of partitioning the population. This, however, as already noted, is complicated. John Dupré and Nancy Cartwright (1988, cf. Cartwright 1979, 1989 and 2001, Dupré 1984) have demonstrated the complexity.

The structure of the paradox lays bare that:

•   a population can be partitioned in a multitude of ways, all consistent with the characteristics of the population,

- there is an entanglement of causal relations that probability claims do not capture,
- to do so, probabilistic representations of causal relations must include methods which will disentangle causal networks,
- to do this, "causal partitions" of populations must be separable from "non-causal partitions" (mere correlations) – background conditions being held fixed.

Achieving the requirement of this last point has proved exceptionally elusive. RCTs certainly do not come close to meeting the requirement of the last point. Hence, there is no clear reason to believe they uncover causal connection. Clinical researchers usually offer as buttressing of RCTs the use of systematic reviews. A systematic review collects and analyses the results from all previous studies on a topic that are considered methodologically sound. The data and analysis are presented in a composite form. The strengths and weaknesses of each are examined. The culmination of the analysis is frequently a meta-analysis. For each study an odds ratio is calculated. The ratio is presented both in terms of a point estimate (a dot on the display), which identifies the most likely estimate of efficacy, and a confidence interval (a line extending to the right and left of the point estimate. The confidence interval gives the range within which we can be confident the evidence of benefit (or not) falls. This aggregation of studies is deemed to satisfy the requirement of replication. The compilation is displayed visually (see Table 7.1). The dot given for each study is the point estimate of the magnitude of the effect of the intervention. The line extending on either side of the dot is the confidence interval – the range within which the value of the effectiveness could fall. The wider the confidence interval – the longer the line – the greater is the uncertainty about the efficacy.

Point estimates can be given for individual studies. In a meta-analysis the confidence intervals will depend on the number of studies and the precision of each study included. That is, the point estimates and confidence intervals for meta-analyses are comparative. Meta-analyses are obviously useful; they compare numerous studies – replications of a sort – and provide a richer, varied perspective on the efficacy of an intervention. There are logical issues regarding principles of valid aggregation if RCTs individually encounter the difficulties identified above; putting ten of them together cannot be expected to remedy those difficulties. Nonetheless, systematic reviews provide a genuine advance over individual studies. There is still no reason, however, to believe that causes have been revealed.

The dots are the best statistical estimate for each study (or group of studies) of the magnitude of the effect and whether it is positive (the left side of the centre – vertical – line) or negative (the right side of the centre line). The line is the range within which we can be confident the magnitude falls.

If RCTs, as the gold standard, do not reveal causes, does that mean that clinical research cannot uncover causal relations? An answer requires an exploration of the alternatives to RCTs. There are other study designs that are frequently

*Table 7.1* An abstract example of the statistical display of a meta-analysis. The dots are the best statistical estimate for each study (or group of studies) of the magnitude of the effect and whether it is positive (the left side of the centre – vertical – line) or negative (the right side of the centre line). The line is the range within which we can be confident the magnitude falls.

| Year of the RCT | # RCTs Patients | # cumulative | ODDS RATIO (Log Scale) |
|---|---|---|---|
| 1971 | 1 | 41 | |
| 1977 | 3 | 80 | |
| 1980 | 5 | 109 | |
| 1983 | 9 | 1008 | |
| 1991 | 14 | 2000 | |
| 2000 | 20 | 5000 | |
| 2006 | 21 | 5300 | |
| 2010 | 30 | 8050 | |
| 2011 | 35 | 10,0000 | |
| | 38 | 13,750 | |
| 2012 | 40 | 20,540 | |
| | 41 | 28,600 | |

Supports Therapy Group        Supports Control Group

used and which we discuss next. In addition, Bayesian methods are increasingly important as a significant alternative to RCTs; we look briefly at those later in the chapter. We close the chapter with an examination of Hill's considerations (often called Hill's criteria) for causal attribution. We end with an exploration of a corollary to the above question, "how significant is an inability to reveal causes in clinical medicine?"

There are a number of methodologies (study designs),[5] other than RCTs, employed in medical research. Some of these are descriptive and some analytic. Some involve primary data collection, others secondary. Some are observational, others experimental. Some are retrospective (looking back in time), others prospective (looking ahead in time). In a retrospective study an outcome is already known; the study looks backwards to explore potential causes for the outcome. An outcome could be the presence or absence of disease. A prospective study is undertaken before an outcome has occurred. A group of individuals is followed into the future to determine the factors that have, or have not, led to an outcome – a particular disease. A study design might be analytic, involve primary data collection, and be experimental and prospective. Hence, study designs can combine, in different ways, these distinctions. Now we move to a more detailed look at these features.

## Descriptive studies

These collect data on incident rates or outcomes and organize the data to answer a question: What is the incidence of multiple sclerosis in various regions or countries? What is the survival rate after surgery to remove a melanoma? *Analytic studies* look for connections – ideally causal – between events: the connection between exposure to second-hand smoke and lung cancer, for example.

## Observational studies

As the name suggests, these studies are based on observations. The researcher does not manipulate any aspect of the context. Observational studies are always descriptive. There are a number of different ways to present the data obtained from the observations. *Case reports (or series)* describe characteristics of an individual case or group of cases. These are useful for new diseases or unusual outcomes. For example, an observational study of veterans returning from combat in Afghanistan and Iraq led to the identification of post-traumatic stress disorder (PTSD). This opened the path to identification and treatment.

## Ecological observational studies

These aggregate information on individuals in different ecological zones. They permit a comparison of rates of exposure with rates of outcomes across regions. Usually, the data used is routinely collected, which means it is a quick and inexpensive methodology. It runs, however, a higher risk of bias than some other methodologies. There is also a risk of committing the ecological fallacy. One commits the ecological fallacy when conclusions about individuals are drawn from group data. There are too many other variables in individual cases to make this inference valid: genetic factors, exercise, other dietary factors, the kind of fat consumed and so on.

In a seven-country study Ancel Keys (1970, 1980) observed variation in cardiovascular mortality rates in post-war Europe. The highest mortality rates were in countries such as Finland (especially, areas like North Karelia). He found a correlation between mortality rates from heart disease and dietary fat intake. Although ground-breaking, there have been numerous criticisms, to which we shall we return in Chapter 9.

## Time-series studies

These studies compare rates of events over time. This is a very useful way of aggregating and displaying data. The rates are plotted against time. For example, we could plot the rate of transient ischemic activity (TIA; a minor stroke) for different ages. Other examples are that we could plot the influenza events by months of the year over many years or we could plot the influenza events by months over many years for those who are immunized and those that are not. Consequently, time series are useful for studying the impact of policy-type interventions, such as an influenza vaccine, or describing rates of occurrence over time of any number of health-related events. This methodology can also use routinely collected data. In those cases, it consequently is cost-effective and easy to implement.

## Cross-sectional studies

As the name implies, a cross-sectional study does for a population what some travel books (DK – Dorling Kindersley – for example) do for buildings. These provide slices of the building. In clinical medicine, these studies assess exposure (or intervention) and outcome at the same point in time by taking a temporal slice of the population. They are used to describe rates of exposure (or intervention) to outcome. They can also describe an association between exposure and outcome. They can be done quickly. The associating of exposure to outcome provides at best a correlation and not a causal connection.

## Cohort studies

These studies involve following a specific group over time. The two first steps are identification of a cohort and choosing a time to start the monitoring. This method assesses exposure at baseline – the beginning of the study period – and measures outcomes over time. The exposure (to a pathogen or a medication, for example) can be controlled during the study. Hence, changes from the baseline allow an inference about the effect of the exposure over time. If the cohort is representative of a relevant population (those with high blood pressure, for instance), the effect of the condition on cardiac events can be assessed, or the effect of medications to lower blood pressure can be assessed, as well as the effect of that lowered blood pressure on the incidence and severity of cardiac events. Ideally, this method can reveal causes but, as we have seen with RCTs, causality is an elusive concept without the employment of a theory. The larger the number in the cohort and the longer the cohort is studied, the more robust the findings. Also, as with RCTs, avoiding confounding is important but difficult.

## Case-control studies

These studies are retrospective; they look back in time. The starting point is grouping individuals with or without a particular disease. The researchers then look back at the history of these individuals. There may be a number of factors that are hypothesized to be relevant to the presence or absence of the disease.

These are what are investigated. In some cases the history is being used to discover differences between those with the disease and those without. This allows a presumptive hypothesis about what might cause the disease or what might prevent the disease.

As with other clinical studies that are looking at inputs and outputs – the connection of events – drawing causal conclusions must at best be tentative until a theory can be applied. Also, as in many other clinical research methods, avoiding bias is important. This method requires extra care.

## n-of-1 studies

These are studies in which a single individual is studied – in clinical research $n$ = the number of individuals in the study or the study group. An individual is followed over time. Ideally, the treatment inferred to be appropriate is prescribed randomly and the patient is blind to when she is receiving the treatment and when receiving a placebo. In clinical practice, this is a useful method for determining the best therapy for a specific patient. Patients are idiosyncratic; for any given treatment, some will respond well, others poorly, some not at all. Hence, this method allows a physician to experiment with a single individual to provide the maximally effective therapy *for that individual*. There are other methods employed but the ones discussed here are among the most common. There are two key elements to all the methodologies discussed, except $n$-of-1 studies: control and statistical power. $n$-of-1 studies require control but are not amenable to statistical power. Statistical power is the number of experimental subjects required to be able to draw robust conclusions. For example, a study that assumes in its design that there will be a statistically significant difference between the outcome for the intervention group and the control group, if there are 5,000 individuals in each group (arm), might discover only a small difference. This might be because there is no significant difference or it might be because the study was underpowered. The same study with 15,000 individuals in each arm might have shown a significant difference.

Do any of these study designs move clinical research closer to identifying causes? Even though each design in specific contexts advances significantly our knowledge of specific and medically important associations, none warrant causal attribution.

We move now to a relatively new[6] set of methods in clinical medicine: Bayesian methods.[7] In Chapter 5, we examined different interpretations of probability. The focus thus far has been on the frequency interpretation on which the statistical edifice of RCTs is built. Bayesian methods are built on a subjectivist interpretation.[8] As previously indicated, on a subjectivist interpretation, probability is an expression of an individual's *degree of belief* (strength of belief) in a proposition (a claim) about events, such as the likelihood of an event occurring under certain circumstances or the likelihood of a causal connection between events. Different *rational* individuals can have different degrees of belief in a proposition even when it is based on the same body of evidence.

This interpretation captures the intuition that different people can have different thresholds of evidence for belief in a proposition.[9] Philosophically, Bayesian methods are, as a set of formal *inferential methods*, consistent with a more general epistemic approach to probability. Subjectivism, broadly construed, is just one subspecies of an epistemic interpretation.

Even though Bayes' theorem, which underlies this approach, was published, posthumously, in 1763, the sophisticated applications required in areas like clinical research were unmanageable until the very recent advances in computing power.

In Chapter 5, we gave an example from Hacking of the application of Bayes' theorem. Here, it is important to explicate why Bayes' theorem is so powerful. An important feature is its inclusion of inverse conditionals. Typically, one asks about the probability of the truth of a hypothesis given the evidence. Bayes' theorem employs the inverse: the probability of the evidence given the hypothesis – $Pr(E/H)$. We encountered this inverse in connection with the hypothetico-deductive (H-D) method; on the assumption that the hypothesis is true, what evidence can we expect to find? Ideally in the H-D method, the evidence can be deduced from the hypothesis: $Pr(E/H) = 1$. A researcher then looks for the evidence. Much more commonly, the evidence is made more probable on the assumption that the hypothesis is true. That probability is expressed as $Pr(E/H) < 1$. In Bayes' theorem, the inverse occurs in the numerator and again in the denominator:

$$Pr(H/E) = Pr(H)\mathbf{Pr(E/H)}/Pr(H)\mathbf{Pr(E/H)} + Pr(\sim H)Pr(E/\sim H)$$

James Joyce (2016) has expressed the value of this clearly:[10]

> Though a mathematical triviality, Bayes' Theorem is of great value in calculating conditional probabilities because inverse probabilities are typically both easier to ascertain and less subjective than direct probabilities. People with different views about the unconditional probabilities of *E* and *H* often disagree about *E*'s value as an indicator of *H*. Even so, they can agree about the degree to which the hypothesis predicts the data if they know any of the following intersubjectively available facts: (a) *E*'s *objective* probability given *H*, (b) the frequency with which events like *E* will occur if *H* is true, or (c) the fact that *H* logically entails *E*. Scientists often design experiments so that likelihoods can be known in one of these "objective" ways. Bayes' Theorem then ensures that any dispute about the significance of the experimental results can be traced to "subjective" disagreements about the unconditional probabilities of *H* and *E*.
>
> When both $\mathbf{P}_H(E)$ and $\mathbf{P}_{\sim H}(E)$ are known, an experimenter need not even know *E*'s probability to determine a value for $\mathbf{P}_E(H)$ using Bayes' Theorem.

The claim here that likelihoods are more "objective" than prior probabilities, where "objectivity" is defined in terms of intersubjective agreement seems right. There are, however, cases in which what is under debate is the appropriate underlying probabilistic distribution with which to model the phenomena; that is, you may want to model a phenomenon with a Gaussian (normal) distribution while someone else may think a Poisson, binomial or Skellam distribution more appropriate (understanding the specific probability distribution is not essential to grasping this point). In the case of appeals to different distributions, the likelihoods of the data given the hypotheses will differ and, what is more, depend crucially upon our subjective prior beliefs about the most appropriate probability distribution. Often jointly accepted scientific practice and community norms resolve these types of problems, but they nevertheless do arise fairly frequently. That said, if the underlying probability distribution is agreed upon, the likelihoods are intersubjectively agreed upon.

The example given in Chapter 5 suffices to illustrate the simple application of Bayes' theorem. Beyond such simple examples Bayesian methods become mathematically complex and powerful. Among the many virtues of Bayesian methods are the convergence in subjective posterior beliefs, and replacements of classical statistical methods of statistical inference.

With respect to the convergence in subjective posterior beliefs, there are proofs showing that agents with different subjective prior probabilities will converge in their posterior probabilities if they update with Bayesian conditionalisation over increasingly large bodies of evidence. That is, agents, who initially disagree over a scientific question will eventually come to an agreement when they faithfully include an ever-increasing body of evidence; this follows as a deductive consequence from Bayes' theorem.

With respect to replacements of classical statistical methods of statistical inference, the focus is on replacing the evidential use of $p$-values and confidence intervals with likelihood methods (see Richard Royall (1997), J.O. Berger (2006), Donald Berry (2012) and Jeffrey Blume (2011)). The likelihood ratio measures the degree of support that some evidence confers on one of two competing hypotheses and follows as a deductive consequence of the law of likelihood:

Law of likelihood:
Evidence $E$ favours $H_1$ over $H_2$ if and only if $Pr(E/H_1) > Pr(E/H_2)$.

Along with many others, we argue that the law of likelihood is an a priori truth: a theorem of mathematics. Embedded in Bayes' theorem is the likelihood ratio: $Pr(E/H)/Pr(E/\sim H)$. In this sense, then, Bayesian methods are consistent with likelihood methods, and so hold the added theoretical virtue of being consistent with the law of likelihood.[11]

Do Bayesian methods provide a justification of causal claims? They can but there is a crucial condition.

As noted above in Chapter 6, Pierre Duhem (1906) and Willard van Orman Quine (1953) taught us that hypotheses inferred from theories always involve a host of auxiliary assumptions. This point is taken seriously by logicians employing Bayes' theorem in inductive inferences. Virtually all hypotheses only make testable predictions contextually; a host of auxiliary hypotheses connect them to evidence. In ideal circumstances, the auxiliary hypotheses are well established (highly probable). They are drawn from the array of scientific knowledge available, including mathematical theorems. As a result, they are often taken for granted. That is a significant danger. There may be a reason to be sceptical of an auxiliary assumption or, more likely, its method of application in supporting the inference. Attention to them is, consequently, important. One also needs to be concerned when an auxiliary hypothesis that rests on knowledge from another theoretical domain is used outside that domain. Using an auxiliary hypothesis from optics to support biological inferences based on the use of a light microscope might be problematic since the required auxiliary assumption might itself be part of the context for an inductive inference in optics; hence, assuming its solidity might be premature.

James Hawthorne (2016) captures the force of this:

> Thus, what counts as a *hypothesis to be tested*, $h_i$, and what counts as auxiliary hypotheses and background information, *b*, and even to some extent what counts as the conditions *c* for an experiment or observation, will depend on the epistemic context – on what alternative hypotheses are being tested by the same experiments or observations, and on what claims are being presupposed or held fixed for present purposes, and on what claims are considered to be the preconditions *c* for the evidential outcome *e*. No statement is intrinsically a *hypothesis*, or intrinsically an *auxiliary* or a *background condition*, or intrinsically an *evidential condition*. Rather, those are roles statements may play in an epistemic context, and the very same statement may play different roles in different confirmational contexts.[12]

Howson and Urbach (2005) discuss the use of Bayesian methods as a formal means by which to resolve the Quine–Duhem problem.[13] We can order in terms of plausibility both the primary hypothesis and the litany of auxiliary hypotheses and test each to find the weakest link – with the ultimate goal of eliminating the most probable culprit of the failed prediction. This underscores a key philosophical point: Causal inferences are probabilistic inferences; there is no magical method that allows us to *observe* causal forces stripped of their metaphysical trappings.

Using Bayesian methods, a causal ascription is on a stronger inferential footing than alternatives but declarations of causality are still probabilistic, albeit within a more robust probabilistic framework and inferential grounding.

Sir Austin Bradford Hill (1897–1991), an English epidemiologist, proposed in 1965 what have become known as Hill's criteria for determining whether or not there is a causal relationship between events. Hill himself never referred to them as criteria. His terms were considerations or viewpoints. He was interested in setting out an array of possible indicators of causality particularly for causes of human disease. Which considerations are important is context-dependent.

That said, he does appear to place special emphasis on his first consideration, *strength*.

That he understands the complexities surrounding the meaning of causation and revealing causal relationships is clear from this passage:

> I have no wish, nor the skill, to embark upon a philosophical discussion of the meaning of "causation". The "cause" of illness may be immediate and direct, it may be remote and indirect underlying the observed association. But with the aims of occupational, and almost synonymously preventive, medicine in mind the decisive question is whether the frequency of the undesirable event B will be influenced by a change in the environmental feature A. How such a change exerts that influence may call for a great deal of research. However, before deducing "causation" and taking action we shall not invariably have to sit around awaiting the results of that research. The whole chain may have to be unravelled or a few links may suffice. It will depend upon circumstances.
>
> Disregarding then any such problem in semantics we have this situation. Our observations reveal an association between two variables, perfectly clear-cut and beyond what we would care to attribute to the play of chance. What aspects of that association should we especially consider before deciding that the most likely interpretation of it is causation?
>
> (p. 295)

Hill's considerations are:

1 Strength

Hill gives three examples. First, the dramatic association between scrotal cancer and the occupation of chimney sweeping. Quoting Doll (1964, p 333), he notes, "the mortality of chimney sweeps from scrotal cancer was some 200 times that of workers who were not especially exposed to tar or mineral oils". The strength of this association makes it reasonable though not certain that there is a causal association.

Second, the association between smoking and lung cancer: "the death rate from cancer of the lung in smokers is nine to ten times the rate in non-smokers and the rate in heavy smokers is twenty to thirty times as great". Again a very strong association.

Third, he cites the, now famous, case of John Snow's analysis of the cholera epidemic of 1854 (Snow 1855): "The death rate that he recorded in the customers supplied with the grossly polluted water of the Southwark and Vauxhall Company was in truth quite low – 71 deaths in each 10,000 houses. What stands out vividly is the fact that the rate is 14 times the figure of 5 deaths per 10,000 houses supplied with the sewage-free water of the rival Lambeth Company." When differences of this magnitude are observed between groups – one with and one without the presumed causative factor – the strength of association is very high and a causal attribution seems warranted.

2   Consistency
Has an association been observed by different people in different circumstances and and at different times? One of his examples returns to smoking
and lung cancer:"the Advisory Committee to the Surgeon-General of the
United States Public Health Service found the association of smoking with
cancer of the lung in 29 retrospective and 7 prospective inquiries".

3   Specificity
The more specific the association, the greater the basis for assuming causation and acting to remove or reduce the cause, "If, as here, the association
is limited to specific workers and to particular sites and types of disease and
there is no association between the work and other modes of dying, then
clearly that is a strong argument in favour of causation."

4   Temporality
His point here is more than the obvious; that is, a cause must precede its
effect. He is probing the need to pay careful attention to temporality. It is
often difficult to determine which of two associated factors is the cause and
which the effect. Does a particular diet lead to a specific disease or does the
early stages of the disease lead to preference for a particular diet? Temporality is especially important in cases where diseases develop slowly.

5   Biological gradient
This consideration is related to dose–response. The example of smoking
and lung cancer exemplifies this. The association is not simply smoking and
lung cancer but the amount of tobacco smoked increases the rate of death
from lung cancer. There is a clearly expressible dose–response curve.

6   Plausibility
A suspected causal relationship is strengthened if there is a biological plausibility. That is, if what we know about biological mechanisms (or other sciences for that matter) makes the attribution of causation to an association
plausible, this increases one's confidence. He is quick to point out, however,
that one must be cautious not to give undue weight to the contrary. If two
things are strongly associated but there is no biological plausibility, it may
still be prudent to act as though the association is causal. The absence of
biological plausibility does not entail that there is no cause–effect relationship. This is different from biological mechanisms making it implausible.
The cases he has in mind are those for which biological mechanisms provide no guidance for either a causal or non-causal judgement.

7   Coherence
This is more like a corollary of "Plausibility" than a distinct point. Hill
makes explicit that all the available relevant knowledge must cohere. He
claims, "the cause and effect interpretation of our data should not seriously
conflict with the generally known facts of the natural history and biology
of the disease". What is not clear is the force of the modifier "seriously".
Some will take all but trivial conflict to be a sign of trouble. Others may be
laxer.

8   Experiment
    If a causal connection is asserted based on the other considerations set out
    here, intervention might be appropriate. The intervention is, in effect, an
    experiment to test the causal hypothesis. Some interventions are rigorously
    structured and the data meticulously recorded and analysed. Sometimes,
    the intervention and observed results are more casual. As Hill expresses it,
    "The dust in the workshop is reduced, lubricating oils are changed, persons
    stop smoking cigarettes. Is the frequency of the association affected?".

9   Analogy
    Other cases of association that have been deemed causal can increase one's
    willingness, at least tentatively, to accept causation in a new but related case:
    "With the effects of thalidomide and rubella before us we would surely
    be ready to accept slighter but similar evidence with another drug or viral
    disease in pregnancy."

Two characteristics can be noted. First, these are not criteria in any normal
sense and Hill was entirely correct to refer to them as considerations. Second,
some considerations are more revealing of potential causes than others. Hill's
ordering of them suggests, though he has never claimed this, that he considered
the earlier ones to have more gravitas than the later ones, but this ordering will
not be deemed by everyone as a descending order of importance. Consider,
for example 8: Experiment, the second to last. Surely this provides some of the
compelling evidence that an association is causal, especially when the experiment is rigorous.

We suspect that the raising of these considerations to the status of criteria (or
a checklist for causality) is a result of clinical medicine's strong desire to be able
to assert causal connections. This impulse is understandable; causal claims con-
fer more confidence on diagnosis and intervention than "mere" associations,
even when the association is very strong. Nonetheless, obtaining knowledge of
causes in clinical medicine remains elusive. Hill's considerations are important
and have broadened the scope of the hunt for causes but they fall short of war-
ranting causal attribution. Their greatest importance has been in providing a
rationale for action, even when a justifiable causal attribution is illusive. As Hill
remarks at the end of the paper:

> All scientific work is incomplete – whether it be observational or experi-
> mental. All scientific work is liable to be upset or modified by advancing
> knowledge. That does not confer upon us a freedom to ignore the knowl-
> edge we already have, or postpone the action that it appears to demand at
> a given time.
>
> (p. 300)

This approaches the edge of incoherence if taken literally, but as a prod against
inaction due to uncertainty, it scores a bulls-eye.

The emphasis on these considerations has resulted in an under-appreciation of several other points that he made in the lecture and the printed version of it (see Phillips and Goodman 2004 for an interesting commentary on this point). One point he convincingly presses is that tests of significance are highly overrated.

> No formal tests of significance can answer those questions. Such tests can, and should, remind us of the effects that the play of chance can create, and they will instruct us in the likely magnitude of those effects. Beyond that they contribute nothing to the "proof" of our hypothesis.
>
> (p. 299)

> Yet I cannot find that anywhere [in his research into working in the cotton-spinning mills] I thought it necessary to use a test of significance. The evidence was so clear-cut, the differences between the groups were mainly so large, the contrast between respiratory and non-respiratory causes of illness so specific, that no formal tests could really contribute anything of value to the argument. So why use them?
>
> (p. 299)

This lays bare a difference between Fisher's justification for randomisation and Bradford Hill's. Both advocated passionately for randomisation. As Peter Armitage (2003) has pointed out, Fisher's (1951) justification was:

> The purpose of randomisation . . . is to guarantee the validity of the test of significance, this test being based on an estimate of error made possible by replication.
>
> (p. 26)

Whereas Hill's (1952) justification was:

> It ensures that neither our personal idiosyncrasies (our likes or dislikes consciously or unwittingly applied) nor our lack of balanced judgement has entered into the construction of the different treatment groups – the allocation has been made outside our control and the groups are therefore unbiased . . .
>
> (p.114)

Fisher considered randomisation essential to a valid application of statistics, especially tests of significance. Hill emphasised the role of randomisation in preventing, or at least reducing, selector bias.

At this point, we have examined RCTs, a number of other research methodologies, Bayesian methods and Hill's considerations. The justification of causal claims in clinical medicine remains elusive. All its frequentist-based methods are not robust enough to warrant causal claims. They do warrant claims of strong association when the studies are robust. Often this is enough to justify confidence in specific medical practices. Bayesian methods provide the closest warrant of a causal claim but the success and credibility of this approach do not depend integrally on causal assertions. Hill's criteria are not really criteria (or a checklist) for determining causal connections and he never proposed that they were.

Our diagnosis of the "causal malady" in clinical research rests on its focus on individual regularities. Interventions and their outcomes are conceived individually, investigated individually and results analysed individually; meta-analyses are still about an individual intervention and outcome, even though there are many studies of this individual association. In Chapter 3, we examined theories and models and provided specific examples drawn from bench medicine. We demonstrated the critical role of theories and models in science. They:

1    integrate knowledge
2    guide hypothesis formation
3    underpin explanation and prediction
4    support counterfactual claims
5    determine relevance of evidence.

Unlike the results of research in clinical medicine, theories and models are holistic structures; every claim is linked to every other claim, some are connected over large logical distances, others connected to claims in the local vicinity. As a result, every claim has the support of every other claim in the interconnected system. This is akin to united we stand, divided we fall. This provides a much more robust approach to separating "causal partitions" of populations from "non-causal partitions" (mere correlations). Theories and large models are causal models.

To capture this point, consider the meta-analysis of the various studies on daily doses of 81mg of acetylsalicylic acid (ASA – aspirin). The result of a meta-analysis can be found in J.S. Berger et al. (2006). Their analysis indicates that most studies had an outcome that supports ASA use. One does not support it. All show only a modest support for ASA use. Interesting though these studies, and the meta-analysis of them, may be, the causal explanation lies elsewhere. Goodman and Gilman's *The Pharmacological Basis of Therapeutics* (2011) explains it this way:

*Mechanism of Aspirin*

The mechanisms underlying the effectiveness of aspirin have been studied extensively. Experimentally, a single oral 100mg dose of aspirin is sufficient to completely block the synthesis of thromboxane $A_2$, the predominant pathway by which aspirin inhibits platelet aggregation. When taken daily, the effect of repeated doses is cumulative. At higher doses, the synthesis of prostacyclin is also inhibited, which could paradoxically lead to thrombosis and vasoconstriction. Currently, there is an increasing focus on the role of inflammation in cardiovascular risk. Aspirin has been demonstrated to reduce C-reactive protein. In the Physicians' Health Study, aspirin was most effective in reducing cardiovascular risk in men with the most elevated levels of C-reactive protein. However, the dose of aspirin required to achieve the maximal anti-inflammatory effect remains unknown.

This explains the mechanism from a physiological and haematological perspective. It explains *why* the RCTs obtained the results they did. It, not the RCTs, is the *causal* story.

The good news for medicine as a whole is that non-clinical medical science does involve constructing theories and models. Disciplines such as immunology, haematology, endocrinology, medical genetics, physiology and biochemistry all develop theories and models and, seldom refer to, or employ, RCTs.

Nancy Cartwright pulls all this together in *Hunting Causes and Using Them* as follows:

> In an RCT, if we are lucky, we find the average difference in effect produced by the treatment in the population sampled. That does not tell us what the overall outcome on this effect in question would be from introducing the treatment in some particular way in some uncontrolled situation, even if we consider introducing it only in the very population sampled. *For that we need a causal model.* Even less does it tell us about "side-effects" of introducing the treatment, either from the treatment itself or from our way of implementing it. These too are crucial in calculating the costs and benefits of a proposed policy. Or, as Heckman argues, suppose one wants to predict what portion of the population will experience a given degree of improvement. *RCTs do not deliver that kind of result. Again, we need a causal model.*
>
> (2007, p. 238, emphasis added)

We think an apt comparison for consideration is with aeronautical engineering. It is apt because aeronautical engineering research and the design and construction of aeroplanes are a complex research and application endeavour. Moreover, errors have serious consequence for the travelling public. In addition, there are regulatory agencies devoted to safety and industries that demand evidence of effective design. Aeronautical research, design and manufacturing do not rely at all on RCTs to demonstrate safety or effectiveness, and nor do regulators and industry assessors rely on them for decision-making. Ratcheting things up a bit, the complexity of a space shuttle (with the computing systems, rocket design, nanotechnical features, electronics and material science, to list but a few) are remarkably complicated. Perhaps there are features of human beings that make them complex in substantively different ways from space craft and aeroplanes. That case has yet to be made. Making it is increasingly difficult given advances in medical engineering with respect to artificial tissues, and materials science related to replacement bone material, circulatory infrastructure and so on.

Moreover, advances in physiology, neurosciences and the like make mysteries of the past less so. The reasons that engineering research emerged from physics and chemistry with no reliance on RCTs, whereas clinical medical research, emerging, sort of, from biology, relies on them extensively is another book.

Notwithstanding, however, the weaknesses of RCTs, their dominance as a research method in clinical medicine and the regulatory approval process is not likely to be muted any time soon. There is too much entrenchment and vested interest. But following Darwin, one can look to new, young and rising clinical researchers, "who will be able to view both sides of the question with impartiality".

## Notes

1 For a 10,000 sample of tosses, there is a 0.988 probability of observing between 4,875 and 5,125 heads.

2 $t = (\bar{x}-\mu)/(s/\sqrt{n})$, which follows a $t$-distribution with $n-1$ degrees of freedom.

3 Pearl 2009.

4 Random assignment to intervention and control groups eliminates (or at least reduces) selector bias. Although we have suggested that pure random assignment is compromised in a few ways, this benefit of using randomization is still one valuable result.

5 This section is indebted to a presentation by Ian Johnson and Vivek Goel.

6 "Relatively new" should not be understood narrowly. Bayesian methods have been employed within clinical medicine for a while now. Notable Bayesian biostatisticians include Adrian Smith (1996), J.O. Berger et al. (2006), David Spiegelhalter et al. (2004) and Steven N. Goodman (2005). Nonetheless, the time period for the use of these methods in clinical medicine is still only several decades.

7 This material on Bayesian methods has benefitted greatly from comments by two outstanding graduate students at the Institute for History and Philosophy of Science and Technology, University of Toronto: Aaron Kenna and Mat Mercuri.

8 There have been Bayesians who championed an *objective* epistemic interpretation; Pierre-Simon Laplace (1812) (on Laplace, see Stigler 1990), Harold Jeffreys (1961), E.T. Jaynes (2003) and Rudolf Carnap (1950) have advanced different forms of objectivism. More recently, philosophers Timothy Williamson (2010) and R.D. Rosenkrantz (1977) advance objective Bayesian epistemic interpretations. Abner Shimony (1970), I.J. Good (2003) and R. G. Cowell et al. (1999) have developed admixtures between subjectivism and objectivism. In any case, the real distinction between Bayesian statistical methods and classical statistical methods is that, unlike the latter, the former express uncertainty about unknown statistical parameters (e.g. the mean response of a target population to a drug intervention) probabilistically, where these probabilities relate, essentially, to the epistemic states of agents.

9 This intuition is not distinctive of Bayesian methods; classical frequentist statisticians do not disagree with this intuition but the basis for it is different. For example, Neyman, Pearson and Fisher were apt to point out that the choices of alpha level and power (Neyman and Pearson) and critical value (Fisher) depended crucially upon the different evidential thresholds of individuals for accepting or rejecting an hypothesis (Neyman and Pearson 1933a and 1953b) or deeming statistical data to count as falsifying a hypothesis (Fisher 1955 and 1956). What is unique about subjective Bayesian methods is that two rational agents with access to the same evidence and considering the same hypotheses can rationally assign different probabilities to the same hypotheses. This is something to which pretty much all classical statisticians would vehemently object.

10  Recall from note 5, Chapter 5 that different writers use different notations: Sometimes, the notation for conditional probability is $\mathbf{Pr}_H(E)$ (the probability of H conditional on E) rather than $\mathrm{Pr}(H/E)$. Hence, Bayes' theorem is written:

$$\mathbf{P}_E(H) = \mathbf{P}(H)\mathbf{P}_H(E) \: / \: [\mathbf{P}(H)\mathbf{P}_H(E) + \mathbf{P}(\sim\!H)\mathbf{P}_{\sim\!H}(E)]$$

11  This also means that Bayesian methods garner any philosophical support proponents of likelihood methods succeed in obtaining for their own methods.

12  He adds:

> In a probabilistic inductive logic the degree to which evidence $ce$ supports a hypothesis $h_i$ relative to background $b$ is represented by the *posterior probability* of $h_i$, $P_\alpha[h_i \mid b \cdot c^n \cdot e^n]$. It turns out that the *posterior probability* of a hypothesis depends on just two kinds of factors: (1) its *prior probability*, $P_\alpha[h_i \mid b]$, together with the prior probabilities of its competitors, $P_\alpha[h_j \mid b]$, etc.; and (2) the *likelihood* of evidential outcomes $e$ according to $h_i$, given that $b$ and $c$ are true, $P[e \mid h_i \cdot b \cdot c]$, together with the likelihoods of outcomes according to its competitors, $P[e \mid h_j \cdot b \cdot c]$, etc.
>
> We suggest that this is not entirely accurate. It seems inaccurate to claim that "the degree to which evidence $ce$ supports a hypothesis $h_i$ relative to background $b$ is represented by the *posterior probability* of $h_i$, $P_\alpha[h_i \mid b \cdot c^n \cdot e^n]$" (see Fitelson 2006).

13  They also argue that Bayesian methods explicate Lakatos' notion of a degenerate research programme.

# 8 Some central measures in clinical medicine

Epidemiology, as the designation indicates, began as the study of epidemics. Over time it transformed into the field that pervades all aspects of clinical medicine. It is common now for departments in medical schools to be called "Epidemiology and Biostatistics", a label that makes clear the significant statistical nature of its activities. This field has imported or developed a number of statistical measures for manipulating data. We now turn to a number of these epidemiological measures, which will be referred to at various points in subsequent chapters.

## Odds ratio

If an event has a probability of p, then the *odds* in favour of it occurring are
p:1−p

That is, if an event has a probability of 0.3, then the probability that the event will not occur is 0.7. The odds are 3:7 that the event will occur. We are usually interested in the odds for a particular group (those exposed to the risk factor). Hence, the probability of the event (let's say a disease) is:

$Pr(D/E)$ Probability of disease given exposure to risk entity, where $D$ is contracting the disease and $E$ is exposure to the pathogen.

The odds then are:

$$Pr(D/E)/(1 - Pr(D/E)$$

This is an expression of simple odds – odds of getting the disease if exposed. The odds ratio is a second measure that compares the odds of getting the disease when exposed to the odds of getting the disease when not exposed. Odds with non-exposure:

$$Pr(D/{\sim}E)/(1 - Pr(D/{\sim}E)$$

As before, the odds with exposure are:

$$Pr(D/E)/(1 - Pr(D/E)$$

The odds ratio combines these:

$$\frac{Pr(D/E)/Pr(\sim D/E)}{Pr(D/\sim E)/Pr((\sim D/\sim E)}$$

Consider the odds ratio of a first coronary and smoking:

| | |
|---|---|
| Pr(coronary/smoker) | = 0.277 |
| Pr(coronary/non–smoker) | = 0.144 |
| Odds ratio   $\dfrac{0.277/0.723}{0.144/0.856}$ | = 2.3 |

We note here that the odds ratio is calculated slightly differently for different kinds of studies.

First, a common epidemiological tool will make clear its application in two different kinds of study design. We will examine more later. The 2 × 2 table used for observational studies is a basic tool (see Table 8.1).

Using this matrix, the difference between different kinds of study can be described. Cohort studies begin with the knowledge of A + C and B + D. That is, the totals of those exposed and those not exposed. These research subjects are followed through time as a group; that is, as a cohort. The goal is to monitor over time the development of disease. At the end of the time period, the four cells are filled in based on the data collected.

Case-control studies by contrast begin by knowing the totals A + B and C + D. That is, disease cases and healthy cases, the latter being the "control". The goal is to find the differences between the groups in terms of previous exposure to the relevant risk factors. Based on that data the cells of the matrix are filled in.

At this point, this comparison of the use of the odds ratio in two different study designs is sufficient to illustrate the difference in the actual calculation of the odds ratio for each kind of study. For cohort studies, the odds ratio is usually expressed:

*Table 8.1* The 2 × 2 table. A, B, C, and D give the number of people in that category. Hence A gives the number of people in the study that have been exposed and have the disease. N is the total number of people in the study.

| | | Exposure status | | Total |
|---|---|---|---|---|
| | | Yes | No | |
| **Disease** | Yes | A | B | A + B |
| **Status** | No | C | D | C + D |
| Total | | A + C | B + D | N |

$$\frac{Pr(D/E)/(1 - Pr(D/E)}{Pr(D/\sim E)/(1 - Pr(D/\sim E)}$$

$$= \frac{Pr(D/E)/Pr(\sim D/E)}{Pr(D/\sim E)/Pr((\sim D/\sim E)}$$

In our example, the odds ratio for first coronary and smoking,

| | |
|---|---|
| Pr(coronary/smoker) | = 0.277 |
| Pr(coronary/non-smoker) | = 0.144 |

$$\text{Odds ratio} = \frac{0.277/0.723}{0.144/0.856} \quad = 2.3$$

For case-control studies, the odds ratio is usually expressed:

$$\frac{Pr(E/D)/(1 - Pr(E/D)}{Pr(E/\sim D)/(1 - Pr(E\sim D)}$$

$$= \frac{Pr(E/D)/Pr(\sim E/D)}{Pr(E/\sim D)/Pr((\sim E/\sim D)}$$

The rationale for this is explored later. Here it is sufficient to note the difference.

## Incidence rate

The incidence rate is the number of new cases/number of persons at risk at time $t$. Symbolically:

$$C(t)/R(t)$$

where $C(t)$ is the number of cases and $R(t)$ is the number of persons at risk, This is a snapshot at a specific time. An incident rate can be over a temporal period:

$$C(t_{0-k})/R(t_{0-k})$$

In addition, incidence rates are usually age-specific and per 1,000 or 10,000, etc.

$$\Sigma(t_{0-k}) \ (C(y_{n-m})/R(y_{n-m})) \times 1{,}000$$

## Average risk

Let $R(t)$ be the average risk for developing a disease among a cohort during the time 0 to $t$ and let $\mu$ be the incidence rate during the period (which we begin by assuming is constant: $\mu = 1$), then, expressed as a natural logarithm:[1]

$$R(t) = 1 - e^{-\mu t}$$

Often the incidence rate is not constant for the period. Hence, an average incidence rate for the period must be calculated and used as the value for $\mu$. For example, the incidence rate for a first coronary event in the risk group of male smokers (an unweighted average over five-year intervals from age 40 to 64) = 13 per 1,000 per year. Hence, per person, the average incidence rate is 0.013 over 25 years. Using the equation $R(t) = 1 - e^{-\mu t}$ :

$$R(t) = 1 - e^{-0.013(25)} = 1 - e^{-0.325} = 0.277$$

Hence, the 25-year average risk is 0.277.

## Rate ratio

The rate ratio = incidence rate for the exposed/incident rate for the unexposed. Let's stay with our smoking and coronary example.

> Incidence rate for male non-smokers of a first coronary is 6.2/1,000
> Incidence rate for male smokers is 13/1,000
> Rate ratio = $\dfrac{13/1,000}{6.2/1,000}$
>
> = 13/6.2 = 2.1

This measure shows that male smokers have a 2.1 times higher rate of a first coronary than male non-smokers.

## Risk ratio

This measure calculates the risk of a disease when exposed compared with those who are not exposed. If $D$ is the presence of disease and $E$ is exposure, the risk ratio is:

$$\dfrac{\Pr(D/E)}{\Pr(D/\sim E)}$$

Hence, if exposure to the risk factor makes no difference to the presence of the disease the risk ratio is 1. If, as in the smoking and coronary example, there is a difference, this ratio calculates that difference, expressing it as a risk of disease.

> Pr(coronary/smoker) = 0.277
> Pr(coronary/non-smoker) = 0.144
>
> Hence:    $\dfrac{0.277}{0.144}$ = 1.924

Therefore, a smoker has an almost double risk of a coronary.

We conclude with three other important epidemiological measures that are widely used in conveying information to clinical practitioners and the general public. They are methods of assessing the effectiveness of interventions: a pharmaceutical, dietary change or lifestyle change, for example. Assessing effectiveness involves comparing two groups: an intervention (experimental) group and a control group. The control group does not receive the intervention, which allows a comparison of the efficacy, or not, of the intervention.

## Absolute risk reduction

The relevant data for both groups is the event rate. That is, the proportion in each group that has the desired (or undesired) outcome (the event). Using this data the two groups are compared. The number of desired outcomes for each group is divided by the total number in each group. This yields the event rate for each group. Then, the event rate for the control group is subtracted from the event rate for the intervention group. The result is the absolute risk reduction. To understand this measure, consider a stylised example. Suppose a new medication is being tested for efficacy. It is claimed that it reduces susceptibility to cervical cancer. There were 10,000 people in each group, which would make it a very large study. The results were:

Event rate for the intervention group: 5,000/10,000 = 0.5
Event rate for the control group: 500/10,000 = 0.05

Hence, the absolute risk reduction is 0.5–0.05 = 0.45, which means that the reduction in risk achieved by the intervention is 45 for every 100 people treated. That is, if 100 people were treated, 45% would be prevented from developing cervical cancer. This example was constructed to have a very high event rate for the intervention group compared with the control group. In most cases the event rates for the two groups are much closer.

An excellent, although still controversial, example of the use of absolute risk reduction is the Canadian clinical trial on mammography. Canadian researchers conducted one of the most extensive and largest trials of the effectiveness of mammography (x-ray diagnosis for breast cancer) during the 1980s. The study began in 1980 with 89,835 women aged 40–59 years. The publication of the first results occurred in 1992. The research team has continued to follow the groups and now has reported on 25 years of data (Miller et al. 2014).

All women who had not had a mammogram in the previous 12 months, who had no history of breast cancer and were not pregnant, were eligible. Women were recruited, "by a general publicity campaign, by reviewing lists and sending personal invitation letters, by group mailings, and through family doctors." The research studied two age groups separately: 40–49 years old and 50–59 years old. The research compared those in a mammography group (intervention group) with a control group (those who did not have mammograms). In the 40–49-year-old group, the women were randomly assigned to a mammography group (the intervention group) or the control group. There were 25,214 women aged 40–49 in the mammogram group and 25,216 in the control group. There were 19,711 women aged 50–59 in the mammography group and 19,694 in the control, which received an annual physical breast examination but no mammography. The results of the first eight years were published in two parts in 1992 in the *Canadian Medical Association Journal (CMAJ)* (Miller et al. 1992a, 1992b).

Let's look at the data reported in the 2014 article (25-year follow-up) since it is much more robust. The various articles to which we have referred have a wealth of data ranging from demographic profile to detection rates. Of interest here is the event rate, which in this study is death from breast cancer.

Event rate (2014) in the intervention group (mammography) = 500 total (deaths per 10,000 = 108.4)
Event rate (2014) in the control group = 505 total (deaths per 10,000 = 110.2)

Hence, the absolute risk reduction = 108.4/10,000 – 110.2/10,000 = –1.8/10,000 (or 0.01084–0.01102 = –0.00018).

That means there is essentially no absolute risk reduction from screening using mammography. These numbers for the two groups are so close that the absolute risk reduction of –0.00018 is irrelevant; mammography neither reduces deaths from breast cancer nor increases deaths from breast cancer.

## Number to treat (NNT)

This is the number of people that need to be treated with an intervention to obtain a single occurrence of the desired outcome. Recall the discussion of PSA tests for prostate cancer. A European study found that to prevent one case of prostate cancer 1,400 men would need to be screened, which would result in 48 men undergoing surgical and/or radiation treatment.

Calculating the NNT is easy once the absolute risk reduction has been calculated. NNT is the inverse of absolute risk reduction. Consider our hypothetical cervical cancer case. The absolute risk reduction was 0.45. The intervention can be expected to reduce the incidence of cervical cancer in 45 out of every 100 people. We want to get the 45 down to 1. Hence, we divide 0.45 into 1 = 1/0.45 = 2.2. Therefore 2.2 individuals need to be treated to have one desired outcome. This is obviously a much more impressive situation than the PSA test.

Returning to the data from the Canadian National Breast Screening Study. The absolute risk reduction is –1.8. Hence, the number to treat (mammography) to obtain the result of avoidance of death from breast cancer is 1 divided by −0.00018 = −5,555.56; consequently, to avoid 1 death from breast cancer, you need to avoid mammography for 5,555.56 persons. Since −0.00018 is insignificant, the correct conclusion is that NNT is irrelevant in this case, since if we were to treat −0.00018 as 0, the NNT cannot be calculated because dividing by 0 is undefined.[2]

## Relative risk reduction

This measure specifies risk reduction as a function of the risk of exposure. It is absolute risk reduction divided by the risk of an event given exposure. If one is exposed to a risk factor such as smoking, the risk of lung cancer increases. For men over 35 in the US who smoke, the risk of dying from lung cancer is about 0.0027. That is, about 27 male smokers over 35 years of age per 10,000 will die of lung cancer. There are, of course, a lot of factors that increase or decrease this risk, such as the amount smoked per day. Hence this is a global number. For men over 35 who are not smokers, the risk of dying of lung cancer is about 0.00015. That is 1.5 non-smokers per 10,000 will die of lung cancer. The event is dying of lung cancer.

Event rate for smokers = 0.0027
Event rate for non-smokers = 0.00015
Absolute risk reduction = 0.0027−0.00015 = 0.00255

Therefore, the absolute risk reduction from not smoking = 0.00255 (or 255 per 1,000: 2,550 per 10,000).

To obtain the relative risk reduction, divide that absolute risk reduction by the risk of exposure. That is:

0.00255/0.0027 = 0.944, which can be expressed as a percentage: 94%
The relative risk reduction from not smoking is 94%

Two studies have raised an important epistemological point. Different presentations of the same data (relative risk reduction, absolute risk difference, number needed to treat) produced different decisions by patients about accepting treatment (Hux and Naylor 1995) and different assessments by physicians about therapeutic efficacy (Naylor et al. 1992). In the Hux and Naylor study, 88% of patients assented to therapy when advised of a relative risk reduction (i.e. 34% reduction in heart attacks). Only 42% assented when given the absolute risk difference (i.e. 1.4% fewer patients had heart attacks). The percentage drops to 31% for number to treat (i.e. treat 71 persons for five years to prevent one heart attack). When the data were extrapolated to disease-free survival (i.e. average gain of 15 weeks), 40% consented. Clearly, the same data from the same research leads to different decisions by patients and, most tellingly, by physicians when different measures are used to convey the information.

# Notes

1 Logarithms are a way of expressing the inverse of exponents $(y = a^x) = (x = \log_a y)$.

The "$a$" in the equation $y = a^x$ determines the slope of the line on a graph determined by the equation. If the slope is set at 1, then $a = 2.71828$. This value of a is designated e, which designates a natural logarithm. Using natural logarithms sets the base of all logarithms as e by setting the slope of the equation at 1. There are mathematical advantages to setting a = e when dealing with logarithms. When the exponent has a minus sign as in $a^{-x}$, the inverse is being given – that is $1/a^x$. In this case, the exponent is $-t$, hence, it is $1/e^{\mu t}$.

2 Sometimes division by 0 is treated as equal to infinity. Although not mathematically correct, that does capture the result that an infinite number of people would have been given a mammogram to save 1 person from death from breast cancer if the absolute risk reduction is 0.

# 9 Reasoning in clinical practice

Prevention, diagnosis, therapy, prognosis, rehabilitation and palliation

Clinical medicine principally focuses on five things: prevention, diagnosis, therapy, palliation and rehabilitation. A sixth important element is prognosis; it is a second-order judgement based on diagnosis, effectiveness of available therapies and the current methods of rehabilitation and palliation. Public health is the dominant domain of prevention. Its efforts are underpinned by clinical research and elements of basic medical science: human genetics, physiology and endocrinology, for example. Diagnosis depends heavily upon knowledge derived from bench medicine, clinical medicine, technology (tests, imaging and the like) and anatomy. It is the process of reasoning from symptoms to potential causes. Therapies include surgery, pharmaceuticals, physiotherapy, lifestyle changes, mechanical devices and prostheses. Rehabilitation aims to return an individual to her pre-disease or pre-injury state of being. If addiction is not considered a disease, it is an addition to this list. Palliation occurs at all stages of medical intervention from the alleviation of symptoms to end-of-life care.

This brief overview might suggest that these elements of clinical medicine are well understood, rational and reliable. This is far from the case. Each element is fraught with complexities, uncertainty, incomplete and questionable research, invalid reasoning and human frailty. In this chapter, we will explore challenges that these pose for clinical practice – challenges that can be exacerbated by a public perception that medicine is a rational and highly successful endeavour. And, by a well-meaning media that over-simplifies the nature and results of research and techniques, and skews reporting towards successes and sensational issues. That clinical medicine is mix of rational and irrational views and actions is politicised internally and externally, is a mix of compelling research and shoddy research, and is complex and riddled with uncertainty is not an indictment. It is a human endeavour and like all human endeavours it has dark aspects. Universities and the activities within them also have dark aspects. Politics is rife with dark aspects, as are commercial activities.

Few will deny that prevention of disease (or more broadly ill health) should be a premier goal of medicine. Preventing tuberculosis is preferable to treating it; preventing HIV/AIDS is preferable to treating it; preventing myocardial infarction is preferable to treating it and the list goes on. Hence, as expected, preventative medicine is an active arena of research and intervention.

Nonetheless, research funding allocations and areas of research emphasis are dominated by developing and employing treatments. Substantial funding of research and interventions aimed at prevention is often triggered by extreme situations, such as epidemics (SARS and Zika, for example).

## Prevention

The taxonomy of preventative medicine has four categories: primordial, primary, secondary and tertiary prevention (see Last 2001). Primordial prevention encompasses actions and measures that prevent the emergence and establishment of the environmental, economic, social and behavioural conditions, cultural patterns of living, etc., known to increase the risk of disease (e.g. improving housing availability, reducing child poverty).

Primary prevention encompasses protection of health by personal and communal efforts, such as enhancing nutritional status, immunising against communicable diseases and eliminating environmental risks, such as contaminated drinking water supplies. Secondary prevention encompasses a set of measures available to individuals and communities for the early detection and prompt intervention to control disease and minimize disability, e.g. by the use of screening programmes. Tertiary prevention measures are aimed at softening the impact of long-term disease and disability by eliminating or reducing impairment, disability and handicap; minimising suffering; and maximising potential years of useful life. Knowing these categories is useful in understanding the sub-specialties in medicine but have a lesser importance in understanding epistemological and metaphysical aspects of preventative medicine.

The success of immunisation in preventing disease is an excellent example of effective prevention. Three other notable examples involve disease transmission. First, major prevention gains have been made through food safety regulations. Many pathogens that infect food have been identified and measures to stop transmission have been put into place. Many measures are now taken at the agricultural source.

For example, trichinosis is a roundworm. It was frequently found in pork; eating undercooked pork allowed its transmission to humans. The first line in interrupting transmission was educating consumers about cooking pork sufficiently that the roundworm was killed. Today, the emphasis is on farming practices that avoid the transmission within the porcine population. Cleanliness is an essential element: replacing soil floors with hard surfaces, for instance – concrete is an excellent choice because it allows a thorough wash-down and sanitising. Rigorous control of food sources is another example of best farming practices. Principally, keep rat populations under control so that pigs do not ingest them; rats are a known vector of trichinosis. Other measures focus on cleanliness in the processing of pork – cleanliness of the facility environment and all equipment used is critical. Inspection allows infected animals to be identified and destroyed before the roundworm can be transmitted, and reduces the probability of infected pork being marketed. Today, because of these "at source" measures, the existence of trichinosis in pork when marketed is rare. The dramatic reduction of salmonella, listeria and tuberculosis in food are other examples of success in dramatically reducing transmission through food.

A second method of reducing transmission employs protective measures: for instance, condoms to reduce HIV/AIDS transmission as well as other sexually transmitted disease (gonorrhoea and syphilis, for example), and bed nets and insect repellents to reduce transmission of malaria. A third method involves pharmaceuticals; the use of anti-malarials is an example. Pharmaceuticals such as Malarone® interrupt the reproductive cycle of *Plasmodium falciparum* and/or kill the adult parasite.

As in lots of areas of medicine, however, these successes can be deceptive. Their success depends on identifying a single – even if complex – pathogen, and understanding its characteristics, lifecycle and method of transmission, and then devising measures to interfere with some metabolic process, its reproduction or transmission. These kinds of "magic bullets" are rare. Diseases whose causes are genetic or environmental or lifestyle-based are exceedingly more complex; also, prevention in the case of the latter two requires government and individual action. Pollution of soil, water and air all loom large as causative factors of disease. As do individual choices about diet (amount and composition), smoking, alcohol consumption, activity level and so on. The largest arena of potential prevention, by far, involves these causes of disease. Regrettably, clarity about the causes and appropriate, effective intervention is illusive.

In the case of these causes, most of preventative medicine relies on the clinical research methods described in Chapter 7. The complexity and challenge of understanding and applying the results of the research are numerous. Results frequently have to be interpreted using assumptions or "supplementary" information. The research on some things is contradictory – over time and at any given time. Even when all research at one time is interpreted as pointing in the same direction, at a later time, new research can up-end previous "knowledge". Consider three examples: breast cancer screening, cholesterol and prostate-specific antigen (PSA) testing. The controversy over breast cancer screening has been discussed in Chapter 8. Suffice it to say here, screening remains controversial and the science seems to point to a null result. Notwithstanding these research results, advice in favour of screening continues to be disseminated. This example illustrates the classic problem with advice regarding disease-detection as quasi-prevention through early detection.

Cholesterol is a lipoprotein. There are two forms: high-density (HDL) and low-density (LDL); there is a sub-category of LDL – very low-density lipoprotein (VLDL). LDL is described colloquially as "bad" cholesterol, HDL as "good" cholesterol. Most recently, clinical medicine has focused on the ratio of HDL to LDL as a predictive tool of risk of an undesirable cardiac-based event.

Interest in the relationship between cholesterol and diet, and cholesterol and cardiovascular disease began in the 1960s. The research of Ancel Keys was a pivotal factor in the view that dietary fat caused increased blood cholesterol and contributed to cardiovascular disease. Keys received his first PhD in

1930 from UC Berkeley in oceanography and biology. A fellowship funded by the National Research Council allowed him to study with August Krogh in Copenhagen. His focus during the fellowship was on fish physiology. He spent some time at Cambridge University before briefly teaching at Harvard University. After Harvard, he returned to Cambridge and was awarded a second PhD in physiology.

His research, based on a seven-country analysis (Yugoslavia, Finland, Greek islands of Crete and Corfu, Italy, Japan, the Netherlands and the United States), was published in 1970 in the journal *Circulation*. The study examined cohorts in each country, which were deemed representative of the culture of the country; in some countries only one cohort was identified (United States and the Netherlands); Yugoslavia had the most with five cohorts. The study began in 1958. His 1970 publication concluded that his hypothesis was correct; that is, that dietary fat intake, especially saturated fats (animal fats), caused elevated levels of cholesterol in blood serum and that cholesterol was a significant factor in cardiovascular disease. Keys and his colleagues followed the cohorts for 49 years. For the first 25 years, the cohorts were examined using the same methods as reported in the original study. From 1984 onwards, additional factors were surveyed in some cohorts, most related to the geriatric status of the members of the cohort by that time.

Keys' work had a profound effect on the dietary advice offered to the public. For some 50 years, the mantra that saturated fats increased the risk of cardiovascular disease was widely believed and widely propagated. Along the way there was controversy about his conclusions and his methodology[1] but only in the last decade or so has the social consensus dissipated. Recent evidence suggests that the assumed causal links between diet and cholesterol, and between cholesterol and cardiovascular disease are significantly less clear than Keys claimed. The conclusion of a 2010 meta-analysis published in *The American Journal of Clinical Nutrition* was:

> A meta-analysis of prospective epidemiologic studies showed that there is no significant evidence for concluding that dietary saturated fat is associated with an increased risk of CHD or CVD. More data are needed to elucidate whether CVD risks are likely to be influenced by the specific nutrients used to replace saturated fat.
>
> (Siri-Tarino 2010)

There are critics of this meta-study just as there were, and are, critics of Keys' work.

A concrete example of the dissolving consensus is the butter vs. margarine advice. For many decades, based on the medical claims of Keys and others, the public was advised to limited the intake of butter – a saturated fat – and favour margarine instead. Saturated fats increase "bad" (LDL) cholesterol and elevated levels of "bad" cholesterol increase significantly the risk of cardiovascular disease. Most margarine is a trans-fatty acid (commonly called trans fats). Margarine and shortening are made from oils that are liquid at ambient temperatures. They are rendered solid at those temperatures by partially hydrogenating them. The oils used in this process are mostly polyunsaturated (olive oil, by contrast, has a high proportion of monounsaturated fats). If a fatty acid molecule contains one double bond, it is monounsaturated; if it contains more than one double bond, it is polyunsaturated. Hydrogenation uses hydrogen to break a double bond between carbon atoms or carbon-based molecules. For example, oleic fatty acid is hydrogenated by the addition of $H_2$ (two atoms of hydrogen). The result is on the right-hand side of Figure 9.1. The double bond on the left-hand side between the CH molecules is broken and two hydrogen atoms are added.

A result of the process of hydrogenating a polyunsaturated fat is a trans fat; the configuration of the hydrogen bonds is changed. A consensus has emerged that trans fats are unhealthy, with a large number of researcher results indicating that trans fats are more health-reducing than saturated fats.

These examples cover two classes of prevention. Breast cancer screening is promoted as a method for early detection of disease, which allows interventions aimed at preventing the disease from progressing. Ideally, the intervention prevents premature death; in other cases of disease diagnosis the prevention is also of death or of disability (mortality or morbidity). Advice about health-promoting diets aims to reduce the risk of disease occurring. In some cases, it aims to increase the probability of physical well-being. In this instance of risk reduction, the aim is to prevent diseases such as coronary heart disease. The example sets out to prevent disease by a lifestyle manipulation – here, diet. In some other cases, pharmaceuticals are employed to reduce risk – statins to lower cholesterol, for example.

The prostate specific antigen (PSA) test was developed to detect cancer of the prostate. An increase in antigen levels was suggestive of the presence of cancer. If the level of antigen is above a certain threshold, a biopsy is required to confirm the presence of disease. In many cases, positive for cancer, surgery is recommended. The surgical procedure involves risks, which could be as dramatic as erectile dysfunction, bowel problems and incontinence. Of course, if death is prevented, these consequences might be deemed trivial by comparison. Prostate cancer, however, is a very slow-developing cancer and is usually asymptomatic until it is quite advanced. A common, and accurate, claim is that most men die with prostate cancer not from prostate cancer. Nonetheless, some do

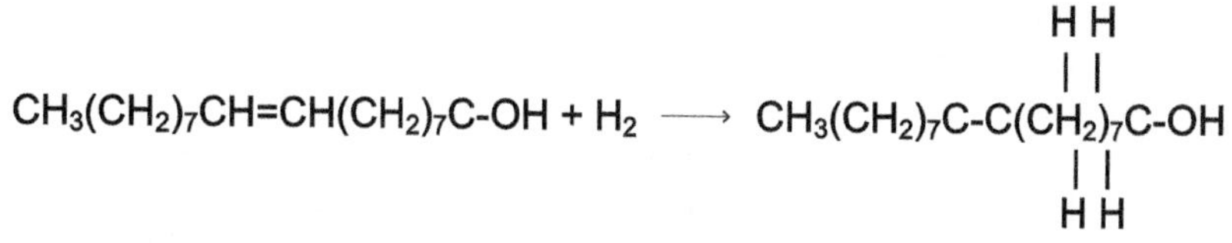

$$CH_3(CH_2)_7CH{=}CH(CH_2)_7C{-}OH + H_2 \longrightarrow CH_3(CH_2)_7\overset{\displaystyle H\ H}{\underset{\displaystyle H\ H}{C{-}C}}(CH_2)_7C{-}OH$$

*Figure 9.1* The hydrogenation of oleic fatty acid.

die from it. The PSA test has a high false positive rate; only 25% of men with an elevated PSA level are found to have cancer when biopsied (Barry 2001). The United States Preventive Services Task Force (Moyer, 2012), using data from a variety of trials, estimated that, for every 1,000 men ages 55 to 69 years who are screened every 1 to 4 years for a decade, 0–1 deaths would be avoided (<0.1%). False-positive test results leading to a biopsy would be found in 100–120 men (10–12% false positive). Of those biopsied for a positive result, 110 would be determined to have cancer and would receive treatment. About half of these will have complications such as erectile dysfunction (their estimate is 29 individuals), urinary incompetence (18 individuals, usually requiring wearing adult diapers) and other life-threatening events in 2–3 others. Given the effects on 4% of men and a death prevention rate of <0.1%, the harm to benefit ratio for this "prevention" is vastly skewed to harm. PSA tests are still recommended to their patients by many physicians. As with mammography, if you are the 1 in 1,000 (or more accurately 1 in >1,000) who cheats death because of the test, all the expense and misery inflicted on others will seem worth it. Rational decisions about resource allocation and harm to benefit ratios would conclude the opposite.

There is another class of risk-reduction interventions. This class aims to mitigate undesirable outcomes that are not related to the prevention of disease: a recommended set of warm-up exercises before running, for example, to prevent muscle damage, torn ligaments or tendons and the like. This attempt at prevention is no less fraught with complexities and uncertainty, as changing advice indicates.

There are important epistemological and logical (and, clearly some ethical) lessons embedded in reflections on these examples of prevention, where there is no "magic bullet" such as vaccination. The first is that although modern clinical research methods are better than anecdotes, intuitions and guesses, they routinely produce conflicting data and interpretations. Consequently, the scientific basis for decision-making is indeterminate. Philosophical analysis sometimes can resolve conflict but it still has great utility even when it cannot affect a resolution. An important goal of philosophical analysis is pointing out conflict and showing that it results from uncertainty. Hence, highlighting that decisions, although usually not arbitrary, rest on a shaky foundation of uncertainty. The landscape is constantly changing and that suggests that regulators and advocates (presumed experts) of this or that prevention strategy should be challenged; it is prudent to recognise that recommendations or regulations are likely to be transient. Dogmatism and strident advocacy contribute to an erosion of public confidence, especially when contrary advice is rendered within a short time frame.

Obesity, for example, is hard to define but there has emerged a consensus definition. Regardless of the "soft" (somewhat arbitrary nature) of such definitions, obesity has increased in North America and some other parts of the world. The most useful definition employs a range for a healthy weight relative to body structure (height, skeletal frame and so on). To fall below that range or above that range is "unhealthy". There are conflicting views about the range and about the nature of the modifier "unhealthy". There are also conflicting views about the causes of obesity ranging from genetic, through overconsumption and sedentary lifestyles, to obese-causing foods. On the latter, high caloric food, processed foods, low-fibre foods and numerous other targets all have expert critics. As is common with a heterogeneous population (genetically and lifestyle), different causes apply to different individuals. The causes are varied and difficult to disentangle, making blanket (one-size-fits-all) advice imprudent, perhaps sometimes dangerous.

These reflections uncover two tensions. First, if one-size-fits-all advice is imprudent because of the complex matrix of potential causes in any single individual, "best practice" in clinical medicine will be to work on the "problem" individual by individual. Leaving aside the challenge of training clinicians to engage in this task – and, thereby, adding to an already large burden of required knowledge – motivating individuals one by one is difficult. A broad-based campaign to highlight a problem, such as obesity, as it is currently understood, and advocacy for a solution that motivates the population to "care" about the problem and more readily accept the need for individual action requires simplification. The simplification often requires a one-size-fits-all approach, rather than complex tailoring to classes of individuals. This is a tension that needs to be recognised and navigated.

Second, advocacy of a preventative measure for one group often has implications for another group. For example, advocacy for a set of preventive measures for obesity can exacerbate the problem of eating disorders, disorders that result in some individuals being unhealthily underweight. This tension also needs to be navigated carefully. Successful advertising focuses on a clear message without much in the way of qualification. Media coverage assumes short attention spans and simple take-away messages. There is, of course, in-depth coverage available but most people make their decisions and order their lives on the basis of soundbites. Therein lies a significant challenge to navigating a complex landscape, which is plagued by the tensions outlined.

The important philosophical observation is just how complex the relevant issues are and, hence, how conflicted and changeable is the advice on disease prevention. Uncertainty abounds and any pretence of certainty in most areas of preventative medicine is folly.

## Diagnosis

The second category of our taxonomy of clinical practice is diagnosis – the process of determining the disease that is causing symptoms. Sometimes a disease that is asymptomatic is detected through investigation – frequently through an investigation of some other ailment or through screening – but this is not properly a diagnosis; it is rather a discovery.

Diagnosis, like other areas of clinical practice, relies on empirical knowledge but its core element is reasoning from symptoms to potential causes. Diagnostic reasoning is a fluid mix of deductive and inductive inferences – reasoning from a specific set of known symptoms to the cause(s) of those symptoms. This may lead directly to an unassailable determination of a cause (or causes) or a determination of what investigations are required to narrow down the potential causes to *a* cause or *the most probable* cause (*C*). Ideally, diagnosis leads to the determination of *a* cause where $\Pr(C) = 1$. This is a rare occurrence; probabilities much less than 1 are common.

A fluid mix of deductive and inductive reasoning is required because some reasoning rests on the statement of symptoms and deductions from the models and theories of anatomy, physiology, haematology and so on. Some other tracks of reasoning will be based on individual or collective experience; in *X* number of cases with symptoms *Y*, the cause has been *Z*. This is an inductive inference. As an example of deduction, symptoms of jaundice (a yellow hue to the skin and the whites of the eyes) along with knowledge of the physiological role of the liver deductively entail that there is a malfunction of the liver, more specifically the liver is failing to metabolise bilirubin (a yellow pigment, which is a by-product of the breakdown – also in the liver – of spent red blood cells). The exact mix of inductive and deductive inference involved will vary by case. In the case of some symptoms, there is no ready-to-hand knowledge to allow a deduction. In others deduction is all that is needed. Moreover, the nature of inductive reasoning is different in diagnosis than in empirical research, both in pattern and goal.

This fundamental importance of reasoning in diagnosis should make the claim of Richard Horton rather chilling. His claim was broader than diagnosis but has a clear bite in the context of diagnosis.

> The skill that physicians lack above all is the ability to reason successfully. By "to reason" I mean interrogating a clinical argument to discover its weaknesses or the basis of its validity. Reasoning is not the skill of switching on a computer, typing in a few key words and printing out several abstracts of randomized trials or systematic reviews . . . Reasoning involves thinking critically and logically about a particular proposition: why this patient with a stenosed coronary artery may require a stent, why this patient with a stroke may require speech therapy. What are the assumptions that underlie these clinical decisions? How far does the available evidence stretch to inform the care of our patients? What are the potential sources of error in the data we are drawing on?

A closer look at diagnosis will sharpen our understanding of what many claim is the core task of a physician. Without accurate diagnosis, appropriate treatment cannot be prescribed and accurate prognosis cannot be offered. Moreover, misdiagnosis is obviously a harm, which to the maximum extent possible is to be avoided. So, is it important to understand in more detail than provided so far exactly what sort of reasoning is involved in diagnosis? How do we know when diagnostic reasoning is valid, or at least logically defensible?

We will initially be concerned with primary diagnosis. This is the reasoning that physicians employ prior to the use of some form of technology (such as blood tests, imaging, etc.). Once we have clarified this process, we will introduce the role that diagnostic testing plays in reasoning. Primary diagnosis begins with the taking of a history, which, of course, includes the presenting symptoms. The symptoms can tightly direct the scope and level of detail of the history or can be mostly the motivation for taking a wide-ranging history. A history can be taken in several ways, but by far the most common way in which a physician begins to make a diagnosis is by a close and careful questioning of a patient. To illustrate this, we will take a simple case.

A five-year-old girl presents to a primary care physician with a fever and lethargy. Children at her age are usually brought to the clinic by parents – sometimes by another adult. Hence, the information will be obtained through a conversation with the parents. A febrile child is a very common occurrence. In fact, children with fevers may be the most common presentation to a primary care physician on a daily basis in virtually every context of practice. The encounter will typically begin with questions about the onset and duration of the fever and then about other associated symptoms such as cough, sneezing, diarrhoea or vomiting, lassitude, appetite and so on. The point of the varied questions is to determine the severity of the illness and each question increases the depth of understanding. In addition to the questions about the most recent events, there will be others about the general health status of the child, including all relevant past illness, allergies, immunisations as well as exploring the home situation and ascertaining the level of anxiety that may or may not be present in the parents. (There is in general a difference between first-time parents and experienced parents.)

After taking the history, a physical examination will be conducted. In this case, vital signs will be measured (temperature, pulse and respirations); a careful examination of the head and neck, auscultation of the lungs and examination of the abdomen will be carried out to see whether there are any signs of infection. The point of the history is to elicit the nature and extent of the patient's symptoms. With a five-year old, the parent(s) will be the source of most information. The physical examination is meant to determine whether there are any signs (physical evidence) of illness. For example, a red inflamed bulging eardrum would give a clue as to the source of the fever, most likely a middle-ear infection. In which case, the physician will inform the parents that the child is most likely suffering from a middle-ear infection. Mild clear discharge from the nose and the presence of sneezing would point in the direction of an upper respiratory tract infection. In which case, the physician will inform the parents that the child is most likely suffering from a viral respiratory illness.

The combined information from the history and physical examination along with knowledge of physiology and the effects on that physiology of infections provides the basis for a diagnosis; that is, a conclusion about the most likely explanation of the constellation of signs and symptoms. Frequently, this exercise suffices and no further steps are required; hence, a clinical diagnosis is offered.

The "most likely" is critical here. This may or may not be expressed as a probability. That is, I am 0.9 certain it is a virus (often expressed to a patient – or the parents – as 90% certain, even though mathematically probability ranges from 0 to 1). Most clinical diagnoses are offered provisionally. Each diagnosis is a differential diagnosis in that there are often a number of possible explanations for the illness. In this case, the child may have a more severe illness such as pneumonia or meningitis. A gurgling sound while listening to the lungs would suggest a chest X-ray is appropriate to confirm or rule out pneumonia. Painful flexion of a stiff neck would suggest investigation of potential meningitis.

Philosophically interesting features emerge from this case. Perhaps more than is obvious even to physicians. A clinical diagnosis is a causal account. That is, it rests upon an architecture of knowledge that has evolved over the centuries and been transmitted to generations of clinicians. Each causal account such as "viral illness" rests upon a taxonomy of disease and collective experience about how various diseases are manifested in humans. There is a body of knowledge deductively and inductively linking a wide range of signs and symptoms to a numerous array of agreed-upon causes of disease.

As we have noted earlier in Chapters 2 and 6, the determining whether something is a disease may be elusive and our notions of cause may be bounded by what is known at any given time. For example, the idea that a virus is the causal agent responsible for the fever that the child is suffering is of relatively recent origin. Viruses as ubiquitous human pathogens were only discovered in the late nineteenth century and knowledge of the wide and diverse number of viruses capable of causing human illness is the product of twentieth-century science. Our understanding of virology continues to evolve. These are observations worthy of philosophical investigation.

Consider an immediate objection to the fever account. Claiming that the child has a viral illness, based on symptoms, signs and other knowledge, does not in any way establish that a virus is the cause of the child's illness. This is an important point to consider; there is a difference between asserting that a virus is the cause and demonstrating that, in fact, the child has a particular virus. In most cases, the diagnosis will be made inferentially based solely on statements and observations obtained during an office visit; no further information will be sought, because background knowledge holds that viral illnesses are common causes of fever in children and are, for the most part, self-limiting in nature. This diagnosis involves inductive reasoning. Inductive reasoning makes the diagnosis probable to some degree but never certain.

This example represents a broad array of clinical encounters. The diagnoses are based on signs and symptoms, are inductive and usually have a high probability – high enough for a clinician to move to management of the illness. One may demand more stringent criteria for diagnosis than this, since a purely clinical diagnosis is one rooted in judgement without any confirmation from sources other than the clinician. From a philosophical perspective, the fundamental epistemic question is, when has sufficient confidence been secured to move from diagnosis to offering a management plan? In the case we have been considering, it would be reasonable for the physician on the basis of her examination to recommend symptomatic management of the child (rest, fluids and perhaps medicine to lower the fever). It is, arguably, unreasonable to demand further information at this stage in order to increase diagnostic certainty.

Understanding why is crucial to the understanding of the purpose of diagnosis. The physician must do something for a patient in danger, but does not know the cause of his illness. For example, she observes the symptoms and if she can find no more likely alternative, judges it to be a case of phthisis (wasting away as is seen in tuberculosis), for example. Now even in her estimation, this judgement is contingent; another observer might perhaps come to a different – perhaps sounder – conclusion. Nonetheless, such contingent belief forms the ground for the employment of certain actions to treat the illness. Philosophically, the judgement (belief) is pragmatic.

The eighteenth-century philosopher Immanuel Kant provides a fundamental insight into the nature of diagnostic reasoning. In the *Critique of Pure Reason* (1781, 1787) he defines pragmatic belief as a form of contingent belief that *provides sufficient ground to take action*. Diagnosis is always differential; there are a wide range of diverse conditions that can manifest with the same set of symptoms and signs. Determining the most probable cause (or perhaps causes) requires differentiating the potential causes and ranking the probability of each. Additional information can change the probabilities. At some point, the information will be pragmatically adequate, at which point a clinician will deem it appropriate to move to treatment/intervention. The clinician and a properly informed patient will monitor the situation. A treatment plan that is not yielding the expected outcome or the appearance of new symptoms will warrant re-diagnosis.

As noted, sometimes the need to move expeditiously is important; the greater the danger to the patient, the greater the need for haste. In a number of cases, the level of certainty of the diagnosis will be high, always recognising that certainty is often unachievable. In many cases, however, danger to the patient will require acting in a situation of undesirable uncertainty. This is the pragmatic balancing of the need to act with the desire, from an ideal perspective of more information, which will potentially increase the level of certainty.

In cases where there is no urgency to act or where the uncertainty of diagnosis is, pragmatically, unacceptably low, additional information can be sought. In this context, modern medicine has a vast array of diagnostic technologies at its disposal. These range from expensive sophisticated technologies to commonly employed (and, many critics claim, often abused) laboratory tests based on biological specimens such as blood, sputum, urine and faeces that are easily obtained and inexpensive to process. The late twentieth century, for example, saw a revolution in terms of imaging technologies with the advent of computerised axial tomography (CAT scan, sometimes simply CT scan), magnetic resonance imaging as well as positron emission scans, all of which augment the information that can be gleaned from radiography. A now pervasive non-radiographic imaging technology is ultrasonography. Each of these technologies rests upon the sorts of biological and mathematical models discussed in other chapters to undergird their utility and applicability. The science behind these technologies is mostly tacit in the practice of medicine in that only very specialised, and hence very few, clinicians will understand the biology, bio-chemistry and physics that explain their function. The clinician's expertise is in interpreting the results yielded by these technologies. This is why the results are useful sources of diagnostic information.

Returning to the narrative of the child with a fever, the course of illness evolves. She returns to the clinic after a few days of symptomatic manage-ment and is much worse. Her parents are concerned because despite the use of antipyretics she remains febrile, listless with poor appetite. Antipyretics are medications to lower temperature: ibuprofen and acetaminophen are common over-the-counter antipyretics; acetylsalicylic acid – ASA or aspirin – is almost never prescribed for children, especially those with a fever, due to the risk of Reye's Syndrome. She also complains of a sore throat. The physician repeats a physical examination and this time finds enlarged tonsillar lymph nodes and exudates on the tonsils. The physician considers the diagnosis of a throat infec-tion caused by streptococcal bacteria. She must decide whether to order a test such as a throat swab to confirm the diagnosis or simply to prescribe a course of antibiotics shown to be effective in treating strep throat.

This decision, though commonly made, is not without complexity. There is much at stake because, as we have frequently noted, all diagnoses have an element of uncertainty and carry the possibility of error. Moreover, even if a physician is correct, there is no guarantee that the treatment will be effective; the effectiveness of treatment is idiosyncratic. Compounding these challenges are the facts that prescribing antibiotics when not indicated is costly, has the potential for adverse effects such as allergic reactions and gastric upset, and also can contribute to the growing problem of drug-resistant organisms. On the other hand, withholding antibiotics, when they are the appropriate treatment, risks prolonged illness and the possibility of complications from the bacteria. Given the clinical symptoms in the case of our child, prescribing an antibiotic is prudent (amoxicillin, cephalexin, or penicillin are effective). A swab to confirm strep throat may also be prudent. That leads to another consideration in diagnosis.

In a perfect world, from a human perspective, all diagnostic tests would be 100% accurate and infallible. However, such a state of affairs does not exist and likely never will. Most diagnostic tests perform variably, with false positives and false negatives. A false positive is a result that is positive for the pathogen when the pathogen is not involved. A false negative is a result that is negative for the pathogen when the pathogen is involved. We examined the 2 × 2 table in Chapter 8; here we use it in a different context. Let us define the cells and then describe their relationships (see Table 9.1).

   a is the true-positive fraction
   b is the false-positive fraction
   c is the false-negative fraction
   d is the true-negative fraction

Table 9.1 A 2 × 2 display of false and true positives and false and true negatives.

|  | *Positive result* | *Negative result* |
|---|---|---|
| Pathogen present | a | c |
| Pathogen not present | b | d |

These kinds of diagnostic tests have properties called sensitivity and specificity.

*Sensitivity* is the proportion of people with a disease who have a positive test for the causal agent ($a/a + b$). It is a measure that represents the proportion of truly positive (diseased) patients in relation to all positive tests. *Specificity* is the proportion of people free of a disease who have a negative test ($d/c + d$). It is a measure that represents the proportion of truly negative (disease-free) patients in relation to all negative tests. Clearly, the better the test distinguishes the two populations, the better it serves for decision-making. A perfectly *sensitive* test would entail that the potential causal pathogen in an ill person with a positive test will be the actual causal agent. A perfectly *specific* test would rule out potential pathogens, meaning the illness of every person with a negative test for a specific pathogen will have a cause other than that pathogen. Most tests, however, must trade off sensitivity and specificity. It is important to note that all tests bear the risk of being falsely positive or falsely negative. Being told that you have a pathogen when you do not in fact have one or similarly being told you do not have a pathogen when you in fact do have one is of immense consequence. What is true of pathogens is also true of other causative factors such as a malfunctioning thyroid or thyroxin feed-back system, where no pathogen need be involved.

An additional measure can be derived from the 2 × 2 table. The "likelihood ratio" is the likelihood that a given test result would be found in a patient with the target disorder compared with the likelihood that the same result would be expected in a patient without that disorder (LR = $a/a + c/b/b + d$).

Returning to our example of a child with a fever and, now observed, inflamed tonsils, let us imagine that the physician orders the throat swab. The "gold standard" for diagnosis of strep throat is to take a swab and see what grows in a bacterial culture. There are a variety of differing culture techniques, all with their own sensitivity and specificity. Bacterial cultures, for all their virtues, take time and the decision to treat must be made quickly. Consequently, bacterial culture has been replaced by more rapid antigen-based methods: rapid antigen detection tests (RADTs). There are several approaches used, based on different molecular technologies. The sensitivity and specificity of these methods have been measured in comparison with the results of bacterial culture. The comparison suggests that RADTs have the best accuracy – lowest false positives and false negatives.[2]

There is an epistemological and logical issue in these comparisons. Comparing one test (RADTs, for example) with a "gold standard" assumes that the "gold standard" is perfect. That is, the performance characteristics noted above are not included in the calculations; any errors of the gold standard are carried forward and neglected. What we find is that there is variability in performance between various rapid tests; they have higher specificity than sensitivity (meaning positive tests rule), but regardless there will be ineliminable misclassifications. What the results also tell us is that despite a large number of studies, there is still abundant uncertainty concerning what is the optimal testing strategy for a very common disease.

In our example, the physician ordered a RADT and it came back positive for group A beta-haemolytic streptococci. An appropriate antibiotic is prescribed. In the large majority of cases, the disease is "cured".

## Treatment

The third element in our taxonomy of clinical practice is treatment. As a defensible generalisation, it can be stated that treatment in modern medicine, in most cases, involves some form of pharmacotherapy. Nonetheless, the spectrum of treatments can range from surgery, advice, dietary changes, physical therapy, counselling and herbal medications delivered by a wide and heterogeneous range of practitioners. Because of its pervasiveness in clinical medicine, for the purposes of this chapter we focus on medical therapy in the form of a pharmaceutical intervention.

In the example of the febrile child, the physician has concluded that the cause is bacterial and an "appropriate" antibiotic is required. The question is, which antibiotic? She decides to consult the Cochrane Collaboration[3] to find out which antibiotic is most likely to be effective in treating strep throat. A systematic review is found with the following results:

Seventeen trials (5,352 participants) were included; 16 compared penicillin with other antibiotics (six with cephalosporins, six with macrolides, three with carbacephem and one with sulfonamides), one trial compared clindamycin and ampicillin. Randomisation reporting, allocation concealment and blinding were poor. There was no difference in symptom resolution between cephalosporins and penicillin.[4] There were no differences between macrolides and penicillin. Carbacephem showed better symptom resolution post-treatment.[5] Children experienced more adverse events with macrolides.[6]

The results tell the physician that despite the high prevalence of strep throat, there are few rigorous clinical trials upon which to base decisions. Symptom resolution, that is, dissipation of fever and absence of sore throat, is achieved with two of the most commonly prescribed antibiotics. There may be a slightly lower risk of relapse with cephalosporins in comparison with penicillin, but a large number of people need to be treated to achieve this modest benefit. She next decides to consult a clinical practice guideline (CPG). CPGs are often regarded as providing authoritative guidance to practitioners regarding treatment decisions. The advice is that patients with acute GAS pharyngitis should be treated with an appropriate antibiotic at an appropriate dose for a duration likely to eradicate the organism from the pharynx (usually ten days). Based on their narrow spectrum of activity, infrequency of adverse reactions and modest cost, penicillin or amoxicillin is the recommended drug of choice for those not allergic to these agents.

Based on all this, the physician prescribes a ten-day course of amoxicillin. This is done on the assumption that:

a   the diagnosis is correct and accurate, and
b   the prescribed therapy is effective in altering the course of the disease and alleviating the symptoms.

Three models of causal reasoning are at play here:

1   Koch's postulates articulated the criteria to determine whether a microorganism has the capacity to produce illness in a host.
2   Randomised trials are a method for reliable causal claims regarding the capacity for a pharmacological agent to produce clinical results.
3   Mechanisms are understood that explain the biological activities of both the microorganisms and the pharmacological agents.

(2) and (3) have in various ways been explained already. Koch's postulates have not. His postulates are more than a century old. Koch published them in 1890. Even though Koch's name is associated with the postulates because he was the one who refined and published them, he developed them six years earlier in collaboration with Friedrich Loeffler. The postulates specify the criteria that must be met to establish that a causal connection exists between a microbial pathogen and a disease. His specific focus was anthrax and tuberculosis. Today his postulates are applied more generally to microbes and disease. The four postulates, which have slightly different formulations in different modern expositions, are:

1   The microorganism must be found in sufficient quantities in all organisms manifesting a specific disease (a stronger but not always expressed condition is that the microorganism must not be found in healthy organisms[7]).
2   The microorganism must be isolated from a diseased organism and grown in pure culture.
3   The cultured microorganism should cause disease when introduced into a healthy organism (usually a laboratory animal).
4   The microorganism must be re-isolated from the inoculated organism and be identified as identical to the introduced microorganism.

A dramatic illustration of the application of these postulates is the discovery that the bacterium *Helicobacter pylori* is a cause of gastritis and gastric ulcers. It was identified by Barry Marshall and Robin Warren, both Australian scientists, in 1982 (Marshall and Warren 1983). At the time, gastric ulcers were not associated with microorganisms. The prevailing view connected ulcers to stress. The most succinct summary of their work is found in the press release of the Nobel Committee on October 3, 2005, in which it announced the awarding of the 2005 Nobel Prize in Physiology or Medicine to Marshall and Warren:

> This year's Nobel Laureates in Physiology or Medicine made the remarkable and unexpected discovery that inflammation in the stomach (gastritis) as well as ulceration of the stomach or duodenum (peptic ulcer disease) is the result of an infection of the stomach caused by the bacterium *Helicobacter pylori*.
>
> Robin Warren (born 1937), a pathologist from Perth, Australia, observed small curved bacteria colonizing the lower part of the stomach (antrum) in about 50% of patients from which biopsies had been taken. He made the crucial observation that signs of inflammation were always present in the gastric mucosa close to where the bacteria were seen.
>
> Barry Marshall (born 1951), a young clinical fellow, became interested in Warren's findings and together they initiated a study of biopsies from 100 patients. After several attempts, Marshall succeeded in cultivating a hitherto unknown bacterial species (later denoted *Helicobacter pylori*) from several of these biopsies. Together they found that the organism was present in almost all patients with gastric inflammation, duodenal ulcer or gastric ulcer. Based on these results, they proposed that *Helicobacter pylori* is involved in the aetiology of these diseases.
>
> (nobelprize.org 2005)

As can be seen, Koch's s (1) and (2) are satisfied. The story of how they demonstrated that their hypothesis also satisfies (3) and (4) is the more dramatic part of the discovery. They failed with studies on lab mice. It is now known that *H. pylori* only affects primates. The medical community rejected their hypothesis. In some desperation, they performed the only ethical experiment on humans available to them. Marshall isolated *H. pylori* from a patient, cultured them and then drank a concoction containing the bacteria. He developed gastritis and vomiting among some other symptoms. He collected *H. pylori* from his stomach. He treated his condition with antibiotics and recovered. They established, using endoscopy, a baseline condition of his stomach before he drank the bacterial concoction. After drinking it, they established a large population of *H. pylori* in his stomach, retrieved and cultured them. After antibiotic therapy, his stomach returned to its baseline condition. This established that their hypothesis satisfies postulates (3) and (4).

This research also illustrates why the more stringent version of postulate (1) often needs to be relaxed. About 80% of the population "carry" the bacterium; only a fraction of those people develop gastric ulcers from it. It also illustrates, yet again, how entrenched ideas can become in medicine and how slowly ideas change.

We focused in the last two sections – on diagnosis and therapy on a febrile child. The example illustrates important features of diagnosis and treatment. Specifically, it illustrates that underlying a simple and common clinical decision are complex interactions of various types of mechanistic, statistical and biological theories and models. The febrile child has all of the important features of diagnosis. In many cases, the complexities of diagnosis are greater but the essence and elements of the diagnostic process are the same, albeit more challenging. Where the febrile child example is somewhat misleading is the "magic bullet" character of its therapy; its value as an example is that it embodies the essential reasoning in diagnosis and recommended therapy. The correct diagnosis of a bacterial infection makes the success of therapy, using antibiotics, very high. It is expected that cure rates with standard antibiotic therapy will be in the 80–95% range. However, this also indicates that even in "easy, magic bullet" cases, treatment failure does occur, and as noted, no physician can be certain which patient will be cured in advance of the course of treatment. The discomforting reality is that a great many therapies are distant from the magic bullet cases, with treatment sometimes amounting to experimentation, or at least trial and error (and one hopes success).

It is in this context that the trial of 1 ($n = 1$) makes sense. It is a quest of a patient and his physician to find the therapy that produces the best outcome. Human populations are physiological and genetically heterogenous. Individuals respond differently to the same therapy under what are, at least ostensibly, the same circumstances. Beyond the domain of the few magic bullet therapies, among which must be counted routine and highly successful surgeries, therapy can be frustratingly elusive.

## Prognosis

The fourth element in our taxonomy is prognosis. Hippocrates praised prognosis, considering it to be a crucial skill for physicians:

> It appears to me a most excellent thing for the physician to cultivate Prognosis; for by foreseeing and foretelling, in the presence of the sick, the present, the past, and the future, and explaining the omissions which patients have been guilty of, he will be the more readily believed to be acquainted with the circumstances of the sick; so that men will have confidence to entrust themselves to such a physician.

Prognosis is prediction, based on diagnosis, therapy and past experience (collectively and individually). It attempts to determine the *likely* course of a disease given its diagnosed cause, available therapies and the success of those therapies. That is, it rests on the logic of causation entailed by diagnosis and appropriate therapy. The greater the degree of certitude in the accuracy of the diagnosis and effectiveness of therapy, the greater should be the physician's accuracy in foretelling what the consequences are for the patient. Nonetheless, prognosis relies on a set of complex considerations around the predictability of the future for a particular patient at a particular time.

For the most part, prognosis relies on past studies of populations with similar clinical circumstances to the case under consideration. Historically, physicians relied on their experience, the experience of colleagues and the collected knowledge of the profession in terms of case reports. Now, prognosis is based upon study designs, either prospective or retrospective cohort studies, or clinical trials that are analysed according to methodologies, such as survival analysis.

Prognosis is usually communicated in probabilistic terms, usually associated with a frequentist interpretation of probability. We commonly read such claims as a person with cancer has a 50% chance of survival for 5 years. What that means is that in a group of people with a particular stage of cancer, one half will still be alive after five years of treatment. This is a measure of mortality, but prognosis can focus on states of pain, quality of life or a wide range of biological markers such as tumour burden or measures of biochemical or haematological parameters. Each of these probability measures will be associated with confidence bounds that speak to the precision with which the estimate is known. It is important to recognise that such population measures fail to be precise with respect to the outcome with any particular person.

Before moving to the final two elements in our taxonomy, a common theme running through diagnosis, therapy and prognosis can be clearly articulated. Clinical practice, like clinical research, is rife with uncertainty. It is one of the most pervasive, but least discussed, aspects of clinical medicine. The causes of uncertainty are numerous. There may be a lack of convincing evidence or inconsistent evidence. There may be multiple interpretations of the data, all consistent with what is known. There may be alternative views about how to apply the evidence from research at the bedside. The chapters of this book, so far, provide a basis for a much more comprehensive list.

Essential on any list of the causes of uncertainty in medicine is the degree to which uncertainty is related to the quality of the science upon which judgements are made. In earlier chapters, we described the variety of ways in which theories and models, biological knowledge and statistics function in order to provide explanations of events. As will be clear now, clinical medicine is built upon a highly heterogeneous set of such considerations. Diagnosis, therapy and prognosis all rely to varying degrees on these considerations, but are never completely dependent on one set of considerations. Later, when we consider evidence-based medicine, we will see how it seeks to base clinical reasoning, for the most part, on statistical considerations and is distrustful of relying on biological accounts of mechanisms.

Whether a physician employs quantitative methods, relies on data from well-designed studies or employs biological knowledge of mechanisms, there is always uncertainty associated with each element of clinical reasoning. A virtue of quantitative approaches is that they permit rather specific and clear statements regarding the extent of uncertainty.

## Rehabilitation

The next element in our taxonomy is rehabilitation. Physiotherapy is a common part of rehabilitation. A person falls in a way that fractures her tibia and fibula just above the ball and socket joint of the ankle. This almost always also involves dislocation of the ankle. After a relocation of the ball and socket and surgery to resolve the fractures, physiotherapy will facilitate a return to normal movement. Many other branches of medicine are involved in rehabilitation. Improvement of cognitive capacity, cessation of drug dependency and reduction or elimination of mental health issues, such as anxiety, are all examples of rehabilitation. The goal is to return a person to that person's normal state of functioning, or to come as close as possible to that state of functioning. It is important that the "normal" state of functioning be relative to the person. There is a wide range of individual differences in capacity to function. To enhance one's base state of functioning, such as training for sprint racing, is not rehabilitation.

The techniques of rehabilitation and the scope of its application have expanded dramatically over the last five decades. Its role in medicine has often been under-appreciated. Indeed, the array of malfunctioning that it addresses and the percentage of the population that benefit from it is very large. On many measures, it has the most successful outcomes of all the elements discussed in this chapter. This raises important questions. Why does the importance of this element receive less public attention? Why does it receive lower levels of research funding? Why do many health jurisdictions not cover the full cost of physiotherapy? There are many parts to complete answers. Part of the answer to each question, for example, involves the internal politics of medicine. Part involves skewed media attention to "dramatic" therapies. Part involves distorted employment of epistemological methods; something we have highlighted in previous chapters.

## Palliation

Palliation is the final element in our taxonomy. It is not last because it is less important; in some respects, it is the most important. In spite of the positive picture often painted of the successes of the diagnosis and treatment of physical disease, reality is far gloomier. Without doubt, there have been tremendous gains; few of us would want to have lived 200 years ago. Nonetheless, in large numbers of cases, diseases resist diagnosis, or therapies are non-existent or, in specific cases, unsuccessful, or diseases are sufficiently advanced at the point of diagnosis that available therapies are doomed to failure. All lead to palliative care of some variety. Add to this the challenges of mental diseases and the need for palliative care grows dramatically. Then there is the reality that none of us will live forever and the end of life can be devastating for many. Palliative care can lighten the burden.

Palliation, of course, covers a very broad territory. A person who obtains physiotherapy to recover mobility in an arm that has been recently broken and now healed is palliation in some sense. It could equally be called therapy. Here we concentrate on the more common use, as applied to those whose prognosis of a return to health is poor.

Palliative care has attracted much attention from bioethicists. Issues ranging from standards of care in institutions and informed consent to socially explosive issues such as assisted dying have generated a wealth of literature. Ethics (theoretical and applied) is a domain of philosophy. Bioethics is a broader field. This is one reason for the remarkable diversity of views on many high-profile issues. As we have noted, philosophy of medicine only tangentially embraces ethics, just as philosophy of biology only tangentially embraces ethics. Its concerns are epistemological, logical and metaphysical – all subfields of philosophy. The ethical issues arising from palliative care seem obvious. The epistemological, logical and metaphysical issues, however, seem in need of a voice.

In some respects, this is because a number of the issues mirror those in all of clinical medicine. How is the best course of action determined for this or that person in his or her circumstances, for example? What studies are there? How reliable are the studies? Can population-level findings be applied in this or that case? The philosophical exploration of these issues will circle back to things already examined. Nonetheless, there will be differences in the specific context of palliation. For many, the end of life is near – unlike the majority of those who seek medical attention. For some others, a long existence of dependence on caregivers lies ahead. The translation of research to these individuals will be different. Research on the appropriate physiotherapy for a successful outcome after a broken ankle in a 18-year-old is not likely to translate into meaningful physiotherapy for a broken ankle, from a tumble out of bed, in someone whose mobility is minimal.

The causal matrix of disease in someone with multiple chronic diseases and taking multiple medications will be different from that in an otherwise healthy 30-year-old with pneumonia. In the former case, it may be difficult to sort out symptoms that arise from the chronic disease from common adverse effects of medication. In the latter case, given fewer interactions at play, sorting out intended from unintended effects is much simpler. Unfortunately, the results of research on highly selected younger populations are applied to older more complex patients without sufficient attention being paid to the justification of such an extrapolation of results.

Many people in palliative care are on multiple medications, especially the elderly. Medications are tested, usually using RCTs, and approved one by one. No systematic research is conducted on the interaction of several medications. Moreover, the elderly are excluded from clinical trials, as are those with diseases in addition to the one being studied. Hence, guidance for those involved in the palliative care of those with co-morbidities is impoverished.

Many in need of palliative care have a sense of despondency, which cannot be lumped with clinical depression found in the general population. It arises from a sense that nothing is working and life is deteriorating. Defining that state of mind requires being attentive to the life that has been lived, the life now being lived and the inability to provide a diagnosis and effective therapy. Definition is a philosophical exercise, maybe best carried out by physicians in this case, but a philosophical exercise all the same. Until something is defined, the object of discussion, investigation and manipulation is vague – that vagueness ensures that, to borrow Galileo's phrase (1623), "one wanders about in a dark labyrinth". Finding the nature and cause of something that is ill defined or only understood intuitively or metaphorically is impossible. Ennui in some individuals during palliation also needs definition. It cannot be assumed that it is the same phenomenon as in a 30-year-old.

Palliation also raises special issues with "informed consent". Informed consent is most often discussed in bioethics but it is a deeply epistemological concept because information is an epistemological category. One technique for countering a claim that a person or organisation is not being open and transparent – often code for a charge of withholding information – is to drown the complainant(s) in information – the more technical the better. That, however, is not the appropriate criterion of "informed" in the concept of informed consent. The information must be intelligible, manageable and relevant. These are all epistemological concepts. The social need to secure informed consent may be an ethical requirement; knowing how to do it is epistemological. This will vary based on the specific characteristics of individuals. It is not that groups cannot be aggregated; it is that the aggregation must be capable of justification, itself an epistemological activity. Treating the mentally challenged person the same as a bright PhD candidate is unjustifiable. Also, treating those in palliative care the same as a 30-year-old with pneumonia is epistemologically unjustifiable.

## Summation

Drawing the threads of this chapter together, prevention, diagnosis, therapy, rehabilitation and palliation involve clinical reasoning (inference). Taken together clinical reasoning is the process of assimilating the information gathered from taking a patient history, performing a physical examination, ordering and interpreting diagnostic tests to make an appropriate diagnosis, management and prognosis for a patient. These elements form the basis of clinical judgement. The philosophically relevant aspects of clinical judgement relate to the status of the reasoning and logic that inform clinical judgement. It is related to the acumen of clinicians in the conduct of their daily tasks. Thus, it is something routinely employed but often not given rigorous scrutiny. The traditional concern for the critical analysis of the adequacy of the relationship between justification and the conclusions they support arises from logic (the codification of inferences).

Discussions of the logic of clinical reasoning have examined its relationship to models of scientific inference. Hence medical reasoning is regarded as analogous to inductive reasoning, the hypothetico-deductive method, or Popperian falsificationism (discussed in Chapters 3 and 6). The inherent fallibility of medical knowledge indicates that the type of reasoning employed by physicians is provisional in nature, pragmatic in orientation and probabilistic in its expression.

Judgements and decisions in clinical medicine, as we have demonstrated in this chapter, rest more on plausibility than certainty; that is, what seems to be true or appropriate in a given set of circumstances. Plausible inferences can carry probative weight that may be quantitative (like probability statements and subject to the probability calculus), or be expressed in qualitative or narrative terms (and hence not subject to the probability calculus). Plausible inferences intend to provide a reasonable guide for sustaining a belief or justifying an action, but may in fact turn out to be erroneous, and in need of revision.

Clinical reasoning should result in decisions that are well supported by the facts of the case and open to scrutiny and revision in light of changing circumstances of the patient's status. In essence the collection of information relevant to a patient is a form of argumentation. Stephen Toulmin (1958) demonstrates that an argument seeks to resolve an undecided issue. Every episode of diagnostic reasoning commences with the undecided issue of what is the matter with the patient. We have seen in the example of a child with a fever that the issue can be easily or more complexly decided depending on the situation and the gravity of the illness.

When attempting to demonstrate the truth or probability of an argument's claim, one may be asked: "What information have you got to go on?" Claims are usually supported by appeal to some facts or other considerations. Broadly considered these can be called data. Data in the case of diagnosis can be direct observation (e.g. the measurement of the child's temperature and the results of the physical examination), appeal to local epidemiology (evidence of respiratory illnesses circulating in the community) or any other form of positive or negative information. Supporting the step between data and the claim is the warrant. Warrants are distinct from the data and the claim and act as a bridge between them. Warrants are often implicit in arguments. The virtue of the Toulmin approach is to make them explicit.

Arguments are liable to rebuttal. Rebuttals are conditions in which the warrant is not applicable and consequently the claim can be overturned. In the case we have used, the argument that the child has a simple respiratory virus is rebutted by the failure of the child to improve with simple supportive measures. A rebuttal calls for a reassessment of the argument in light of new or additional information that casts doubt on the adequacy of the initial argument.

When introduced in argument, information can either be "warrant-using" or "warrant-establishing." Warrant-using information acts as the basis for a claim and attempts to answer "What information do you have to go on?" In the clinical context, warrant-using information relates to the individual patient and is obtained through the patient interview, physical examination and investigative tests. Warrant-establishing information serves as the backing or justification of the warrant used to make the leap from the data to the claim. Essentially, this form of information is used to answer "How did you get there?" According to the Toulmin model of argumentation (see Figure 9.2), clinical decisions require warrants even in the absence of research data that may certify the warrant. Clinicians often find themselves in situations where there is little, if any, research data available, or substantive disagreement about the interpretation of the research data.

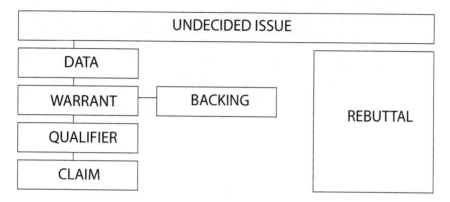

*Figure 9.2* A schematic of Toulmin's model of argumentation.

Douglas Walton (1998), in *The New Dialectic: Conversational Contexts of Argument*, provides a typology of argument contexts relevant to the different contexts of clinical reasoning. For Walton argumentation is dialectical, a fundamentally social process conducted in diverse contexts between individuals with potentially differing interests. The context of argumentation strongly influences the adjudication of argument adequacy and soundness. In medicine argumentation occurs to serve a variety of goals. What is warranted in one context may be regarded as unwarranted in another. Three types of dialogue will be illustrated.

The first, persuasion dialogue, is likely ubiquitous in clinical practice. The process is dyadic and can involve a patient attempting to persuade the health care provider or vice versa. However, there will also be a set of value commitments that are not reducible to empirical data and may not be expressed. In the case with the child with a fever, parental anxiety may be a potent influence driving the dialogue. The parents may desire therapy that the physician may not believe is in the child's best interest (or vice versa). They each proffer their reasons for their perspective. Research evidence will likely be offered in support of the disparate views, and likely will serve as the basis of the legitimacy of the physician's standpoint. The parents can trump even a sophisticated and compelling meta-analysis by declining to initiate therapy. The exchange of views is intended to serve a maieutic function; that is, the opposition of perspectives should elicit greater explicitness concerning the shortcomings of the rival perspective.

The second, inquiry dialogue, has the goal of producing solid inferences, with clear concepts of burden of proof articulated *a priori*. The effort is collective, exhaustive, with clearly specified questions and criteria stipulated in advance to determine the acceptability of evidence. Considerable effort is made to ensure that all acceptable evidence is included and evaluated according to the pre-established standards. It is the dialogic context where research evidence is necessary. In our example, we showed how the results of studies in the diagnosis and treatment of strep throat, while informative, leaves considerable unanswered questions relevant to therapeutic success and prognosis. It illustrates the point that even summarising the best possible evidence does not eliminate uncertainty.

In the third, negotiation dialogue, commitment to the truth or falsity of premises is subordinate to the exchange, purchase or movement of items of value. Rather than the marshalling and adjudication of the burden of evidence, negotiation involves trade-offs and bargaining. Negotiation is rooted in interests and not in the pursuit of truth per se. The question in assessing evidence in this dialogue context is the reasonableness, fairness and justice of the trade-offs. This type of trade-off is illustrated by recent developments in concordance research. In this vision of the physician–patient relationship, a dialogue is established and a process of partnership develops through discussion. Negotiation is an important element of this as there may be trade-offs between the goals of the provider and the patient. Evidence of the effectiveness and potential adverse effects associated with drug therapy may be subordinated to the beliefs of parents regarding the necessity and wisdom of taking an antibiotic.

The typology of argument contexts established by Walton is useful in that it directs attention to the type of dialogue in question and establishes that the weight of evidence is relative to that context of application. As demonstrated in the discussion of the Walton model above, what is plausible and reasonable to do in a clinical encounter is determined by the context of that clinical encounter.

Clinical judgement is the concern for integrating the totality of considerations undergirding reasoning in clinical practice relevant to the care of an individual patient. Most clinical encounters result in incomplete understanding of the patient's problems. Diagnoses are often provisional, and if definitive, seldom met with certainty that treatments will be effective. Prognosis is always hedged with statements of uncertainty. It is this situation that likely prompted Osler to call medicine the art of probability and the science of uncertainty. Uncertainty arises from lack of evidence, conflicting interpretations of evidence, inability to access evidence in a timely manner, concerns about the application of aggregate statistical data to individual cases, lack of clarity regarding patient preferences and values. In any clinical case therefore uncertainty plays a role.

H. Tristram Engelhardt, observed:

> an adequate assessment of the significance of clinical judgment is a complex endeavor in the epistemology of medicine. It involves . . . a fundamental critique of medical knowledge and the methods of clinical knowing. It is, moreover, much more than simply an enterprise in epistemology. Clinical judgments in their rich and full sense are freighted with values, including ethical and moral values. Evaluation and explanation properly and inextricably are bound together in medicine in general and in clinical judgment in particular . . . Ideas, concepts, and notional presuppositions and structures, including value judgments, fashion the actual practice of medicine. Medicine more than most endeavors of knowledge and technology

is involved in the entire range of human values and the whole gamut of levels of reality (i.e., from subcellular processes to psychological and socio-logical interactions). In studying medical knowledge, in analyzing clinical judgment, one thus addresses a first instance of knowing and doing, the better comprehension of which is likely to illuminate our understanding of science and technology in general. That is, understanding medicine may shed light on areas of science and technology where the interplay of facts and values may not be as salient, or the consequences of different views of science and technology as immediately or as intimately intrusive.

(Engelhardt 1979,
pp. xxii–xxiii)

## Notes

1 Keys was regarded as the international expert. Those submitting contrary studies fre-quently had those studies peer reviewed by Keys, who summarily dismissed them.
2 Meta-analysis of the comparisons between rapid detection methods and throat cultures are instructive. A total of 60 pairs of sensitivity and specificity from 48 studies were included. Overall summary estimates for sensitivity and specificity of RADTs were 0.86 (95% CI 0.83 to 0.88) and 0.96 (95% CI 0.94 to 0.97), respectively, and estimates for paediatric data were similar. Molecular-based RADTs had the best diagnostic accuracy. Considerable variability exists in methodology between the studies. There were insuf-ficient studies to allow meta-regression/subgroup analysis within each test type.
3 The Cochrane Collaboration is an international organization. Its aim is to make available high-quality meta-analyses/systematic reviews. Clinical researchers and many clinical practitioners consult it frequently to assist them in making the best decisions based on the best evidence available.
4 In Chapter 3, some measures of association used in clinical trials were introduced. Both the odds ratio (OR) with 95% confidence intervals as well as the "number needed to treat" are reported as quantitative measures to describe the magnitude of benefit from treatment. Intention-to-treat (ITT) analysis; $N = 5$; $n = 2{,}018$; odds ratio for absence of resolution of symptoms (OR) 0.79, 95% confidence interval (CI) 0.55 to 1.12. Clinical relapse was lower with cephalosporins ($N = 4$; $n = 1{,}386$; OR 0.55, 95% CI 0.31 to 0.99); overall number needed to treat to benefit (NNTB) 50), but found only in adults (OR 0.42, 95% CI 0.20 to 0.88; NNTB 33).
5 $N = 3$; $n = 795$; OR 0.70, 95% CI 0.49 to 0.99; NNTB 14, but only in children ($N = 2$; $n = 233$; OR 0.57, 95% CI 0.33 to 0.99; NNTB 8.3).
6 $N = 1$, $n = 489$; OR 2.33; 95% CI 1.06 to 5.15.
7 The reason this condition is frequently relaxed or omitted is that sometimes the presence of the organism in certain numbers is sub-clinical in some individuals but not in others, and some infected individuals may have a genetically based immunity to the disease.

# 10 Medicine from first-person perspectives

## Phenomenology, narrative of knowledge and qualitative approaches to knowledge creation and use in medicine

> But facts do not make history; facts do not even make events. Without meaning attached, and without understanding of causes and connections, a fact is an isolated particle of experience, is reflected light without a source, planet with no sun, star without constellation, constellation beyond galaxy, galaxy outside the universe – fact is nothing.
>
> (Russell Banks 1997, p. 339)

In medicine, in addition to the various models and theories we have thus far considered, there is a wide range of methods that generate knowledge relevant to medicine derived from the social sciences and humanities. In this chapter, we will provide an overview of some of the more common approaches, found in the traditions of phenomenology, narrative and qualitative research. These are distinct from the modes of knowledge we have considered so far as they are primarily non-quantitative in approach (that is, do not rely upon mathematics or models of the sort described in Chapter 3). They are focused on meaning, are expressed in natural language and are intended to illuminate the lived experience of those engaged in health care: patients, health care providers such as physicians, nurses and allied health providers and others such as care-givers or policy-makers.

As a consequence, it is useful to think of these approaches as having two dimensions. One is the way in which greater attention to, or facility with, these techniques improves the practice of medicine. The other dimension is the extent to which these techniques generate legitimate knowledge in and of themselves. We will explore both dimensions in this chapter.

Phenomenology is a branch of philosophy that is concerned with the study of structures of consciousness as experienced from the first-person point of view. This approach to the creation of knowledge is quite distinct from that of mathematical models we have explored thus far. Rather than the formal language of probability and statistics or other mathematical means of expression, phenomenology relies more on the use of natural language.

With respect to consciousness and the first-person point of view, phenomenology directs attention to the experiential dimensions of health and the delivery of health care. Mathematical models may not be able to render accounts of what is experienced in the course of both illness and well-being in such a manner as to be intelligible to a broad population or in a manner that captures the unique and particular experience of an individual. It is usually the manifestation of some disturbance of function (mental or physical) in the life of a person that leads one to believe something may be wrong and assistance should be sought to prevent, explain, meliorate, palliate or remove the disturbance. Proponents of phenomenological approaches argue that approaches to medicine that are reliant on the natural sciences (the so-called biomedical model) overlook the subjective experience of persons suffering from illness or the experience of those providing care. Something essential to a complete understanding of illness and well-being is lost.

It is only recently that phenomenological approaches have been incorporated into medical thinking. Here, we outline the different ways in which phenomenology and related approaches can make contributions to the philosophy of medicine. We take an expansive view of phenomenology that includes various non-quantitative, narrative and other approaches to the generation of reliable knowledge in medicine. As such, the focus is more on the epistemic claims made by these approaches.

Phenomenology as a branch of philosophy did not originate as a means to explain or explore medical phenomena. Phenomenology is closely associated with Continental traditions of philosophy, particularly the work of the German philosopher Edmund Husserl. Husserl produced a large body of work, which sought to explore the structure of consciousness and intentionality. He completed his doctoral studies in mathematics and sought to ground phenomenology as a pure science; one that grounds all other sciences. Husserl's work evolved significantly over his career, but a consistent theme was articulating how the structure of consciousness operates as a means of grounding inferences.

Husserl argued that philosophy is rooted in the experiencing subject, best understood by the intentionality of consciousness to an object. Husserl advanced a method of "eidetic reduction", also known as "bracketing", as a means to opening up the contents of first-person experience to philosophical exploration. In this manner, the contents of consciousness are made explicit.

He is particularly recognised for his concern with the notion of embodiment. In contrast to the tradition of naturalism, Husserl grounds reflection in a *lived* body; a life that is experienced in a unique way by the embodied experiencer. From this perspective, what is missing in biomedical accounts is how events are "directly" experienced from within. The idea that consciousness is related to that which is "directly experienced from within" is an important bridge to looking at ways in which the human experience of both pain and suffering, as well as the experience of medical care itself, can be accessed and explored in a philosophical manner.

Martin Heidegger, a student of Husserl, adapted the notion of phenomenology to be explicitly focused on the question of the ontology of being (*Dasein*). Heidegger's philosophy, like that of Husserl, is quite complex (and, to novice students, often opaque). The main difference in their philosophies is that for

Heidegger, the central issue of concern is the examination of the question of "being"; that is, what it means "to be" as opposed to what it means "to know".

Heidegger's later philosophy was concerned with the effects of technology on humanity. With respect to medicine, the concern is that with an increasing emphasis on technology, the importance of "being" is eclipsed. Science and technology have increasingly shown the capacity to intervene in nature and alter it without any accompanying discourse on the consequences of this for our self-understanding. Technological rationality "frames" being in a way that the wider dimensions of human experience are no longer considered. Modern medicine is highly dependent on technology at the expense, in the view of many, of the human dimensions of diagnosis, treatment and palliation of illness and disease. Technology has demonstrated increasing capacity for intervention and the alteration of life forms, down to the molecular level without sufficient attention to the humanities and social science perspectives.

Gadamer's philosophy derives from that of Husserl and Heidegger and he is the only one of the three that has written explicitly about health and illness. Gadamer's philosophy is concerned with the nature of understanding, and hermeneutic understanding in particular. In his philosophy, hermeneutic understanding centres on *human* meanings that are expressed in language (especially narratives) and are embedded in a variety of forms of expression: mythologies, art, language and, broadly understood, religious constructs, for example. This is opposed to a Cartesian approach to knowing. Gadamer argues that our understanding of our lived being (our "life world") emerges from our historical circumstances, creating a particular temporal horizon within which we engage with the world. Part of coming to understand the life world is to encounter our prejudices or pre-understandings, which are contained in the vast textual and scientific knowledge held collectively. Those prejudices or pre-understandings are below the surface of textual and scientific knowledge.

His focus on the nature of understanding, and hermeneutic understanding in particular, is the reason that he is chiefly known for his contribution to hermeneutics, or the theory of interpretation. As indicated, in Gadamer's philosophy interpretation is the fundamental activity of human understanding. Such understanding cannot be reduced to any simple set of formulae or rules, but rather evolves dialogically in response to the thing being understood. The dialogic nature of understanding means that interpretation is always conducted in a mediation between the part and the whole, between the instance and some general rule. This mediation cannot be prescribed in any systematic way.

Gadamer refers to health as an enigma. Health, as a state of being, as opposed to illness, is best appreciated by its absence. That is, when one is healthy one is not aware of experiencing symptoms or discomfort. The intrusion or disruption caused by symptoms destroys one's feeling of wholeness. From this emerges the realisation of illness.

Phenomenological approaches have been extensively used to illustrate the subjective experience of illness; that is, from the perspective of one who suffers. Only the person experiencing such phenomena as pain, or shortness of breath, for example, can lay claim to understanding what that experience is for her or him. Clinical techniques that quantify such experiences, either through scales or other such measures, which are commonly used to make comparisons between cases, cannot adequately capture, or express, such experiences. They assume that the quality of pain or other such fundamentally subjective and highly heterogeneous experiences can be suitably abstracted from the person and made comparable via quantification. This would be adequate for the measurement and evaluation of disease, but would not be adequate for understanding illness, which in phenomenological terms is always a lived experience. Illness, then, is not simply a dysfunction of the corporeal body, a disturbance in body chemistry or the presence of a pathogen in a biological system, but is a transformation of the experience of a person.

Phenomenologists maintain that illness cannot be objectively understood and described either by physical facts or by the mechanisms and models that, as we noted in earlier chapters, are powerful methods for giving general accounts of biological phenomena. Furthermore, such accounts are radically inadequate in providing a full account of the meaning of health and illness. Havi Carel captures this well and argues that phenomenological approaches are distinct from other first-person approaches:

> Phenomenology, in its embodied understanding of human beings, differs from other first person approaches such as certain narrative approaches and qualitative interviews. This is particularly important when we come to think of actual research methods that may arise out of this approach. So, for example, a narrative approach focuses on verbal and written self-reports, and qualitative interviews are conducted while sitting down and conversing with the interviewee or by using questionnaires. In contrast, embodied phenomenological research methods glean information about the experience of illness in ways that go beyond verbal accounts. They may use "walking with" exercises, videotaping (thus including nonverbal information about bodily movement and gestures), and reports relating sensual and perceptual experiences (e.g., looking at changes to sense of taste). Such phenomenologically informed research may also focus on the body of the carer and use phenomenological methods to examine health professionals' visceral responses to the ill person.
>
> (Carel 2011)

This illustrates the uses of phenomenology to illuminate the lived experience of diagnosis, embodiment of symptoms and encounters between physicians and patients. She argues that phenomenological approaches provide evidence built upon "standpoint epistemology", a term coined by Sandra Harding in the context of feminist epistemologies. Helen Longino has summarised this view:

> There is no one position from which value free knowledge can be developed, but some positions are better than others. Standpoint epistemologies

notice systematic distortions in description and analysis produced by those occupying social positions of power. Traditional Marxists identified the standpoint of the bourgeoisie as producing such distortions, whereas feminists have identified the standpoint of men (of the dominant class and race) as equally distorting.

. . .

Most standpoint theorists locate the epistemic advantage in the productive/reproductive experience of the oppressed whose perspective they champion.

(Longino 1993)

Of relevance here is the degree to which a specific standpoint fundamentally affects the assessment of knowledge claims. The biomedical standpoint of physicians distorts the claims of knowledge and expertise. The standpoint of the patient is equally distorting, as also is the standpoint of the physician in the physician–patient interaction. A dialogic approach recognises the distortion of standpoints and navigates a course among them.

There are limited means to answer questions about the experience of day-to-day living with a significant health condition, or capture expertise gained by this lived experience. Neglecting the first-person experience – the standpoint of the patient – will diminish the capacity to understand how treatments are experienced or felt or remembered. Given that illness and its treatment can dramatically change the life world of patients there is a need to capture how these events result in changes to the self and one's self-understanding in ways that quantitative "quality of life" measures cannot capture.

Phenomenology focuses primarily on first-person accounts. Other approaches permit the exploration of first- and third-person perspectives. Narrative is another source of knowledge relevant to the understanding of medicine. As Rita Charon has written:

A scientifically competent medicine alone cannot help a patient grapple with the loss of health or find meaning in suffering. Along with scientific ability, physicians need the ability to listen to the narratives of the patient, grasp and honor their meanings, and be moved to act on the patient's behalf. This is narrative competence, that is, the competence that human beings use to absorb, interpret, and respond to stories. . . . Narrative competence enables the physician to practice medicine with empathy, reflection, professionalism, and trustworthiness. Such a medicine can be called narrative medicine.

(2001, p. 1,897)

Narrative knowledge leads to local and particular understandings about one situation by participants or observers and hence renders a rich and detailed account of human existence. Narrative thus has the capacity to contribute to medical knowledge in the doctor–patient encounter; patient histories, a genre of narrative, are the chief means by which physicians come to know the temporal course and nature of a patient's understanding. Narrative competence is required of clinicians as a means of gaining credible and reliable knowledge of patients.

Charon argues that narrative has additional epistemic value in the education of clinicians and in fostering self-reflective practice. In this manner, it enhances clinicians' self-knowledge. Narrative enhances intersubjective understanding; that is, the ability to contemplate what it is like for a person to suffer from or experience an illness of a particular type, one from which the physician has not suffered.

One criticism of narrative as knowledge is that it does not open to critical scrutiny. That is, there is a sense in which a narrative text must be understood in its own light and may be immune to criticism. Cheryl Misak takes issue with this account of narrative. While conceding that narratives have a descriptive function that is valuable in its own right, she maintains that narrative accounts have the status of evidence, but they must be subject to critical scrutiny. As she writes:

> Narratives are not simply chronological accounts of events, but rather, they are accounts that give coherence or shape to events and are thus burdened with interpretation, motivation and other dents to what we think of as objectivity.
>
> (2010, p. 394)

Misak uses her experience of a life-threatening illness to advance several important insights regarding the status of first-person accounts as a particular form of knowledge crucial for an adequate account of knowledge in medicine. Misak experienced multi-organ failure as a consequence of an infection and spent several weeks in an intensive care unit where she required full life support. From this experience, she draws several important lessons relevant to medical knowledge.

First, she notes that patient experience is a non-ignorable dimension of understanding illness and disease as well as illuminating how care is experienced. Some phenomena can only be understood "from the inside"; that is, by accounts given by those who have experienced grave illness. In this respect, she is agreeing with phenomenologists. She notes that there is an urgent need for these accounts to be taken seriously, for both ethical and epistemic reasons. The ethical reasons relate to how critical illness changes agency (the ability to act to bring about a particular result; that is, to be an agent) and perhaps undermines the capacity for autonomous reasoning. The epistemic reason relates to how illness challenges our self-understanding. Any robust conception of medicine must engage with the subjective experience of those who are afflicted with illness. The subjective cannot be "drummed out" of adequate accounts of medical knowledge.

Where Misak perhaps differs from phenomenologists and those advocating for narrative-based approaches is in the importance of critical scrutiny of narrative claims. As she states:

> My argument will be that we can learn something important from narrative evidence, but only if we take narratives to be subject to critical scrutiny.

The view that narratives are not criticizable, but that they are nonetheless somehow legitimate and important in our deliberations, is a poor view indeed.

(2010, p. 393)

Narrative for Misak is indispensable in medicine since it is the foundation from which diagnosis and understanding a patient's predicament emerge. This is generally regarded as requiring critical scrutiny. Hence, most clinicians will probe and refine the patient history. It is interpreted, re-interpreted and reconstructed. Second, in keeping with advocates of narrative-based approaches, narrative plays an essential role in educating health professionals. But Misak also argues that narrative has an important research function: it is a critical source of new knowledge. Because narratives are interpretive in nature they often conflict. But conflicting interpretations are not unique to narrative forms of evidence. It is often the case that more quantitative forms of evidence such as systematic reviews and randomised trials are subject to competing interpretations amongst a community of inquirers.

Misak argues that narrative accounts can be judged in ways that other theories or explanations are evaluated. They must have some form of internal coherence, be consistent with other forms of evidence and have explanatory power. The evidentiary status of narratives is rooted in their contestable nature. Claims made in narratives are open to dispute and revision and therefore are like other forms of evidence.

Phenomenological and narrative approaches in medicine permit the documentation and exploration of events in the life world. Rather than relying on mathematical models and other forms of quantitative reasoning, these approaches rely upon the use of natural language, either through stories or deep reflections.

The most common way in which first-person accounts appear in medicine is in the history a patient gives to a physician. The history is usually given in natural language and is a descriptive account of the changed or altered function or sensation that gives rise to symptoms. Most phenomenological accounts, as noted above, focus on the experience of illness. These illnesses may be experienced suddenly or be more chronic in nature.

Pain is one of the most commonly experienced symptoms. The experience of pain is characteristically phenomenological and is unique to each sufferer. Although there are a variety of ways of reporting pain in a structured way using techniques like visual analogue scales, pain is always experienced subjectively and communicated through the use of language.

We have so far canvassed phenomenology and narrative as two techniques of using linguistically and interpretively oriented approaches focused on meaning to both generate and interpret experience in medicine. Both of these approaches tend to be "unstructured" in the sense that they are not reliant on the idea of a design or protocol to generate data that can then be interpreted. Lived experience and written texts require the techniques of phenomenology and narrative in order to provide interpretations that are coherent (even if challengeable). The lived experience of a person or reading a story or account of an illness or clinical encounter resembles observational approaches outlined earlier as there is no intervention on behalf of those seeking to use the information. It is either reported by the one experiencing the phenomenon or is in a form that requires reading.

These fundamentally discursive accounts are for the most part not necessarily structured for the creation of new knowledge. That is, they may not be explicitly intended for the purpose of asking and answering a research question. We will now consider a set of techniques that are employed in research with the explicit purpose of creating new knowledge or insights relevant to medicine.

The set of techniques go under the broad category of qualitative methods. The idea of qualitative research is not unique to medicine. Indeed, most of the methods and forms of analysis originate from the social sciences and have been adapted to health research. Phenomenology and narrative approaches emerged from the humanities – philosophy and literature in particular.

Qualitative research typically takes the form of an explicit protocol that sets out the research question, the type of data to be collected and the manner of its analysis as well as consideration of the strengths and limitations of the approach. In this sense it parallels the sorts of protocols common to other forms of research employed in clinical medicine. Interviews are the most common means of collecting qualitative data. Interviews involve researchers talking, usually face to face with participants. Unlike surveys or other forms of data collection, interviews are typically open-ended without pre-specified responses. Interview data is usually from a transcript or notes taken by the data collector.

Interviews can take many forms, including: (1) *structured interviews*, which follow a set list of questions usually focused on a theme to gather specific information from participants; (2) *semi-structured interviews*, which use an interview guide listing a set of issues to be explored but permit flexibility to explore themes that emerge in the interview or (3) *unstructured interviews*, in which the interviewer does not have a pre-specified set of questions, but rather the process is driven by the participant. In each of these forms, as much as possible, the data is collected in the words of the participant. Interview data will illuminate how participants view and interpret their experiences with little emphasis on such issues as quantities. Participants are encouraged to explore their values, attitudes and beliefs. Lurking in these are the prejudices or pre-understandings we mentioned earlier. Only concerted examination of values, attitudes and beliefs will unearth unconscious elements of our conscious articulation of what we claim to know, how we understand ourselves and how we understand the context of our life experiences.

A revealing example is Donald Rumsfeld's famous parsing of knowledge claims, widely available on YouTube. It is incomplete; something any logician would immediately detect. Rumsfeld said:

> Reports that say that something hasn't happened are always interesting to me, because as we know, there are known knowns; there are things we know we know. We also know there are known unknowns; that is to say we

know there are some things we do not know. But there are also unknown unknowns – the ones we don't know we don't know. And if one looks throughout the history of our country and other free countries, it is the latter category that tends to be the difficult one.

There are four combinations of what is known or unknown and that we know or do not know is known or unknown. There are indeed known knowns, known unknowns and unknown unknowns, but there are also unknown knowns. That is, things that we do not know we know. This knowledge resides in our unconscious or subconscious, and affects profoundly the conscious knowledge we profess and to which we adhere. The psychoanalytic philosopher Slavoj Žižek put it well:

> In March 2003, Rumsfeld engaged in a little bit of amateur philosophizing about the relationship between the known and the unknown: "There are known knowns. These are things we know that we know. There are known unknowns. That is to say, there are things that we know we don't know. But there are also unknown unknowns. There are things we don't know we don't know." What he forgot to add was the crucial fourth term: the "unknown knowns," the things we don't know that we know – which is precisely, the Freudian unconscious, the "knowledge which doesn't know itself," as Lacan used to say.
>
> If Rumsfeld thinks that the main dangers in the confrontation with Iraq were the "unknown unknowns," that is, the threats from Saddam whose nature we cannot even suspect, then the Abu Ghraib scandal shows that the main dangers lie in the "unknown knowns" – the disavowed beliefs, suppositions and obscene practices we pretend not to know about, even though they form the background of our public values.
>
> (2005, n.p.)

The unknown knowns underlie our prejudices and pre-understandings – things we know in advance of conscious knowledge and that interpret for us the meaning of conscious experience and knowledge. Uncovering the unconscious knowns requires commitment and techniques. Interviews are one of those techniques.

In medical research, interviews may involve key informant interviewees chosen for their particular set of expertise or experience. For example, studies devoted to exploring the dimensions of leadership in medicine would typically select identified medical leaders. Interview studies may also look for broader representative samples of patients with a particular illness. Further sampling could relate to age and gender if such factors are thought to illuminate different experiences relevant to a deeper understanding of the condition and its effects on the lives of those afflicted.

Focus groups are a means of collecting data from groups in situations where the researchers hypothesise that group dynamics will add deeper understanding or illuminate different aspects of the question being researched. Focus groups are typically moderated and are scripted in terms of the questions asked. Focus groups are useful in situations where there may exist power differentials between the participants and other groups or where the use of language, belief structure or other cultural characteristics of groups is of interest.

Observational techniques include varieties of research associated with anthropology or sociology such as ethnography and participant observation methodologies. In these methodologies, the researcher observes participant(s) in their own environment, or in the environment being studied. Sometimes the researcher "embeds" into the culture or institution in order to get a deeper understanding of the practices, beliefs and actions of the group under study. Data collection through observation can be structured or unstructured, with the observer as a collaborative participant (participant observation) or external to the environment. In medical research, there are a wide range of locations in which this sort of research has been conducted including waiting rooms of doctors' offices, operating rooms, lecture halls, board rooms and so on.

Texts are common sources of data for the exploration of health and illness. This can take the form of literary accounts published in novels or essays or archival research that examines materials that are usually but not necessarily deposited in official or private libraries or archives. Increasingly, online resources such as blogs, social media and other forms of communication are being used as sources for health research. The advance of the internet has enabled research to be conducted entirely online for recruitment, data collection and analysis. Increasingly visual analysis is playing a role in health research through the study of films, videos, photographs, paintings and other visual media.

A variety of methods comes together in case studies. In case study methodology, in-depth understanding of a particular context is sought that might combine document analysis, direct observation and various modalities of interviewing. The idea here is less to provide "generalisable" knowledge than to provide highly detailed insights into organizations or social interactions within particular contexts.

Thus far we have canvassed three distinct but related approaches to illuminating experience and meaning in medicine. We must now answer the question of how these modalities fit with an overarching philosophy of medicine that situates itself in the philosophy of science. The approaches we have considered allow for values and the perspectives of humans to be integrated with the more object-related accounts we have considered. They form a bridge between the subjective and the objective dimensions of medical science and clinical medicine. Each of these domains is seeking to make claims to knowledge, thus making epistemological claims.

In philosophy, there has been a long-standing contrast between the human and physical sciences, the *Geisteswissenschaften* and *Naturwissenschaften*. There is a long and divisive debate in the social sciences and philosophy about the relationship between positivism and constructivism, between reductionism and holism. These debates have been extensively documented elsewhere and a resolution has yet to emerge. Here we simply note that this tension also exists in philosophy of medicine.

The issue of the epistemic status of phenomenological and narrative approaches and qualitative research methods relates to whether they are legitimate and reliable sources of knowledge or evidence that provide either explanation or understanding relevant to medical science or the practice of medicine. In this sense, the question becomes to what extent are they evidential and what is the function of the evidence produced. In a broad sense, we can distinguish between the explanatory and predictive roles that such evidence can play. It is likely the case that phenomenological and narrative approaches and qualitative research methods will be weak in terms of generating robust predictions since the primary goal of such methods is not the creation of models of the sort outlined earlier. The approaches are likely explanatory to the extent that one regards interpretations as providing an explanation or understanding of a particular kind relevant to medicine.

Toulmin (1976) identifies a set of contrasting distinctions within which to situate medical knowledge. His distinctions are also applicable to evidence as related to the broader field of health care. Rather than viewed as dichotomies (either/or), these distinctions should be seen as poles of contrast, recognising that there is a dynamic tension between the two poles of the distinctions and interaction between them.

- Abstract and concrete
- Mathematical and historical
- Theoretical and practical
- Pure and applied
- General and particular
- Collective and personal
- Descriptive and prescriptive
- Predictive and interpretive
- Algorithm and judgement
- Inference and decision
- Disinterested and interested.

The terms on the left side characterise the type of evidence that the natural sciences produce. The epistemic commitments of the left side have been described in earlier chapters. Much of basic science and epidemiological approaches to medical knowledge aspire to these standards as epistemic goals. They rely on abstraction of particular details, which allows a more general or universal application. The results of the mathematical predictions are thought to hold true regardless of whether the individual making the predictions is alive or present to witness the event. Predictive capacity and explanatory power are the hallmarks of this vision of science.

The terms on the right side illustrate the knowledge of the particular that can be explored using the methods and approaches we have discussed in this chapter – methods associated with the humanities and social sciences. Clinical encounters are concrete, dealing with this individual at this particular time, in a specific embodiment of language and culture, and within a historical horizon of knowledge. The salient features of this form of evidence are its narrative structure and contextuality. The concern is with the understanding of meaning rather than quantities or properties of objects. Epistemologically, it is also rooted in empiricism. It is empirical because it relates to the lived experience of patients and clinicians. The approaches outlined above do not make claims about the causal structure of events. They do permit the exploration of how agents may interpret or believe whether and how causation is at play in their life worlds.

The important point to establish in this analysis is that medicine relies on both sorts of claims. Both are required to make sense of the clinical and biological aspects of health, well-being and illness. The task of an adequate philosophy of medicine is to bridge the concrete and particular, and the abstract, mathematical and general. Each has its required role and method.

# 11  Neurosciences and diseases of the mind

Diseases of the mind are the least well understood of all medical conditions and are the most stigmatised. Three professions diagnose and treat disease of the mind: psychiatry, clinical psychology and social work. There is another group of therapists, whose training is often separate from these professions; those specially trained in psychoanalysis. Only psychiatry is recognised as a medical specialty and in the English-speaking world, of those who treat persons with mental disorder, with some exceptions, only psychiatrists can prescribe controlled medications (those requiring a prescription).

The standard diagnostic tool is the DSM (Diagnostic and Statistical Manual). The complexity of this field can be seen in the array of classifications in the DSM. Diagnoses can range from syndromes – a collection of symptoms of which some subsets suggest a tentative diagnosis – to symptoms that seem to be ameliorated by a pharmaceutical therapy.

The title of this chapter signals that something different is involved. That something is "mind": diseases of the mind, or mental diseases/disorders. What is this entity called "mind" that has now entered the medical arena and, more generally, the health care arena? The answers to this question are numerous and the concept of mind has a long history. The first comprehensive Anglo-European account of mind that is extant is found in Aristotle's *De Anima*[1] (written around 350 BCE). In that work, he claims that mind (nous) is a part of the soul (psyche). Aristotle holds that the soul is inseparable from the body, which suggests that mind is also inseparable.[2] René Descartes introduced the major break from this view.

In his *Meditations on First Philosophy*, Descartes divided the body and the soul/mind. For him the body was material and the mind immaterial. The body and mind interacted as separate, and different kinds of, substances, through the pineal gland, which he described as "the principal seat of the soul". The pineal gland is located deep in the brain. Melatonin is the only hormone that it is known to produce but there is much that is unknown about this gland. Few at the time accepted Descartes' pineal gland view and after his death anatomical advances made it less and less tenable. His separation of body, as matter, from mind, as immaterial, however has had a lasting impact. This view is known as dualism (or more precisely, substance dualism – two kinds of substances).

A number of views about how to conceptualise the relationship of these two substances have been advanced, and a number of views that reject this dualism have been advanced.

The philosopher, mathematician and logician Gottlieb Leibniz[3] more or less accepted the duality of substances – although he was not a Cartesian (follower of Descartes) – but he postulated that there was no interaction between the substances. At the point of the origin of a specific body and its mind, a pre-established harmony was created (by God) such that mind and body were in perfect harmony, giving the appearance of interaction. They are, however, entirely causally disconnected. This view also had few supporters.

There are still dualists today. There is something attractive and intuitive about the idea that minds exist. After all, we can reflect on our feelings, we can have hopes, and experience failure and loss, and we can "feel" physical pain. In short, we are conscious. This seems to take us beyond the physical. There are others that contend that, however intuitive the existence of mind might seem, there is nonetheless only one kind of substance and that is matter. There is no independent entity "mind". These views are called materialist. Mind is the same substance as the body.

Two influential materialist views are mind–brain identity, and mind as supervening on the body (in effect, the brain). The first view is easy to understand: mind and brain are identical. The classic analogy is the morning star and the evening star. In antiquity, these were identified and studied as different objects. Today, we know they are the same object and are not a star. Both are the planet Venus. Hence, although believed to be different and studied (trajectory, seasonal variation and the like) as separate entities, they are now known to be the same entity.

Similarly, even though the mind and brain have been considered separate entities and we have studied them as separate entities, it is becoming clear that they are the same entity. We are seeing different manifestations of that entity. A somewhat more contentious analogy but still illustrative is lightning and thunder. Lightning is an atmospheric electrical discharge, either from cloud to cloud or earth to cloud. Sometimes we see lightning but hear no thunder. Sometimes we hear thunder and have seen no lightning. Nonetheless, lightning is the primitive. Thunder is simply the effect of lightning producing an increase in pressure and temperature. That produces a rapid expansion of the air. This expansion creates a sonic shock wave. That sonic shock wave is thunder. The light and sound are properties of the same phenomenon. Hence, thunder is not a separate thing. The mind is similar, except it is the consequence of the activity of the neurons in the brain. At this point, you likely see the relevance of this view to the knowledge neuroscience is shedding on our mental activity.

The other materialist view – mind is supervenient on the brain – is a little more complex. Within philosophy, supervenience in its contemporary use captures an invariant relation between two things or characteristics. If one thing supervenes on another thing, any change in the thing on which it supervenes results in corresponding change in the thing that supervenes. Donald Davidson brought supervenience into the context of the relation of mind and body. In his 1970 article "Mental Events", he writes:

> Although the position I describe denies there are psychophysical laws, it is consistent with the view that mental characteristics are in some sense dependent, or supervenient, on physical characteristics. Such supervenience might be taken to mean that there cannot be two events alike in all physical respects but differing in some mental respect, or that an object cannot alter in some mental respect without altering in some physical respect.
>
> (1970, p. 214)

Whether Donaldson's concept of mental events supervening on physical events actually commits him to psychophysical laws – laws that govern the interaction of mind and brain – has been much discussed. The important idea for a materialist view is that for every mental property there is a physical property such that the physical property determines the mental property. Essentially, any change in the mental properties requires a change in the physical properties and any change in the physical properties results, in principle, in a determinable change in the mental properties. Hence, mental properties are entirely dependent on physical ones.

This view allows us to accept that there are two different kinds of properties, even though one kind (mental) is entirely dependent on the other (physical). This makes more sense of consciousness. We do experience pain but that experience is completely determined by the physical – i.e., neural activity. The mental and the physical are not "identical" the way the mind–brain view suggests – although it might be recast with some modification to embrace consciousness. The supervenience view, up front, recognises that something beyond the physical is being described but allows one to hold steadfastly to the view that the physical determines the mental. The mind is not a separate entity. Eliminate the physical and the mental goes with it.

Sigmund Freud approached the issue of mind from a different angle. Freud began his career as a neurologist but increasingly focused on mental disorders rather than neurological ones. He first became interested in mental disorders through the study of hysteria, which he initially encountered through his association with Josef Breuer. Breuer told Freud that when he encouraged a hysterical patient to talk uninhibitedly about the symptoms, they occasionally became less dramatic and/or frequent. Freud's two major contributions to explaining this were the introduction of the concept of the "unconscious" and, connected to it, forgotten trauma, which had caused the symptoms. The unconscious became a powerful concept. Much of what we think and do flows from things that are hidden from us in the unconscious. In a poetic passage that powerfully makes his point about the unconscious, Freud situates its discovery and importance as among the great scientific revolutions:

> In the course of centuries the *naïve* self-love of men has had to submit to two major blows at the hands of science. The first was when they learned

that the earth was not the centre of the universe but only a tiny fragment of the cosmic system of scarcely imaginable vastness. This is associated with Copernicus . . . The second blow fell when biological science destroyed man's supposedly privileged place in creation and proved his descent from the animal kingdom and his ineradicable animal nature . . . But human megalomania will have suffered its third and most wounding blow from the psychological research of the present time which seeks to prove to the ego that it is not even master in its own house, but must content itself with scanty information of what is going on unconsciously in its mind.

(1919, *Introductory Lectures on Psychoanalysis*)

Hence, for Freud, there are two clear facets to mind: the conscious mind and the unconscious mind. Much of mental illness is explained in terms of the goings on in the unconscious mind – especially illnesses such as neurosis, hysteria, obsessive-compulsive behaviour and the like. A lot, however, that goes on in the subconscious is "normal" mental activity; it's just that we are not aware of it. Abnormal unconscious mental activity (mental illness) constitutes a small portion of mental activity. In these cases, some defect of the operation of the mind might be the cause or it might be a "repressed" experience. That is one to which we no longer have access because the unconscious is blocking conscious knowledge of it as a coping strategy to suppress the pain of a trauma. Nonetheless, it is determining thoughts, behaviours and actions. Because we are not conscious of this cause, we cannot control it, nor do we understand it as the cause of the thoughts, feelings and behaviours.

Freud also introduced other features of the mind, as he constructed. For example, there are three dimensions to personality: Id, Ego and Superego. The Id is a carnal force, driven by the desire for pleasure. Unconstrained, the Id would drive an individual, from birth, to immediately satisfy desire. The Ego, which develops in the first three or so years of life, brings reality to bear. It constrains the Id by recognising that others have needs and desires. With this comes a recognition that more needs and desires can be satisfied by social cooperation than complete selfishness. The Id and the Ego are often in tension. The Superego, which has emerged by around age five, is best thought of as conscience. It is the moral part of personality.

Perhaps the most well-known, and controversial concept Freud introduced, is the Oedipal complex, named after the ancient Greek play *Oedipus Rex* by Sophocles. In the play, Oedipus, the king of Thebes, unknowingly marries his mother. This results from his being abandoned when he was a child. Also, robbers had killed his father. Oedipus, prompted by the blind seer Teiresis' revelation, came to believe that he was the abandoned child and that he had killed his father, and now was married to his mother. Freud used the theme of this tragic play to capture his view that children – and some individuals into adulthood – have a love and sex desire for their opposite-sex parent. The emphasis has been on a boy's love and sexual desire towards his mother. A failure to resolve this leads to internal conflict and mental disorder. As this brief outline indicates, Freud had a complex and well-developed theory of the mind and of the stages of mental development.

Freud had learned hypnosis earlier in his career and it became an early tool for reaching into the unconscious but he more-or-less abandoned hypnosis by 1896 and had introduced two new methods: psychoanalysis and the interpretation of dreams. Psychoanalysis allows the patient to introspect under the guidance of the analyst, thereby recovering hidden aspects of one's past and confront them. Dreams provide a path for the unconscious to reveal one's past, especially in terms of fears, frustrations, traumas and a wealth of other factors. Dreams, however, need to be interpreted and that is another role of the analyst. With this psychoanalysis, psychiatry and a branch of psychology were born. Freud was a medical doctor – he held an MD – and, hence, psychiatry became a speciality of medicine, with psychoanalysis as an important tool. Psychology was a nascent discipline earlier than psychoanalysis and, although influenced by it, developed as a discipline outside the medical arena.

The early evidence for the existence of mind was our shared experience of thinking and feeling, and our ability to will our bodies to behave in certain ways. These subjective experiences still exist but two trends have emerged to challenge this. The first is the tradition descended from Freud. The concept of an unconscious that causes thoughts, feeling and behaviours, and is beyond our conscious control, is a part of modern psychiatry and other professions: social work, theology, clinical psychology and so on. Moreover, psychoanalysis is still used as a tool for exploring the unconscious and providing therapy for a range of mental disorders. Other tools have been introduced as well, such as introspection. In many respects, introspection is a kind of psychoanalysis. It is the technique of looking inside oneself. The individual can perform it alone (that is, without professional or other help) or with professional help.

The second trend is much more recent: neuroscience. Freud and, following him, psychiatry took the reality of mind as a given without much attention to the kind of thing mind was. Today, neuroscience is providing evidence that whatever it is that we call mind, it is intimately connected to the brain. Modern psychiatry has been influenced by these discoveries, as we shall see. This connects back to the philosophical issue of mind–brain and to the view that the mind and brain are the same thing or, more precisely, mental processes are identical to brain processes. And, it connects to the view that mental processes are supervenient on brain processes. The more we discover through neuroscience, the more these views seem to better capture the nature of, and connection between, mind and brain than dualistic views. Recall strong dualism claims that there are two separate *entities*. Some claim that both entities are material; others claim that mind is immaterial. A weaker dualism claims that there are two different kinds of processes: mental and physical. Whether neuroscience is eroding the basis of process dualism is explored later. Its discoveries, as we shall see, have certainly made entity (ontological) dualism less compelling.

With these two trends in mind, we can return to the two opening paragraphs of this chapter. Diseases of the mind are approached by both of the trends. The DSM can be more closely associated with the first. On this approach, mental disorders/mental illnesses are classified by symptoms, and therapies are designed to ameliorate the symptoms. There need be no overt commitment to Freud's views or others in the psychoanalytic tradition for that matter (Adler, Jung, for example). One need not be committed to a dualist view of mind and body, or a materialist one. Modern psychiatry focuses on complexes of symptoms and treatments. Some psychiatrists will be dualists, some materialists. Some complexes of symptoms will be syndromes such as hyperactive attention deficit disorder. These are indicative of a mental disorder but the disorder can have a variety of causes and manifestations, which differ among individuals. Nonetheless, the name of the collection of symptoms captures the fact that there are common features to the symptoms and causes. Some complexes of symptoms are more definitive, such as addiction or erectile dysfunction. The causes may be compound and different in different individuals but the symptoms are narrow in range and clear in diagnosis. In the Preface of DSM-5 (the latest edition), the authors state:

> Although DSM-5 remains a categorical classification of separate disorders, we recognize that mental disorders do not always fit completely within the boundaries of a single disorder. Some symptom domains, such as depression and anxiety, involve multiple diagnostic categories and may reflect common underlying vulnerabilities for a larger group of disorders.

This makes clear the difficulty of classifying mental disorders. Even a cursory reading of the DSM, or some sections of it, will make clear the complexity of mental disorders. Moreover, an examination of the sequence of editions of the DSM will show how fluid the symptoms, classifications, diagnosis and treatment of mental disorders are. The most recent edition of the DSM was published in 2013. As the preface also states, the DSM is used by a wide variety of practitioners: "psychiatrists, other physicians, psychologists, social workers, nurses, counsellors, forensic and legal specialists, occupational and rehabilitation therapists, and other health professionals".

Compared with the symptoms, diagnosis and treatment of physical disorders, this is a very different landscape. Things like a fracture of the tibia, a melanoma, anaemia and heart palpitation are much easier to detect and treat than almost any mental disorder. Not only are the symptoms more definitive but also modern diagnostic tools are more sophisticated – even though they are frequently used inappropriately and excessively. Treatments are also well understood. A third-stage melanoma (an aggressive skin cancer) may elude treatment because of its advanced stage and the likelihood of metastasis (the spread of the malignancy to other areas of the body) but our understanding of what is happening is rich and the quest for new therapies is structured and guided by robust theoretical knowledge. A first-stage melanoma is different; the success of therapy is very high.

Consider a person who sees a physician with abdominal pain and reports recent vomiting and loss of appetite. As in many cases of a collection of general symptoms, there are a number of potential causes. This means the physician has to make a differential diagnosis – one that rules out some possible causes and indicates what additional information should be sought. One obvious question is the location of the pain. The person says, "the right side, low down". The physician asks the patient to point to the area. The person points to the lower right quadrant of the abdomen below the belly button. The physician presses in that area. There is tenderness. The physician suspects appendicitis. The Merck Manual give the classic symptoms as:

Classic signs of appendicitis are

- Right lower quadrant direct and rebound tenderness located at the McBurney point (junction of the middle and outer thirds of the line joining the umbilicus to the anterior superior spine)

Additional appendicitis signs are pain felt in the right lower quadrant with palpation of the left lower quadrant (Rovsing sign), an increase in pain caused by passive extension of the right hip joint that stretches the iliopsoas muscle (psoas sign), or pain caused by passive internal rotation of the flexed thigh (obturator sign). Low-grade fever (rectal temperature 37.7 to 38.3° C [100 to 101° F]) is common.

In more than 50% of patients, one or more of these symptoms may be absent. Consequently, further investigation using imaging may be necessary: a CT (computerised tomography) or ultrasound. Given the need for speedy intervention if the cause is appendicitis, it is often prudent to presume appendicitis, even without using imaging, when a number of the symptoms are present. An appendix that ruptures introduces significant complications. The treatment is a course of antibiotics and surgery to remove the appendix.

Appendicitis is a good case study because diagnosis is more complicated than a fractured tibia but less complicated than some other physical disorders, such as liver diseases. What this case illustrates is that with physical disorders, there is a determinable cause. It may take a skilled diagnostician to ask the appropriate questions, to perform an informative physical examination and to request the relevant tests, but the cause can be identified with considerable accuracy. False positive diagnoses and false negative diagnoses do occur but are uncommon. Once the diagnosis has been made, the treatment is uncontroversial and successful in almost all cases. Complications occur when there are other disorders along with the appendicitis or the appendix has ruptured. But even then, the treatment regime is clear.

Now consider a person who sees a physician and reports that he has difficulty concentrating, remembering details and making decisions, is tired most of the time and has decreased energy. These symptoms can be caused by a number of things; hence, again, a differential diagnosis is required. The cause could be physical: viruses, medications and illnesses. Those need to be ruled out or confirmed. If no physical cause is found, the presumptive diagnosis is "depression". Unlike appendicitis, where there are suggestive physical symptoms and imaging techniques to confirm the cause, and, in the final analysis, surgical investigation and treatment, there is no diagnostic test for depression. It is diagnosed based on the presence of a collection of symptoms, many of which are subjective, in that the physician (perhaps a psychiatrist) cannot observe these: a feeling of guilt and worthlessness, a feeling of hopelessness and long-term sadness, for example.

Hence, diagnosis of depression is very different from diagnosis of appendicitis. Moreover, the treatment is much less clear. Different mental health professionals will have different approaches. In some cases, medications may be employed (e.g. selective serotonin uptake inhibitors (SSRIs) such as Celexa or Prozac), in others psychoanalysis and in yet others electroconvulsive treatment. An additional complication is that some people respond better to some approaches than others and some respond poorly to all the current treatment regimens; there is no uniformity or predictability. These two examples draw out significant differences between mental and physical disorders. These differences have led to very different attitudes. Individuals with physical disorders evoke sympathy and support. Individuals with mental disorders are frequently stigmatised and blamed for their condition. There is a sense that depressed individuals should "get a grip" or "pull themselves together". Much of this is a result of the subjective nature of the symptoms and the lack of any clear sense of causes. It is amplified by the unpredictable success and extensive array of therapies. It is also, arguably, because most people have not really accepted something like the Freudian unconscious. That is, they either reject or are unaware that there can be a part of our mind that causes us to think, feel and behave in ways over which we have no conscious control.

As neuroscience advances, it becomes clearer and clearer that there is a vast amount of brain activity that is beyond our control. This is not because there is an entity of some kind identified as mind but because the brain is complex and most of its activity is not represented in conscious thought. The early evidence of this came from work that mapped areas of the brain and the things that specific areas seemed to control, or sensations and thoughts to which they give rise. The work of Sperry on epileptic seizures led to a landmark discovery: the two hemispheres of the brain "communicate" via the corpus callosum – a complex of neural fibres that join the two hemispheres. He discovered that cutting the corpus callosum eliminated or reduced the incidence and intensity of seizures, thus demonstrating that the seizure generalises in the brain via the corpus callosum. The symptoms of victims of accidents or strokes gave evidence that a region of the left hemisphere controls the muscles of the right side of the body and vice versa.

Schizophrenia serves as an excellent example of the increasing role of neuroscience in the understanding of mental disorders, as well as the increasing acceptance that almost all – some would claim all – mental disorders will be shown to be physical in cause. Hence, a materialist view of mind is emerging as the dominant view.

Schizophrenia comes from two Greek words: *skhizein* (to split) and *phrenos* (in this context, mind). The Swiss psychiatrist Eugen Bleuler coined it in 1908. Contrary to a common view, it does not mean two different personalities. As Bleuler used it, and as it used today, it is a disorder in which mental functions are split (fragmented). The symptoms vary, are numerous and can wax and wane but hallucinations, delusions, disordered thinking and attention deficit are among the most distinctive.

Until recently, the cause of the disorder was described in terms of a theory of mind such as Freud's (or Adler's, Jung's, Bleuler's and so on) and treatment was psychoanalysis or some other treatment that a particular of theory of mind justified. Today, it is know that the disorder is largely a brain disorder. It is the result of an imbalance of chemical reactions in the brain. The chemicals are known as neurotransmitters (e.g. dopamine and glutamate). These chemicals are involved in brain cell communication and it is that communication process that is compromised in people with schizophrenia. A microscopic (light and electron) examination of brain sections (very thin slices of brain tissue) reveals that there are small but important differences in the brain cells of those with schizophrenia; their distribution and characteristics are different. Moreover, the brains of schizophrenics often have less grey matter and the fluid-filled vesicles (ventricles) in the brain are larger in many schizophrenics. More is being discovered about the differences in the structure and functioning of the brain in schizophrenics. Enough is known now to make acceptance that this is a brain disorder compelling.

There is also a genetic dimension. A disorder (physical or mental) that has a higher incidence in families with the disorder in previous generations suggests a genetic component. Schizophrenia has a ten-fold greater incidence in families with a close relative with the disorder. More suggestive is the relationship in identical twins. If one twin manifests the disorder, there is about a 50% chance the other twin will develop it. A lot more work needs to be done to discover the genetic mechanism. Currently, several genes have been targeted as important but this is a quantitative disorder; that is, one with multiple interacting genes causing a trait. Just as the structure of the brain is complicated and its functioning is equally complex, so one can expect the genetic determinants of these structures and functions to be complex. Evidence of this complexity at the genetic level comes from research that has found higher rates of genetic abnormalities at many genetic locations in the genome of schizophrenics. These genetic abnormalities likely predispose an individual to develop schizophrenia but that predisposition may well require environmental triggers.

The research on more and more mental disorders is leading in the direction of a physical basis (genetic and brain-based). This not only steers research, diagnosis and treatment into a materialist domain but also will begin to erode the stigma surrounding mental disorders. After all, if this materialistic approach is correct, schizophrenia and a host of other mental disorders are no different from Parkinson's or cystic fibrosis; they all have physiological causes and are not defects of an immaterial mind, or manifestations of weakness of will or personality.

This increased focus on the brain has led to a number of new models. One of particular philosophical interest is the connectionist model. This model views the brain as a network of neural pathways. Any model of the brain has to explain input, processing, outputs and memory (learning). The first three are explained by the web of neurons (see Figure 11.1). Some neurons are sensory neurons. These are input neurons. Others – a vast web of them – are processing neurons. These constitute the inner workings of the brain. The third kind of neuron is output neurons. These, for example, innervate muscles. The processing neurons give rise to inner sensations: thoughts, desires, consciousness, a sense of self and so on.

At any given time, some synapses are open (connected); some are closed (transmission across them is blocked). This mirrors computer switches – some on, some off. This allows the application of propositional logic – the basis of computer language. Propositional logic has two primitive operators: "not" and "and". All the other operators can be defined in terms of these two; for example, "A or B" is logically equivalent to "not (not A and not B)". "A or B" is defined as either A is True or B is True or both A and B are True. The only condition under which A or B is false is if neither A nor B is True[4]. These equivalences can be seen in a truth table (Table 11.1).

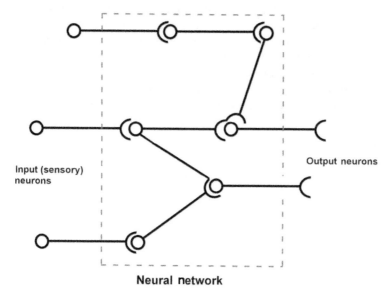

**Neural network**

*Figure 11.1* A simplified neural network.

*Table 11.1* A truth table showing the equivalence of *A* or *B* and Not (not *A* and not *B*).

| A | B | Not A | Not B | A and B | A or B | Not A and not B | Not (not A and Not B) |
|---|---|-------|-------|---------|--------|-----------------|------------------------|
| T | T | F | F | T | **T** | F | **T** |
| T | F | F | T | F | **T** | F | **T** |
| F | T | T | F | F | **T** | F | **T** |
| F | F | T | T | F | **F** | T | **F** |

The Truth value (T or F) is the same for "*A* or *B*" and "not (not *A* and not *B*)".
The operator "if *A* then *B*" means that whenever *A* occurs, *B* must occur; *A* never occurs without *B*. The truth table (which does have one odd feature[5]) shows that "If *A* then *B*" is equivalent to "not (*A* and not *B*)" (see Table 11.2).

*Table 11.2* A truth table showing the equivalence of If *A* then *B* and Not (*A* and not *B*). If *A* then *B*, known as material implication, is a common way of expressing a causal relationship (e.g. if I release my grip on this ball then it will fall to the ground).

| A | B | Not A | Not B | If A then B | A and not B | Not (A and not B) |
|---|---|-------|-------|-------------|-------------|-------------------|
| T | T | F | F | **T** | F | **T** |
| T | F | F | T | **F** | T | **F** |
| F | T | T | F | **T** | F | **T** |
| F | F | T | T | **T** | F | **T** |

The various logical operators can be used to describe the logic of the gates (switches in computers and synapses in neural networks). The various arrays of gates allows the flow of electrochemical activity in the case of neural networks and electrical current in the case of computers. It also allows memory (in neural networks and computers); different arrays are different memory structures. That mind is supervenient on the brain is clear on this model. It is worth noting an emerging research program: Research Domain Criteria (RDoC). It integrates many dimensions: genomics, analysis, self-reporting and so on.

## Notes

1  The earliest discourses of the Buddha (ca. 450 BCE) provide a complex account of the mind and predate Aristotle but had little influence on Anglo-European ideas. The contributions of the Arabic work were extensive but were unknown until the late middle ages and were very much influenced by Aristotle.
2  Except for a confusing and much debated passage in *De Anima* iii 5, his writings assume that the soul is inseparable from the body. In *De Anima* iii 5 he seems to suggest that although the mind is a faculty of the soul, it is separable from the body. In *De Anima* iii 5 he discusses the *active mind* or *active intellect*. For the most part, Aristotle's influence on later thinking was that mind, psyche and body are inseparable.
3  Leibniz and Newton independently and simultaneously developed the infinitesimal calculus – what today we simply call calculus or differential calculus and integral calculus.

The notation used today is Leibniz's. Newton's concept of "fluxions" was too unwieldy and his methods of proof less elegant than Leibniz's. Leibniz also set the groundwork for the development of mathematical logic – the logic on which the writing of today's computer algorithms depend.

4  Often in ordinary language, the exclusive sense of "or" is used. $A$ or $B$ means either $A$ or $B$ are True but not neither and not both. Logic uses the inclusive meaning, where $A$ or $B$ is True when $A$ and $B$ are True.

5  Intuitively, one might think that if $A$ is False then "If $A$ then $B$" must be False. Its best status is "indeterminate" because $A$ is not the case. But in a bi-valued logic, it has to be T or F. Since the only case where "If $A$ then $B$" is clearly false is when $A$ actually does occur (is T) and $B$ does not (is F). Hence, in the other cases it is deemed to be true because it is not clearly false. There are also internal consistency reasons for making this decision.

# 12 The varieties of modern medicine

Evolutionary medicine, evidence-based medicine, precision and personalised medicine and alternative medicine

Arthur Caplan argued in 1992 that the philosophy of medicine does not exist because there was not an established canon of key textual sources or "a set of distinctive or defining problems". In this book, thus far, we have set out some of the defining problems facing the philosophy of medicine as a branch of the philosophy of science. One important issue is whether a unified philosophy of medicine is possible – one that encompasses bench science and clinical medicine. Is unification possible and at what conceptual and methodological price? If it is not possible or the conceptual and methodological price is too high, is a middle ground between unity and isolation possible? That is, is there something similar to the essential theoretical connections between quantum theory and relativity theory, which fall considerably short of a unified physics, possible in medicine?

Unification is a common ideal in science; how close can medicine come to a coherent and unified theoretical account? Currently there is an array of different approaches advanced on which to centre or base medicine with respect to one or more of the core epistemological considerations we have outlined. Relevant considerations include the degree to which such constructs are applicable in the current context of clinical medicine, the degree to which the ideas cohere with accepted scientific norms and the extent to which they provide a means to grow medical knowledge and improve practice in the future.

It should be noted that the current rapid growth of research and technological innovation, and the increase in the number of providers of health services with associated traditions of research and practice mean that the central role of medicine and physicians is under challenge. For the purpose of this chapter, we will continue to use the term medicine as a global descriptor of those activities related to understanding health and well-being, illness and disease in human populations.

We will survey some of the leading descriptions of medicine that seek to provide an account for grounding both medical science and clinical care. We argue that attempts to ground medicine on singular foundational ideas will likely fail, and that a pluralistic vision of medicine likely best serves to account for the many diverse scientific and humanistic practices relevant to medicine.

Current accounts of medicine engage with epistemological considerations in various ways. These can broadly be construed as accounts of medicine on a spectrum in terms of the orientation to the sciences. We discuss approaches that are explicitly based in biology and molecular science, statistical approaches, those oriented to privileging first-person accounts or social processes and those that abjure reliance on orthodox accounts of medical practice or science.

We consider evidence-based medicine, Darwinian/evolutionary medicine, precision/personalised medicine, person-/patient-centred medicine, values-based medicine, narrative-based medicine and complementary and alternative medicine. Each of these accounts provides arguments and reasons for the utility and applicability of the approach on conceptual or empirical grounds. Although many exponents claim compatibility with other accounts, there is typically more focus on distinguishing the virtues of the particular account over more inclusive theorising.

## Evidence-based medicine (EBM)

In the late twentieth century, evidence-based medicine assumed prominence as the pre-eminent approach to the practice of clinical medicine. In 1992, EBM was announced as "a new paradigm for medical practice". It sought to reduce reliance on intuition and unsystematic clinical experience, place less emphasis on pathophysiologic rationale as sufficient grounds for clinical decision-making. Instead, EBM required physicians to be skilled at efficient literature searching and the application of critical appraisal tools to evaluate clinical literature. EBM is "the conscientious explicit and judicious use of best parent evidence in making decisions about the care of individual patients" and that the practice of evidence-based medicine is "integration of individual clinical experience with the best of external clinical evidence from systematic research and patient values and expectations" (Sackett et al. 1996).

EBM most closely sets out some of the criteria identified by Caplan to demarcate a philosophy of medicine. There are a set of core texts and a set of defining problems. Moreover, it is an explicitly normative (prescriptive) account in that it provides explicit and clear directions about how one *ought* to practise medicine and criteria for determining which sorts of considerations *should* be included and excluded in the practice of medicine. Furthermore, there are clear claims that one is a better physician by following EBM.

There are essentially five steps to the practice of EBM. These steps are supported by a hierarchy of evidence that directs clinicians to the most reliable form of evidence. The first step involves the formulation of a focused question that arises out of the encounter between a patient and a clinician. As we noted in the chapter of first-person accounts, patients might not always come in with a focused question. A patient will usually have complaints, and the task of the clinician is to take the information gleaned from a history and physical examination. For example, if an otherwise healthy woman wondered whether she should take low-dose aspirin® (81mg) daily to prevent stroke, the focused question would be "Will daily aspirin reduce the risk of thrombotic stroke in a 62-year-old woman?"

In EBM, a focused question takes the form of a PICO, which stands for "population, intervention comparison and outcome". The virtues of PICO are that one must be explicit about all dimensions of the question in order to acquire maximal informational content. Populations should be as clearly specified as possible (gender, age group, etc.), and interventions clearly described (medication at a particular dose for a specified duration of time, physical therapy, etc.). The comparison group is important, and data for comparison is often derived from the placebo group in a randomised controlled trial. This permits quantification of the unit of benefit ascribed to the intervention. Finally the outcome should be clearly understood, relevant to the patient and be relevantly influenced by the intervention. It is clear that PICO attempts to provide answers to specific causal questions. They are not well-suited to the exploration of values or psychic distress.

The second step in the practice of EBM is to find the best evidence. This entails efficient searching of databases in the clinical trials literature. In the early days of EBM, it recommended that all clinicians have the skills and abilities to conduct thorough and systematic literature reviews on their own and to foster a familiarity with the primary literature. However, as it has evolved and as the volume of health-related research has grown, clinicians are increasingly directed to "filtered" or pre-appraised sources of clinical evidence found in summaries or synopses of the literature. The Cochrane Collaboration, which supports the creation and dissemination of systematic reviews is a good example of an endorsed repository of evidence.

The third major step of EBM is the critical appraisal of the literature. Critical appraisal entails the close examination of the evidence to determine the applicability of the evidence found in the search to the particular patient problem. EBM relies upon grading evidence on a hierarchy to make recommendations, giving priority to study designs that minimise measurement error and statistical bias. Hence RCTs, and the meta-analysis of RCTs, are considered the highest forms of evidence. Physicians are also directed to search the "filtered" literature first before embarking on searching the unfiltered literature.

As a result of steps 1–3 a physician is now in a position to make a decision regarding a diagnostic or treatment strategy that integrates patient values and expectations. The final step is for the physician to evaluate the effect of the decision on both the patient's well-being and on the physician's practice.

The advent of EBM has triggered both positive acceptance and critical reaction. It is not an overstatement that much of the renewed interest in the philosophy of medicine is a result of the rapid ascendance of EBM in clinical medicine and the reaction to it by critics. EBM has become a staple in medical curricula at the undergraduate and postgraduate levels. There are extensive EBM resources in textbooks and on the internet for use by practising clinicians.

However, critics argue that the concept of evidence in EBM has not been well defined or articulated. The idea that evidence can be placed in a hierarchy has been questioned, particularly in light of the multiplicity of proposed hierarchies. There is an ongoing debate as to the role that mechanisms play in medicine. According to EBM they are lower on the hierarchy than well designed clinical trials. That the evidence hierarchy is itself a theoretical construct which requires independent justification is an issue that has not yet been resolved by proponents of EBM.

## Darwinian/evolutionary medicine (DEM)

Evolutionary medicine traces its lineage to the discovery, by Charles Darwin, of natural selection and its role in the theory of evolution as an overarching explanatory theory of biology. It uses the concepts of evolutionary biology to provide an account of disease as well as how adaptation over time through the mechanism of natural selection provides an explanation of health and disease. Evolutionary accounts demonstrate how natural selection adjusts virulence levels to whatever is optimal for the pathogen. It provides an account, in evolutionary terms, of why bodily defences, such as fever, cough, and anxiety, are required. An evolutionary account is not necessarily normative in terms of desired outcomes of medical interventions. An evolutionary view of medicine sees the human organism as a product of natural selection, well adapted in many ways but also flawed in other ways that give rise to recognisable diseases.

Proponents of evolutionary medicine argue that evolutionary biology is a unifying principle that provides an explanatory framework for organising knowledge from other basic sciences that is relevant to the practice of medicine. The power of evolutionary thinking in medicine comes from its ability to understand the human organism as a product of evolutionary processes.

Currently, there is no clear application of evolutionary principles in clinical practice but it is argued that, like understanding concepts in other sciences such as mathematics, physics and biochemistry, such understanding will make clinicians able to make better medical decisions. Evolutionary applications in medicine can be understood to apply to two subfields of evolutionary biology (phylogeny and adaptation) in five distinct areas where natural selection affects human biology: human genes, human traits, pathogen traits, pathogen genes, and somatic cell lines such as those in cancer and the immune system. Using an evolutionary approach applies to every biological system in humans at every level of function.

For example, Neese outlines six ways that evolution explains vulnerability to disease:

1   Pathogens evolve faster than hosts, and co-evolution arms races shape protective defences that can harm hosts.
2   There is a mismatch between our bodies and the modern environment.
3   Trade-offs have net benefits despite substantial costs.
4   There are constraints on what natural selection can shape.
5   Selection does not shape health and longevity, but maximal reproductive success.
6   Protective responses can seem like diseases, but they are actually useful defences.

It is evident from this account that while evolutionary medicine will help provide a broad account of disease, rooted in a fundamental and universal theory of biology, it will do little, in its current form, to provide an adequate account of the experience of illness. As well, there is limited application to the core tasks of clinical medicine, such as diagnosis, therapy and prognosis. This may change rapidly in the future.

### Precision/personalised Medicine (PPM)

Precision/personalised medicine is closely related to evolutionary medicine in the sense that they are premised on the claim that diagnosis, treatment and prevention strategies can be based upon and tailored to the particular biological profile of individual patients. The advent of large-scale biologic databases deriving from the human genome sequence, and adjunct methods for analysing the biological characteristics of patients as represented by the "omics" revolution (proteomics, metabolomics, epigenomics, microbiomics and so on), as well as the growing technological capacity to rapidly collect and access such information aided by the revolution in computational technology, promises to transform the practice of medicine.

Precision medicine recognises that, throughout history, medical practice has been, as noted in Chapter 9, fraught with uncertainty and is largely imprecise. It is argued that the new tools of molecular biology permit richer and deeper understanding of the underlying mechanisms that give rise to diseases. This reliance on mechanistic reasoning permits greater accuracy in both diagnosis and treatment. Thus, the approach fits squarely within the types of scientific inquiry discussed earlier. Biological science provides the high-level models within which mechanisms are described which in turn provide accounts of disease. Diagnosis and treatment therefore follow logically on the basis of the models.

This precision approach is also personalised because it utilises the techniques outlined above to provide an account of the particular patient's unique biological profile to tailor therapy to the specific genetic, epigenetic, microbiomic signature of that patient. It is argued that this approach simplifies the process of managing the extreme biological complexity that underlies human disease, which leads to uncertainty of diagnosis and management. Precision/personalised approaches are less dependent on making inferences based upon aggregate information and there will accordingly be less heterogeneity to address.

Precision medicine holds the most promise for advances in cancer and infectious diseases as these are areas in which molecular advances relevant to health and disease have advanced the most. As yet, it does not prescribe how to best practise medicine or articulate a means to adjudicate claims to knowledge in medicine.

### Patient-centred medicine (PCM)

Patient-centred medicine orients the goals of medicine away from the biological account and analysis of disease and illness to a focus on the interpersonal relationships between patients and physician. Its advocates see PCM as a necessary counterbalance to the depersonalising nature of other accounts of medicine. It places emphasis on the central importance of the patient in the pursuit of care.

PCM contains the following elements:

- It explores the patient's main reason for the visit, concerns, and need for information.
- It seeks an integrated understanding of the patient's world – that is, their whole person, emotional needs, and life issues.
- It finds common ground on what the problem is and mutually agrees on management.
- It enhances prevention and health promotion.
- It enhances the continuing relationship between the patient and the doctor.

## Values-based medicine (VBM)

Values-based medicine is related to patient-centred medicine, and to a lesser extent narrative medicine, in the attention to language and the importance of first-person engagement over the creation of reliable knowledge. It takes as a point of departure the fact that in clinical medicine there will be legitimately differing values at play. Some of these values may conflict. Some of the valuations may reside in the differential weight and interpretation given to various types of knowledge or disputes as to the legitimacy of certain claims to knowledge.

Values-based practice is seen by proponents as complementary to many elements of evidence-based practice in that it connects best evidence, derived from research and clinical experience, with the particular values, positive as well as negative, of the individual. Bill Fulford (2004) has articulated ten principles for values-based medicine as a counterpoint to evidence-based medicine.

These include the "two foot" principle that holds that clinical decision-making must be equally grounded in both the "facts" of the case as discerned by research methods and the "values" as espoused by patients and communities. In VBM medicine, the "first call" principle holds that the perspectives of the patient and community take priority in decision-making. In contrast, EBM searches for evidence first before considering the perspective of patients.

Increases in scientific discoveries result in increasing need to take values discourse seriously. As well, values tend to be "invisible" in discourse, but are diverse and often divergent. As a result, there is a need to make values explicit, abjure approaches that specify unique rules that lead to correct answers and create processes that support the articulation of divergent views. VBM thus privileges process over outcome. Fulford argues that value blindness and value myopia are responsible for many failings of effective decision-making in medicine. Value blindness is the failure to recognise values when values are at play, and value myopia is the false presumption of shared values. Fulford argues that philosophical techniques such as ordinary language approaches and analytic philosophy provide a robust set of analytic tools to address difficulties that arise in the integration of values to practice.

## Complementary and alternative medicine (CAM)

CAM refers to diagnostic and therapeutic approaches that either emerge from indigenous communities and rely on indigenous epistemologies (also known as traditional medicines) or are based on theories that eschew current dominant scientific theories or approaches to evaluation. CAM modalities fall into five categories:

1   Alternative medical systems
2   Mind–body interventions
3   Biologically based treatments
4   Manipulative and body-based methods
5   Energy therapies.

As the name implies, alternative medical systems represent a category that extends beyond a single modality, and refers to an entire system of theory and practice that developed separately from conventional western medicine. Examples of these systems include traditional Chinese medicine, ayurvedic medicine,[1] homeopathy and naturopathy. Mind–body interventions strive to enhance harmony and balance within the person through the use of techniques such as meditation and relaxation. Biologically based approaches assert the effects of "natural" substances such as vitamins, herbs and other forms of natural substances. Manipulation therapies include massage, chiropractic and osteopathy. Energy-based approaches seek to harness energy fields to bring about healing.

It is evident that CAM represents a heterogeneous set of approaches. Some represent comprehensive theories of medicine that provide accounts of how disease arises and include normative accounts of diagnosis and therapy. Some modalities are amenable to, and have been subjected to, rigorously designed randomised control trials with positive effect. Hence, the precise differentiation of a CAM from an orthodox medical approach is not entirely straightforward. As a result, boundaries between them are not fixed.

Does medicine need to be "based" or "centred" on anything? Each of the accounts of medicine described above seeks to provide some form of grounding that secures the epistemological foundation of medicine. Each account emphasises some particular commitment to a form of knowledge as critical to the foundation. These commitments can be ordered on a spectrum in terms of the types of science that inform the approach to theories of disease and subsequently to the diagnostic, therapeutic, prognostic and preventative needs attendant to the model. Each account seeks to differentiate itself from other forms of medicine by addressing weaknesses identified in each of the others.

PPM/DEM are strongest in terms of commitment to biological sciences as foundational, EBM is strongest in terms of commitment to statistical approaches. EBM, as noted, downgrades the sort of knowledge generated by the models and mechanisms proposed by biological science. "Basic" science is regarded as an unreliable guide to inference in clinical medicine.

PCM and VBM point in the direction of first-person approaches and weigh the knowledge generated by the social sciences and humanities as being either complementary or more foundational than biology or epidemiology. From the perspective of PCM/VBM neither PPM nor EBM can provide an adequate account of what it means to be ill, experience suffering or well-being. As the goals of medicine are to respond to the needs of humans suffering from illness or at risk of illness, only by integrating human experience including values in some integral way will we provide an adequate theory of medicine.

CAM proposes to base clinical care on a wide range of practices with varying allegiance to conventional approaches to understanding biological phenomena or evaluating therapeutic efficacy. Some types of CAM, such as homeopathy, are based upon theories of molecular action and therapeutic intervention that abjure well-accepted and established physical laws. Others rely on harnessing life forces that are not amenable to detection with current technologies.

Given the wide variety of rival formulations of medicine, it is worth asking whether any of these can work in isolation from the other, and whether it even makes sense to consider medicine as having a base or a centre that is somehow foundational.

Each of the conceptions of medicine seeks to provide arguments to support the preferred type of evidence that is required to enable legitimate inferences. There has been some engagement between proponents of VBM/PCM and EBM and lesser engagement with PPM and the other forms. Part of this relates to the relatively new emergence of PPM as an identified approach to medicine. Yet PPM must challenge some of the core tenets of EBM, particularly the role that biological mechanisms play in diagnosis and treatment.

Given the important role that the term evidence has played in recent discussions in the philosophy of medicine, we will examine the evidential status of each variety of medicine. Evidence, although invoked frequently in current discussions about medicine, is seldom defined. Evidence is often invoked as something that supports or justifies beliefs about states of affairs relevant to the health and well-being of a patient. In modern health research, data can be either quantitative or qualitative. We have seen that methodologies exist for both forms of data collection that can be published as original research. Narratives and other first-person accounts can also be published as research. Thus the scope of research evidence is quite wide indeed. Quite clearly, we are seeing that evidence in some way is related to data, or grounds for belief, and claims made about having evidence are also claims to knowledge, and thus fall under the purview of epistemology.

Evidence in the form of published research studies has certain significant properties that are important to understand. Rather than articulating a definition that all forms of evidence should possess, it may be more helpful to characterise properties of evidence and link these to how evidence functions in medical science and clinical practice. Three properties are salient. First, evidence is provisional, defeasible (open in principle to revision and disagreement) and emergent. All evidence can be contested and is subject to modification and revision in light of new evidence. There will be changes in what counts as evidence over time, in light of the growth of scientific knowledge.

*Helicobacter pylori* and peptic ulcer disease is again an excellent example to illustrate this point. Peptic ulcers occur when the protective lining of the stomach deteriorates causing a hole in the lining of the stomach wall. It typically presents with central abdominal pain which can be quite severe, and a decrease in appetite. It can result in perforation of the stomach, obstruction of the stomach preventing food passing into the small intestine, haemorrhaging and death.

The understanding of ulcers has evolved over time both in terms of causation and treatment. There are good descriptions of the signs and symptoms of ulcer disease dating back centuries. From the mid-nineteenth century to the late-twentieth century numerous causes were postulated such as overstimulation of the stomach, psychological issues, personality traits such as anxiety or a Type A personality, genetics, and toxins. All were posed as candidate explanations.

Diagnostic capacity has improved over time. In the nineteenth century to the early twentieth century diagnosis was primarily clinical and based upon the history and physical examination, with little laboratory support. With the advent of radiology, ulcers could be detected by imaging with the aid of contrast media such as barium. More recently, with endoscopy, ulcers can be directly visualised and biopsied.

Treatments were naturally linked to causes. Since the mid-nineteenth century, treatments have evolved. They focused on rest and stringent dietary regimens initially. As alcohol and tobacco became well understood to be associated with ulcers, prohibitions on their use became common. Psychotherapy was recommended as an adjunct to diet as a means of addressing the psychological causes of ulcer disease. In the mid-twentieth century, severe disease was amenable to surgical intervention either through the removal of the ulcer, or cutting the nerve that leads to the production of acid in the stomach. Medications to reduce pain such as antacids were commonly prescribed, and in the 1980s the first medication that could reliably suppress the production of gastric acid (cimetidine) became a standard of therapy and one of the largest-selling drugs of its time.

However, it is instructive to return to the discussion of peptic ulcers and *Helicobacter pylori* to illustrate important philosophical points about medicine. On one level, establishing an infectious cause for a common chronic disease marks an important, indeed highly significant, contribution to medical science. In clinical medicine eradication of the bacteria with the use of antibiotics provides a cure in a high proportion of patients with demonstrated infection. Randomised controlled trials showed very large treatment effects. Furthermore, the treatment is well tolerated, of short duration and is cost-effective as well. Improved quality of life in patients receiving therapy is also well documented.

The story of *Helicobacter pylori* is instructive to our understanding of evidence and its relation to medical science and medical practice as well as providing key insights into medical epistemology. It shows how medical knowledge is provisional and defeasible. Current knowledge acknowledged, it remains intelligible why clinicians would use rest, surgery or medications to treat ulcers in the absence of clear knowledge of the infectious origin of the disease. But, it would no longer be reasonable to use such modalities now as we have good reason to believe we have a better explanation and treatment. We would also be remiss to claim the story has come to a happy ending. There are ulcers that do not have an infectious cause. Moreover, many people have the infection and do not develop ulcers. Finally, an all-too-common experience of late, the bacterium itself is demonstrating the capacity to develop resistance to the antibiotic. Thus, our understanding of peptic ulcer disease continues to develop and there is no doubt more to be learned in the future regarding diagnosis, treatment and prognosis.

From the narrative regarding peptic ulcer disease three general observations can be made:

1   Medical science evolves over time.
2   Multiple lines of evidence derived from different types of scientific inquiry.
3   Knowledge acquisition is required to move from biological understanding to integration with clinical practice.

Also, the peptic ulcer disease example provides some general lessons. There has been a long, slow accumulation of observations, which led to the generation of multiple explanatory accounts linked to diagnostic and therapeutic strategies. The line of reasoning that led to the current explanatory model started with the observations of a trained pathologist (spirochetal organisms seen on biopsy slides). A critical mechanism, the enzyme urease, was shown to permit the existence of bacteria in an environment thought unable to sustain bacterial life forms. Auto-experimentation satisfied Koch's postulates to demonstrate the infectious nature of the disease. Clinical trials demonstrated the effectiveness, safety and acceptability of antibiotics to eradicate the bacteria and eliminate the symptoms of distress and reduce dramatically the complications of the disease.

Which of these models was most important? If one is wedded to PPM then the basic science discoveries would be most important, and EVM could provide an account of how the urease enzyme and bacteria evolved to exist in a particular ecological niche. EBM supporters would favour the clinical trial data as being most relevant to clinical practice. VBM/PCM supporters would argue that the quality of life considerations are most important.

However, in the case of peptic ulcer, while each component is necessary, no individual element is sufficient to provide a satisfactory account. The bigger question is why there is a need to put qualifiers to the practice of medicine in the first place.

Medicine is an integration of plural inputs (mechanisms, models, narratives) with differential weights not amenable to pre-specifying which one is more important than the other. In a very strong sense the question of which takes precedence over the other is a meaningless one as none of the currently proposed visions can account for all aspects of the medical enterprise.

The variety of the forms of knowledge that support medicine has been recognised for some time. Stephen Toulmin in the inaugural issue of *The Journal of Medicine and Philosophy* in 1976 recognised the need to acknowledge this as an irreducible facet of medical epistemology:

> The complexity of the tasks facing an epistemology of medicine should not surprise us. For in one way or another, medicine is a mirror of all human life. In some ways, it is no doubt a distorting mirror: it magnifies ills and distresses and ignores the richness and variety of joys and satisfaction. But there is no way in which we can legitimately disregard that complexity. By painting a picture of medicine as an art only, or, alternatively, as a science only, we may temporarily succeed in distracting attention from it: *tamen usque recurret.* An exclusive concentration on the craft aspects of medicine would merely slow down the fruitful interaction of clinical practice with scientific physiology; the converse oversimplification, of treating the physician as a pure "biomedical scientist," has already recoiled on the profession, from the hands of a frustrated, uncomprehending, and overoptimistic public. To restore a proper balance, we need to reinstate a proper sense of medical understanding as raising problems about the epistemology of a multivalued enterprise.
>
> (pp. 48–49)

How are these diverse elements drawn together? Peter Galison, in his book *Image and Logic*, sets out a conceptual framework for interdisciplinary understanding in a complex scientific culture. Examining the history of particle physics in the twentieth century, he argues that physics has advanced due to the interactions of heterogeneous disciplines, including theorists, experimenters, engineers, mathematicians, statisticians, architects and colleagues, all making contributions at various times to the vision and practice of science. Galison's analysis is a profound one in that it recognises diversity of scientific disciplines, the contexts in which they operate and interact, and the manner in which knowledge and research change and evolve. As he writes:

> My question is not how different scientific communities pass like ships in the night. It is rather how, given the extraordinary diversity of the participants in physics–cryogenic engineers, radio chemists, algebraic topologists, prototype tinkerers, computer wizards, quantum field theorists – they speak to each other at all. And the picture (to the extent one simplifies and flattens it) is one of different areas changing over time with complex border zones that sometimes vanish, coalesce and even burgeon into quasi autonomous regions in their own right.
>
> (1997, p. 63)

Medicine similarly has a breath-taking diversity of participants and an even wider ambit of disciplines. Galison quotes the American philosopher C.S. Peirce, who regarded the progress of science as trusting the multitude of arguments (and methods) rather than a single method, so that:

> Its reasoning should not form a chain which is no stronger than its weakest link, but a cable whose fibres may be ever so slender, provided they are sufficiently numerous and intimately connected. With its intertwined strands, the cable gains its strength, not by having a single golden thread that winds its way through the whole. No one golden strand defines the whole.
>
> (1997, pp. 843–844)

None of the varieties of medicine provides a golden thread. The task of understanding knowledge in health care is to understand and appreciate how the intertwining disciplinary threads relate to, and give strength to, the modern enterprise of medicine. In this vision, the contexts of practice, experiences and narratives of practitioners and patients, the basic and clinical sciences, values and societal perspectives are all conceived as integral elements of a larger process. The landscape will no doubt change as sciences evolve, but there is no clear reason, at this point, why any particular pursuit should be regarded as foundational or more central to the goals of modern medicine.

## Note

1 Ayurvedic medicine is one of the world's oldest holistic ("whole-body") healing systems. It was developed more than 3,000 years ago in India. It is based on the belief that health and wellness depend on a delicate balance between the mind, body, and spirit. Its main goal is to promote good health, not fight disease.

# Bibliography

Armitage, P. (2003) "Fisher, Bradford Hill, and Randomization," *International Journal of Epidemiology*, 32(6): 925–928.

Ashcroft, R.E. (2004) "Current Epistemological Problems in Evidence Based Medicine," *Journal of Medical Ethics,* 30: 131–135.

Banks, R. (1997) *Affliction.* Toronto: McLelland and Stewart.

Barry, M.J. (2001) "Clinical Practice. Prostate-specific-antigen Testing for Early Diagnosis of Prostate Cancer," *New England Journal of Medicine*, 344(18): 1,373–1,377.

Bedard, P.L., Krzyzanowska, M.K., Pintilie, M. and Tannock, I.F. (2007) "Statistical Power of Negative Randomized Controlled Trials Presented at American Society for Clinical Oncology Annual Meetings," *Journal of Clinical Oncology*, 25(23): 3,482–3,487.

Bell, J.L. (2015) "The Axiom of Choice," in *The Stanford Encyclopedia of Philosophy*. (Summer Edition), E.N. Zalta (ed.). URL = https://plato.stanford.edu/entries/axiom-choice/.

Berger, J. (1983) "The Frequentist Viewpoint and Conditioning," in L.M. Le Carn and R.A. Olshen (eds.), *Proceedings of the Berkeley Conference in Honor of Jerry Neyman and Jack Kiefer* (Vol. 1). Monterey, CA: Wadworth.

Berger, J.O., and Wolpert, R.L. (1988) *The Likelihood Principle* (2nd ed.). Institute of Mathematical Statistics Lecture Notes – Monograph Series.

Berger, J.S., Roncaglioni, M.C., Avanzini, F., Pangrazzi, I., Tognoni, G. and Brown, D.L. (2006) "Aspirin for the Primary Prevention of Cardiovascular Events in Women and Men: A Sex-Specific Meta-analysis of Randomized Controlled Trials," *Journal of the American Medical Association*, 295(3): 306–313.

Berry, D. (2012) "Bayesian Approaches for Comparative Effectiveness Research," *Clinical Trials*, 9(1): 37–47.

Bluhm, R. (2005) "From Hierarchy to Network: A Richer View of Evidence for Evidence-based Medicine," *Perspectives in Biology and Medicine*, 48: 535–547.

Bluhm, R. (2009) "Some Observations on 'Observational' Research," *Perspectives in Biology and Medicine*, 52(2): 252–263.

Bluhm, R. (2010) "The Epistemology and Ethics of Chronic Disease Research: Further Lessons from ECMO," *Theoretical Medical Bioethics*, 31: 107–122.

Bluhm, R. (2017) "Evidence-based Medicine, Biological Psychiatry, and the Role of Science in Medicine," in J. Poland and Ş. Tekin (eds), *Extraordinary Science and Psychiatry: Responses to the Crisis in Mental Health Research (Philosophical Psychopathology)*, Cambridge: The MIT Press, pp. 37–57.

Blume, J. (2011) "Likelihood and its Evidential Framework," in *Handbook of the Philosophy of Science: Philosophy of Statistics* (Vol. 7), pp. 493–507.

Bolie, V.W. (1960) "Coefficients of Normal Blood Glucose Regulation," *Journal of Applied Physiology*, 16: 783–788.

Borgerson, K. (2009a) "Valuing Evidence: Bias and the Evidence Hierarchy of Evidence-based Medicine," *Perspectives in Biology and Medicine*, 52: 218–233.

Borgerson, K. (2009b) "Why Reading the Title Isn't Good Enough: An Evaluation of the 4S Approach of Evidence-based Medicine," *International Journal for Feminist Approaches to Bioethics*, 2: 152–175.

Bovens, L. and Hartmann, S. (2002) "Bayesian Networks and the Problem of Unreliable Instruments," *Philosophy of Science*, 69(1): 29–72.

Boyer, C.B. (1991) *A History of Mathematics* (2nd ed.), Uta C. Merzbach (rev. ed.). New York: John Wiley & Sons.

Brody, Howard (1980) *Placebos and the Philosophy of Medicine: Clinical, Conceptual and Ethical Issues*. Chicago: University of Chicago Press.

Bromberger, S. (1966) "Why Questions," in R.G. Colodney (ed.), *Mind and Cosmos*. Pittsburgh, PA: University of Pittsburgh Press.

Boorse, C. (1977) "Health as a Theoretical Concept," *Philosophy of Science,* 44: 542–573.

Boorse, C. (2011) "Concepts of Health and Disease," in Fred Griffith (ed.), *Philosophy of Medicine*. Amsterdam: Elsevier, pp. 13–64.

Braude, H.D. (2012) *Intuition in Medicine: A Philosophical Defense of Clinical Reasoning*. Chicago: University of Chicago Press.

Braunwald, E., Fauci, A.S., Kasper, D.L., Hauser, S.L., Longo, D.L. and Jameson, J. L. (eds) (2001) *Harrison's Principle of Internal Medicine* (15th ed.). New York: McGraw-Hill.

Caplan, A.L. (1992) "Does the Philosophy of Medicine Exist?" *Theoretical Medicine*, 13(1): 67–77.

Carel, H. (2011) "Phenomenology and Its Application in Medicine," *Theoretical Medicine and Bioethics*, 32: 33–46.

Carrell, J.L. (2004) *The Speckled Monster: A Historical Tale of Battling Smallpox*. New York: Penguin (Plume).

Carnap, R. (1950) *Logical Foundations of Probability*. Chicago: University of Chicago Press.

Cartwright, N. (1979) "Causal Laws and Effective Strategies," *Noûs*, 13(4): 419–437.

Cartwright, N. (1983) *How the Laws of Physics Lie*. New York: Oxford University Press.

Cartwright, N.(1989) *Nature's Capacities and their Measurement*. New York: Oxford University Press.

Cartwright, N. (2001) "What Is Wrong with Bayes Nets?" *The Monist*, 84(2): 242–264.

Cartwright, N. (2007) *Hunting Causes and Using Them: Approaches in Philosophy and Economics*. Cambridge: Cambridge University Press.

Cassell, E.J. (2004) *The Nature of Suffering and the Goals of Medicine* (2nd ed.). New York: Oxford University Press.

Chang, H., 2011, "The Philosophical Grammar of Scientific Practice," *International Studies in the Philosophy of Science*, 25(3): 205–221.

Charon, R. (2001) "Narrative Medicine: A Model for Empathy, Reflection, Profession, and Trust," *Journal of the American Medical Association*, 286(15): 1897–1902.

Chou, R. (2011) "Screening for Prostate Cancer: A Review of the Evidence for the US Preventive Services Task Force," *Annals of Internal Medicine*, 155: 762–771.

Cold Spring Harbor Laboratory (1961) *Biological Clocks*. Series title, *Cold Spring Harbor symposia on quantitative biology*, Vol. 25, Cold Spring Harbor: Long Island Biological Association, Biological Laboratory.

Cowell, R.G., Dawid, P., Lauritzen, S.L. and Spiegelhalter, D.J. (1999) *Probabilistic Networks and Expert Systems*. Dordrecht: Springer-Verlag.

Darwin, C. (1859) On *the Origin of Species*. London: John Murray.

Davidson, D. (1970) "Mental Events," in L. Foster and J.W. Swanson (eds), *Experience and Theory*. London: Duckworth.

Desai, D. and Dhanani, H. (2003) "Sickle Cell Disease: History and Origin," *The Internet Journal of Hematology*, 1(2): 1–3.

Diamond, J. (1999) *Guns, Germs, and Steel: The Fates of Human Societies*. New York: W.W. Norton & Company.

Dobzhansky, T. (1973) *The American Biology Teacher*, 35: 125–129.

Doll, R. (1964) *Medical Surveys and Clinical Trials: Some Methods and Applications of Group Research in Medicine*, L.J. Witts (ed.). London: Oxford University Press.

Doll, R. and Hill, A. Bradford (1954) "The Mortality of Doctors in Relation to their Smoking Habits," *British Medical Journal*, 328: 1,529–1,533.

Duhem, P. (1906) *La theorie physique: Son objet et sa structure*, Paris: Chevalier et Riviere. Translated by P.P. Wiener, *The Aim and Structure of Physical Theory*, Princeton, NJ: Princeton University Press, 1954.

Dupré, J. (1984) "Probabilistic Causality Emancipated," *Midwest Studies in Philosophy*, 9: 169–175.

Dupré, J. and Cartwright, N. (1988) "Probability and Causality: Why Hume and Indeterminism Don't Mix," *Noûs*, 22(4): 521–536.

Edelstein-Keshet, L. (1988) *Mathematical Models in Biology*. New York: Random House.

Engelhardt Jr., H.T. (1979) "Introduction" in H. T. Engelhardt Jr., S. Spicker, and B. Towers (eds), *Clinical Judgment*. Dordrecht: D. Reidel Publishing Company.

Fisher, R. (1955) "Statistical Methods and Scientific Induction," *Journal of the Royal Statistical Society. Series B (Methodological)*, 17(1): 69–78.

Fisher, R.A., Sir (1956) *Statistical Methods and Scientific Inference*. New York: Hafner Publishing Company.

Fisher, R.A. (1958) "Cigarettes, Cancer and Statistics," *Centennial Review*, 2: 151–166.

Fitelson, B. (2006) "Logical Foundations of Evidential Support," *Philosophy of Science*, 73(5): 500–512.

Fulford, K.W.M. (2004) "Ten Principles of Values-based Medicine," in J. Radden (ed.), *The Philosophy of Psychiatry: A Companion*. New York: Oxford University Press, pp. 205–223.

Fuller, J. (2013) "Rationality and the Generalization of Randomized Controlled Trial Evidence," *Journal of Evaluation in Clinical Practice*, 19(4): 644–647.

Gadamer, H.-G. (1996) *The Enigma of Health: The Art of Healing in a Scientific Age*. Translated by Jason Gaiger and Nicholas Walker, Cambridge: Polity Press.

Galileo, G. (1623) *Il Saggiatori* Rome: Giacomo Mascardi. Reprinted in English translation in C.D. O'Malley and S. Drake (eds), *Controversy on the Comets of 1618*. Philadelphia: 1960.

Galison, P. (1997) *Image and Logic: A Material History of Microphysics*. Chicago: University of Chicago Press.

Gillies, D. (2000) *Philosophical Theories of Probability*. Abingdon, Oxon: Routledge.

Gödel, K. (1930) "Die Vollständigkeit der Axiome des logischen Functionenkalküls," *Monatshefte für Mathematik und Physik*, 37: 349–360.

Gödel, K. (1931) "Über formal unentscheidbare Sätze der Principia Mathematica und verwandter Systeme," *Monatshefte für Mathematik und Physik*, 38: 173–198.

Good, I.J. (2003) *The Estimation of Probabilities: An Essay on Modern Bayesian Methods*. Cambridge, MA: MIT Press.

Goodman, L.S. and Gilman, A. (2011) The *Pharmacological Basis of Therapeutics* (12th ed.). New York: McGraw-Hill Medical.

Goodman, S.N. (2005) "Introduction to Bayesian Methods 1: Measuring the Strength of Evidence," *Clinical Trials*, 2(4): 282–290.

Hacking, I. (2001) *An Introduction to Probability and Inductive Logic*. Cambridge: Cambridge University Press.

Hacking, I. (2006) *The Emergence of Probability: A Philosophical Study of Early Ideas about Probability, Induction and Statistical Inference* (2nd ed.) Cambridge: Cambridge University Press.

Hawthorne, J. (Winter 2016) "Inductive Logic," in E. N. Zalta (ed.), *The Stanford Encyclopedia of Philosophy*. URL = https://plato.stanford.edu/archives/win2016/entries/logic-inductive/.

Hempel, C.G. (1965) *Aspects of Scientific Explanation*. New York, NY: Free Press.

Hempel, C.G. (1966) *Philosophy of Natural Science*. Englewood Cliffs, NJ: Prentice-Hall.

Hempel, C.G. and Oppenheim, P. (1948) "Studies in the Logic of Explanation," *Philosophy of Science*, 15: 135–175.

Hill, A.B. (1952) "The Clinical Trial," *New England Journal of Medicine*, 247: 113–119.

Hill, A.B. (1965) "The Environment and Disease: Association or Causation? " *Proceedings of the Royal Society of Medicine*, 58(5): 295–300.

Hippocrates (circa 400 BCE) *The Book of Prognostics*. Translated by Francis Adams. The Internet Classics Archive. URL = http://classics.mit.edu/Hippocrates/prognost.1.1.html (accessed 2 April 2017).

Höfler, M. (2005) "The Bradford Hill Considerations on Causality: A Counterfactual Perspective," *Emerging Themes in Epidemiology*, 2: 11.

Howick, J. (2011) *The Philosophy of Evidence-Based Medicine*. BMJ Books, Oxford: Wiley-Blackwell.

Howson, C. (2002) "The Logic of Bayesian Probability," in David Corfield and Jon Williamson (eds), *Foundations of Bayesianism. Applied Logic*, Vol. 24. Dordrecht: Kluwer Academic Publishers, pp. 137–160.

Howson, C. and Urbach, P. (2005) *Scientific Reasoning: The Bayesian Approach*. Chicago: Open Court.

Huff, D. (1954) *How to Lie with Statistics*. New York: W.W. Norton & Company (reissued as Norton paperback in 1993).

Hux, J.E. and Naylor, C.D. (1995) "Communicating the Benefits of Chronic Preventive Therapy: Does the Format of Efficacy Data Determine Patients' Acceptance of Treatment?" *Medical Decision Making*, 15: 152–157.

Jaynes, E.T. (2003) *Probability Theory: The Logic of Science*. Cambridge: Cambridge University Press.

Jeffreys, H. (1961) *Theory of Probability* (3rd ed.). Oxford: Clarendon Press, Oxford.

Jenner, E. (n.d.) *Three Original Publications on Vaccination against Smallpox* [e-book]. Hoboken, NJ: Generic NL Freebook Publisher. Available from: eBook Collection (EBSCOhost), Ipswich, MA.

Joyce, J. (Winter 2016) "Bayes' Theorem," in *The Stanford Encyclopedia of Philosophy*. E.N. Zalta (ed.)., URL = https://plato.stanford.edu/archives/win2016/entries/bayes-theorem/.

Kant, I. (original 1781, Norman Kemp Smith translation 1929) *Immanuel Kant's Critique of Pure Reason*. London: Macmillan and Company Ltd.

Kauffman, S. (1995) *At Home in the Universe: The Search for Laws of Self-Organization and Complexity*. Oxford: Oxford University Press.

Kauffman, S.A. and Johnsen, S (1991) "Co-Evolution to the Edge of Chaos: Coupled Fitness Landscapes, Poised States, and Co-Evolutionary Avalanches," *Journal of Theoretical Biology*, 149(4): 467–505.

Keynes, J.M. (1921, 2004) *A Treatise on Probability*. Dover Publications, Inc.

Keynes, J.M. (1923) *A Tract on Monetary Reform*. London: Macmillan and Co., Limited.

Keys, A. (ed.) (1970) "Coronary Heart Disease in Seven Countries," *Circulation*, 41(4S1): 1–198.

Keys, A.(1980) *Seven Countries: A Multivariate Analysis of Death and Coronary Heart Disease*. Cambridge, MA: Harvard University Press.

Kincaid, H. (2011) "Causal Modelling, Mechanism and Probability in Epidemiology," in P.M. Illari, F. Russo and J. Williamson (eds), *Causality in the Sciences.* Oxford: Oxford University Press.

King, L.S. (1982) *Medical Thinking: A Historical Preface.* Princeton: Princeton University Press.

Koch, R. (1880) *Investigations into the Etiology of Traumatic Infective Diseases.* London: The New Sydenham Society.

Kravitz, R.L., Duan, N. and Braslow, J. (2004) "Evidence-Based Medicine, Heterogeneity of Treatment Effects, and the Trouble with Averages," *The Milbank Quarterly,* 82(4): 661–687.

Last, J.M. (ed.) (2001) *A Dictionary of Epidemiology* (4th ed.). Oxford: Oxford University Press.

Leonard, T. and Hsu, J.S.J. (1999) *Bayesian Methods: An Analysis for Statisticians and Interdisciplinary Researchers.* Cambridge: Cambridge University Press.

Lewis, D. (1973a) "Causation," *Journal of Philosophy,* 70: 556–567.

Lewis, D. (1973b) *Counterfactuals.* Cambridge, MA: Harvard University Press.

Lewis, D. (1979) "Counterfactual Dependence and Time's Arrow," *Noûs,* 13: 418–446.

Laplace, P.-S. (1812) *Théorie Analytique des Probabilités.* Paris: Mme Ve COURCIER, Impriment-Libraire pour les Mathématique, quai des Augustins, No 57.

Lind, J. (1753) *A Treatise of the Scurvy. In Three Parts. Containing an Inquiry into the Nature, Causes and Cure, of that Disease. Together with a Critical and Chronological View of what has been Published on the Subject.* Edinburgh: Sands, Murray and Cochran for A. Kincaid and A. Donaldson.

Lloyd, E. (1988) *The Structure and Confirmation of Evolutionary Theory.* New York: Greenwood Press (reprinted Princeton University Press, 1994).

Löwenheim, L. (1915) "Über Möglichkeiten im Relativkalkül," *Mathematische Annalen,* 76: 447–470. Translated as "On Possibilities in the Calculus of Relatives" in Jean van Heijenoort, 1967. *A Source Book in Mathematical Logic, 1879–1931.* Cambridge, MA: Harvard Univiversity Press, pp. 228–251.

Mackie, J.L. (1974, 1980) *The Cement of the Universe: A Study of Causation.* Oxford: Clarendon Press.

Malinas, G. and Bigelow, J. (2016) "Simpson's Paradox," in *Stanford Encyclopedia of Philosophy,* E.N. Zalta (ed.). URL = https://plato.stanford.edu/entries/paradox-simpson/.

Marshall, B.J. and Warren, J.R. (1983) "Unidentified Curved Bacilli on Gastric Epithelium in Active Chronic Gastritis," *Lancet,* 321 (8336): 1,273–1,275.

McClintock, B. (1929) "A Cytological and Genetical Study of Triploid Maize," *Genetics,* 14(2): 180–222.

McClintock, B. (1950) "The Origin and Behavior of Mutable Loci in Maize," *Proceedings of the National Academy of Sciences of the United States of America,* 36(6): 344–355.

Mees, C.E. Kenneth (1934) "Scientific Thought and Social Reconstruction," *Transactions of the American Institute of Electrical Engineers,* 53: 381–387.

Mendel, G. (1865) "Versuche über Pfanzenhybriden," *Verhandlungen des Naturforschenden Vereins in Brünn,* 4: 3–47 (Fisher's reprinting and modification of Bateson's English translation is used in this book), Bateson, W. (1909) *Mendel's Principles of Heredity.* Cambridge: Cambridge University Press).

Miller, A.B., Baines, C.J., To, T. and Wall, C. (1992a) "Canadian National Breast Screening Study: 1 Breast Cancer Detection and Death Rates among Women aged 40–49 Years," *Canadian Medical Association Journal,* 147: 1,459–1,476.

Miller, A.B., Baines, C.J., To, T. and Wall, C. (1992b) "Canadian National Breast Screening Study: 2 Breast Cancer Detection and Death Rates among Women aged 50–59 Years," *Canadian Medical Association Journal,* 147: 1.477–1,488.

Miller, Anthony B., Wall, C., Baines, C.J. Sun, P., To, T. and Narod, S.A. (2014) "Twenty Five Year Follow-up for Breast Cancer Incidence and Mortality of the Canadian National

Breast Screening Study: Randomised Screening Trial," *British Medical Journal (BMJ)*, 348: g366.

Misak, C. (2010) "Narrative Evidence and Evidence-Based Medicine," *Journal of Evaluation in Clinical Practice*, 16: 392–397.

Morgan, M.S. and Morrison, M. (eds.) (1999) *Models as Mediators: Perspectives on Natural and Social Science*, Cambridge: Cambridge University Press.

Moyer, V.A. (on behalf of the U.S. Preventive Services Task Force) (2012) "Screening for Prostate Cancer: U.S. Preventive Services Task Force Recommendation Statement," *Annals of Internal Medicine*, 157(2): 120–134.

Morrison, M. (2000) *Unifying Scientific Theories: Physical Concepts and Mathematical Structures*. Cambridge: Cambridge University Press.

Morrison, M. (2007) "Where Have All the Theories Gone?," *Philosophy of Science*, 74(2): 195–228.

Murphy, E.A. (1997) *The Logic of Medicine* (2nd ed.) Baltimore: The Johns Hopkins University Press.

Murray, J.D. (2002) *Mathematical Biology* (3rd ed.). New York: Springer.

Nagel, E. (1961) *The Structure of Science: Problems in the Logic of Scientific Explanation*. New York: Routledge & Kegan Paul.

Naylor, C.D., Chen, E. and Strauss, B. (1992) "Measured Enthusiasm: Does the Method of Reporting Trial Results Alter Perceptions of Therapeutic Effectiveness?" *Annals of Internal Medicine*, 117: 916–921.

Neyman J. and Pearson, E.S. (1933) "On the Problem of the Most Efficient Tests of Statistical Hypotheses," *Philosophical Transactions of the Royal Society of London: A*. 231: 289–337.

nobelprize.org (2005) "The Nobel Prize in Physiology or Medicine 2005,"press release 3 October. URL = http://www.nobelprize.org/nobel_prizes/medicine/laureates/2005/press.html.

Oresme, N. (1968) *Nicole Oresme and the Medieval Geometry of Qualities and Motions: A Treatise on the Uniformity and Difformity of Intensities Known as "Tractatus de configurationibus qualitatum et motuum"*. Edited with an introduction, English translation and commentary by M. Clagett. Madison, Milwaukee, and London: University of Wisconsin Press, 1968.

Papineau, D. (1994) "The Virtues of Randomization," *British Journal for the Philosophy of Science*, 45: 437–450.

Pearl, J. (2009) *Causality: Models, Reasoning, and Inference* (2nd ed.). Cambridge, UK; New York: Cambridge University Press.

Pearson, K. (1900) *The Grammar of Science*. Cambridge, MA: MIT Press.

Phillips, C.V. and Goodman, K.J. (2004) "The Missed Lessons of Sir Austin Bradford Hill," *Epidemiologic Perspectives and Innovations*, 1: 3.

Popper, K. (1963) *Conjectures and Refutations*. London: Routledge & Kegan Paul

Prigogine, Ilya and Nicolis, G. (1977) *Self-Organization in Non-Equilibrium Systems*. Hoboken. NJ: Wiley.

Pylarinius, J. (1716) "Nova et Tuta Excitandi per Transplatationem Methodus: Nuper Inventa et in Usum Tracta," *Philosophical Transactions*, 29: 393–399.

Quine, W.V. (1953) "Two Dogmas of Empiricism," in *From a Logical Point of View*. New York: Harper Torchbooks.

Quine, W.V. and Ullian, J.S. (1978) *The Web of Belief*. New York: McGraw-Hill Education.

Ramsey, F.P. (1926) "Truth and Probability," in Ramsey (1931) *The Foundations of Mathematics and other Logical Essays*, Chapter VII, R.B. Braithwaite (ed.). London: Kegan, Paul, Trench, Trubner & Co., New York: Harcourt, Brace and Company, pp.156–198.

Reinhart, A. (2015) *Statistics Done Wrong: The Woefully Complete Guide*. San Francisco: No Starch Press.

Rosenkrantz, R.D. (1977) *Inference, Method, and Decision*. Dordrecht-Holland: D. Reidel.

Royall, R. (1997) *Statistical Evidence: A Likelihood Paradigm*. New York: Chapman & Hall.

Russell, B. (1913) "On the Notion of Cause," *Proceedings of the Aristotelian Society*, 13: 1–26.

Sackett, D.L., Rosenberg, W.M.C., Muir Gray, J.A., Haynes, R.B. and Richardson, W.S. (1996) "Evidence Based Medicine: What It Is and What It Isn't," *BMJ*, 312: 71.

Salmon, W. (1984) *Scientific Explanation and the Causal Structure of the World*. Princeton, NJ: Princeton University Press.

Salmon, W. (1998) *Causality and Explanation*. New York: Oxford University Press.

Salsburg, D. (1993) "The Use of Statistical Methods in the Analysis of Clinical Studies," *Journal of Clinical Epidemiology*, 46(I): 17–27.

Scott, S. and Duncan, C.J. (2001) *Biology of Plagues: Evidence from Historical Populations*. Cambridge: Cambridge University Press.

Shimony, A. (1970) "Scientific Inference," in *The Nature and Function of Scientific Theories*. Pittsburg: University of Pittsburgh Press.

Simpson, E.H. (1951) "The Interpretation of Interaction in Contingency Tables," *Journal of the Royal Statistical Society (Series B)*, 13: 238–241.

Siri-Tarino, Patty W. et al. (2010) "Meta-analysis of Prospective Cohort Studies Evaluating the Association of Saturated Fat with Cardiovascular Disease," *American Journal of Clinical Nutrition*, 91(3): 535–546.

Skolem, T. (1920), "Logisch-kombinatorische Untersuchungen über die Erfüllbarkeit oder Beweisbarkeit mathematischer Sätze nebst einem Theoreme über dichte Mengen," *Videnskapsselskapet Skrifter, I. Matematisk-naturvidenskabelig Klasse*, 4: 1–36.

Smith, A. (1996) "Mad Cows and Ecstasy: Chance and Choice in an Evidence-based Society," *Journal of the Royal Statistical Society A*.

Snow, J. (1855) *On the Mode of Communication of Cholera* (2nd ed.). London: John Churchill

Spiegelhalter, D.J.K., Adams, K.R. and Myles, J.P. (2004) *Bayesian Approaches to Clinical Trials and Health-Care Evaluation*. John Wiley & Sons.

Steel, D. (2011) "Causal Models, and Social Mechanisms," in I.C. Jarvie and J. Zamora-Bonilla (eds), *The Sage Handbook of Philosophy of Social Science*. London: Sage.

Stigler, S.M. (1900) *The History of Statistics: The Measurement of Uncertainty before 1900*. Cambridge: Harvard University Press, Ch. 3.

Suppe, F., ed. (1977) *The Structure of Scientific Theories*. Urbana: University of Illinois Press.

Suppe, F. (1989) *The Semantic Conception of Theories and Scientific Realism*. Urbana: University of Illinois Press.

Suppes, P. (1970) *A Probabilistic Theory of Causality*. Amsterdam: North-Holland Publishing Company.

Svenaeus, F. (2013) "Naturalistic and Phenomenological Theories of Health: Distinctions and Connections," in H. Carel and D. Meacham (eds), *Phenomenology and Naturalism: Exploring the Relationship between Human Experience and Nature*. Cambridge: Cambridge University Press, pp. 221–238.

Tarski, A. and Vaught, R.L. (1957) "Arithmetical Extensions of Relational Systems," *Compositio Mathematica*, 13: 81–102.

Toulmin, S. (1958) *The Uses of Argument*. Cambridge: Cambridge University Press.

Toulmin, S. (1976) "On the Nature of the Physician's Understanding," *Journal of Medicine and Philosophy*, 1: 32–50.

Thompson, R.P. (1986) "The Interaction of Theories and the Semantic Conception of Evolutionary Theory," *Philosophica*, 37: 28–37.

Thompson, R.P. (1987) "A Defence of the Semantic Conception of Evolutionary Theory," *Biology and Philosophy*, 2: 26–32.

Thompson, R.P. (1989) *The Structure of Biological Theories*. Ithaca, NY: State University of New York Press.

Thompson, R.P. (2007) "Formalisations of Evolutionary Biology," in M. Matthen and C. Stephens (eds), *Philosophy of Biology*, Elsevier, Amsterdam, pp. 485–523.

Thompson, R.P. (2010) "Causality, Mathematical Models and Statistical Association: Dismantling Evidence-Based Medicine," *Journal of Evaluation in Clinical Practice*, 16: 267–275.

Thompson, R.P. (2011a) "Causality, Theories and Medicine," in P. McKay Illari, F. Russo and J. Williamson (eds), *Causality in the Sciences*. Oxford: Oxford University Press, pp. 25–44.

Thompson, R.P. (2011b) "Theories and Models in Medicine," in Fred Gifford (ed.), *Philosophy of Medicine*. Amsterdam: Elsevier, pp. 115–136.

Thompson, R.P. (2014) ""Darwin's Theory and the Value of Mathematical Formalisation" in R.P. Thompson and D. Walsh (eds), *Evolutionary Biology: Conceptual, Ethical and Religious Issues*. Cambridge: Cambridge University Press.

Thompson, R.P. (2015) *A Remarkable Journey: The Story of Evolution*. London: Reaktion Books Ltd.

Timonius, E. and Woodward, J. (1714) "An Account, or History, of the Procuring the Small Pox by Incision, or Inoculation; As It Has for Some Time Been Practised at Constantinople," *Philosophical Transactions*, 29(339): 72–82.

Tressoldi, P.E. et al. (2013) "High Impact = High Statistical Standards? Not Necessarily So," *PLoS ONE*, 8(2): e56180.

Upshur, R. (2003) "Are All Evidence-based Practices Alike? Problems in the Ranking of Evidence," *Canadian Medical Association Journal*, 169: 672–673.

Von Mises, R. (1928) *Wahrscheinlichkeit, Statistik, und Wahrheit*. Berlin: J. Springer. English edition (2nd ed.): *Probability, Statistics and Truth*. 1961, Crows Nest, New South Wales, Australia: Allen and Unwin.

Walton, D. (1998) *The New Dialectic: Conversational Contexts of Argument*. Toronto: University of Toronto Press.

Whitehead, A.N. and Russell, B. (1910–1913) *Principia Mathematica* (3 volumes). Cambridge: Cambridge University Press.

Williamson, T. (2010) *In Defense of Objective Bayesianism*. Oxford: Oxford University Press.

Winther, R.G. (Winter 2016) "The Structure of Scientific Theories", in *The Stanford Encyclopedia of Philosophy*. E.N. Zalta (ed.). URL = https://plato.stanford.edu/archives/win2016/entries/structure-scientific-theories/.

World Health Organization (1946) "Preamble to the Constitution of the World Health Organization," adopted by the International Health Conference, New York, 19–22 June, 1946; signed on 22 July 1946 by the representatives of 61 States (Official Records of the World Health Organization, no. 2, p. 100) and entered into force on 7 April 1948.

Worrall, J. (2002) "*What* Evidence in Evidence-Based Medicine?" *Philosophy of Science*, 69(S3): S316–S330.

Worrall, J. (2007) "Why There's No Cause to Randomize," *British Journal for the Philosophy of Science*, 58: 451–488.

Worrall, J. (2010a) "Do We Need Some Large, Simple Randomized Trials in Medicine?" in M. Suárez, M. Dorato and M. Rédei (eds), *Epsa Philosophical Issues in the Sciences: Launch of the European Philosophy of Science Association*. London, UK: Springer, pp. 289–302.

Worrall, J. (2010b) "For Universal Rules, Against Induction," *Philosophy of Science*, 77(5): 740–753.

Worrall, J. (2010c) "Evidence: Philosophy of Science Meets Medicine," *Journal of Evaluation in Clinical Practice*, 16(2): 356–362. ISSN 1356–1294.

Worrall, J. (2011) "Causality in Medicine: Getting Back to the Hill Top," *Preventive Medicine*, 53(4–5): 235–238.

Zermelo, E. (1904) "Neuer Beweis, dass jede Menge Wohlordnung werden kann (Aus einem an Herrn Hilbert gerichteten Briefe)," *Mathematische Annalen*, 59: 514–516. Translated in J. van Heijenoort (ed.), *From Frege to Gödel: A Source Book in Mathematical Logic, 1879–1931*. Cambridge, MA: Harvard University Press, 1967, pp. 139–141.

Žižek, S. (2005) "The Empty Wheelbarrow: Intellectuals Have to be Most Critical when Rulers Insist the Choice is Clear," *Guardian*. URL = https://www.theguardian.com/comment/story/0,,1417982,00.html (accessed 30 February 2017).

# Index